INDEPENDENT LEARNING PROJECT FOR ADVANCED CHEMISTRY

ILPAC

ADVANCED PRACTICAL CHEMISTRY

second edition

REVISED BY ANN LAINCHBURY JOHN STEPHENS ALEC THOMPSON

JOHN MURR

D1421884

Acknowledgements

Our thanks are due to the University of London Entrance and Schools Examination Council for permission to use experiments which appeared in practical examinations:

Experiment 4.10 (1979), Experiment 4.11 (1974), Experiment 8.7 (1978 and 1979), Experiment 11.3 (1973 and 1980), Experiment 11.11 (1980), Experiment 12.5 (1977).

Experiment 9.8 is based, with the kind permission of Longman Group Ltd., on an experiment that appeared in *An Experimental Introduction to Reaction Kinetics* by M. A. Atherton and K. Lawrence (ISBN 0582 32145 X).

Original material produced by the Independent Learning Project for Advanced Chemistry, sponsored by the Inner London Education Authority and published as ILPAC volumes S1–S4, P1–P5, O1–O4 and I1–I6.
Taken from the second edition, published as ILPAC volumes 1–12 with additional material by Ann Lainchbury, John Stephens and Alec Thompson.

First edition published in 1985
by John Murray (Publishers) Ltd., a member of the Hodder Headline Group
338 Euston Road
London NW1 3BH

Reprinted 1989, 1990, 1992, 1994, 1995, 1996.
Second edition 1997.
Reprinted 1999 (twice), 2000, 2001 (twice), 2002, 2004 (twice), 2005

Design by John Townson/Creation.
Layouts by Wearset Ltd, Boldon, Tyne and Wear.
Illustrations by Barking Dog Art.

Typeset in 10/12 pt Times and Helvetica.
Printed and bound in Great Britain by Athenaeum Press Ltd., Gateshead, Tyne and Wear.

A catalogue record for this book is available from the British Library.

ISBN 0 7195 7507 9

CONTENTS

PREFACE

The experiments in this book are collected from the ILPAC books (Independent Learning Project in Advanced Chemistry). ILPAC was originally produced by an Inner London Education Authority team to cover the requirements of all the major Examination Boards, and all the materials were tested in schools and colleges both inside and outside London. A first edition of ILPAC was published by John Murray in 1983, followed by a revised and updated second edition in 1995 and 1996.

An important feature of the complete ILPAC scheme is that it enables students to work more effectively on their own and at their own pace. This is reflected in the way in which the procedures for the experiments are written: the style is personal and direct, and the instructions are far more detailed and precise than is usually the case in practical books.

However, the phrase 'independent learning' must not be interpreted too literally. It is not intended that students should be left unsupervised while they do practical work: rather, it is envisaged that a single teacher will be better able to supervise a number of different experiments going on at the same time without having to spell out detailed instructions to everyone.

An important feature of this book is the provision of specimen results, with detailed calculations where appropriate, and answers to the 'consolidation' questions which follow each experiment. These are available for use by teachers in the *Advanced Practical Chemistry Resource Pack*.

INTRODUCTION

The ILPAC Units from which these experiments are taken are organised into four blocks: Starter, Physical, Inorganic and Organic. The Starter Block Units are concerned mainly with introductory physical chemistry. The area of each experiment (physical, inorganic or organic) is indicated by the appropriate letter following the title of the experiment in the Contents list (pages iii and iv).

The order in which these experiments are listed is identical to that in the ILPAC Units, and could provide a logical teaching sequence within each section. It is envisaged that the material in Experiments 1.1 to 3.6 might be covered first (they come from the Starter Block Units). Thereafter, experiments in the three areas can be 'dovetailed'.

Many of the experiments may be used either for practical assessments or as preparation for practical examinations. In particular, Experiments 2.2, 7.7 and 9.7 are suitable for the assessment of planning skills, since we do not give the usual requirements lists or detailed instructions, while Experiments 4.10, 4.11, 8.7, 11.3, 11.11 and 12.5 are useful in preparing for practical examinations which include the investigation of 'unknown' substances.

■ International hazard symbols

 Corrosive

 Oxidising

 Explosive

 Radioactive

 Harmful or irritant

 Toxic

 Highly flammable

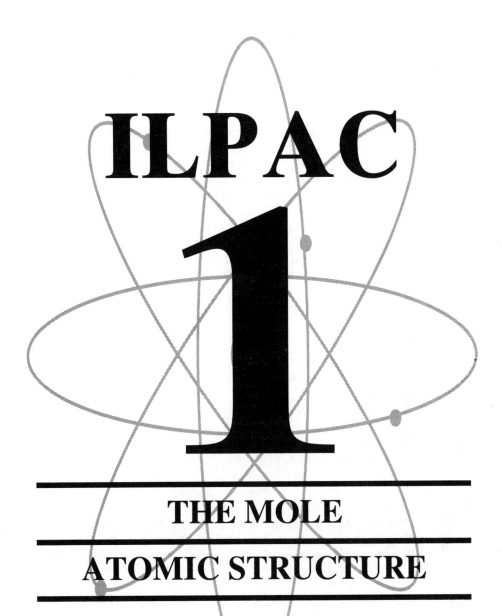

ILPAC

1

THE MOLE

ATOMIC STRUCTURE

EXPERIMENT 1.1 Determining the Avogadro constant

Aim The purpose of this experiment is to estimate the value of the Avogadro constant and to compare this estimate with the accepted value.

Introduction When a solution of oleic acid (more correctly called *cis*-octadec-9-enoic acid), $C_{17}H_{33}CO_2H$, in pentane is dropped onto water, the pentane evaporates leaving behind a layer of oleic acid one molecule thick. For this reason, this experiment has been called 'The Monomolecular Layer Experiment'.

You use a loop of hair or thread to contain the oleic acid and to give a measure of the surface area. By making certain assumptions about the shape of the molecule and its alignment on the surface, you can get a reasonably accurate value for the Avogadro constant.

The experiment has two parts. In the first, you calibrate the pipette. This gives the volume of one drop of solution. In the second part you determine how many drops of solution are required to just fill the loop with a layer of oleic acid molecules. Then we lead you, step by step, through the calculation.

Requirements ■ safety spectacles
■ measuring cylinder, 10 cm^3
■ teat pipette and adaptor (for small drops)
■ trough
■ human hair or cotton thread, 40–50 cm
■ scissors
■ petroleum jelly or Vaseline
■ oleic acid solution in pentane (0.05 cm^3 of oleic acid per dm^3)

HAZARD WARNING

Pentane is extremely flammable and harmful by inhalation. Therefore you **must**:
■ **keep the stopper on the bottle when not in use;**
■ **keep the liquid away from flames.**

Procedure 1. Fill the teat pipette with oleic acid solution and deliver it drop by drop into the 10 cm^3 measuring cylinder. Count the number of drops which must be delivered from the pipette to reach the 1 cm^3 mark. Enter your value in a copy of Results Table 1.1.

Results Table 1.1

Number of drops to deliver 1 cm^3 of solution	Number of drops delivered to make monomolecular layer	Diameter of monomolecular layer/cm

2. Tie the hair or cotton thread in a loop. Use a reef-knot (Fig. 1.1), rather than an overhand knot, so that the loop will make a flat circle. Cut the ends as close to the knot as possible. Hair is preferred because it does not need greasing but if you are using thread, thoroughly but lightly grease it with petroleum jelly. It is most important that no part of the thread escapes greasing. Run the knotted thread through your fingers several times before wiping off the excess.

Figure 1.1

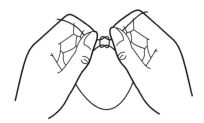

3. Fill the trough with water and float the loop on it, making sure that the entire circumference is in contact with the surface. Look very carefully for 'bridges' or submerged loops and move them into the surface with a clean glass rod or a pencil point.
4. Using the same pipette, add the oleic acid solution dropwise to the middle of the loop until it is filled. At first you will probably see the loop expand to a circle and then retract again.
   Before the loop is filled, it 'gives' when you push it gently from the outside with a pencil (Fig. 1.2).
   When the loop is filled, it will slide across the surface, only denting very slightly when pushed gently with the pencil (Fig. 1.3).

Figure 1.2

Figure 1.3 (right)

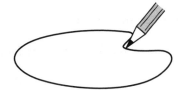 

Count the number of drops required to fill the loop and record this in a copy of Results Table 1.1.
5. Measure the diameter of the loop and complete Results Table 1.1.
6. If you have time, repeat the whole procedure. However, you must use a fresh hair or thread, and wash out the trough thoroughly to obtain a clean surface.

Calculation

1. Calculate the volume of 1 drop delivered from the teat pipette using the value in column one of Results Table 1.1.

$$\text{Volume of 1 drop} = \underline{\quad\quad} \text{ cm}^3$$

2. Calculate the volume of oleic acid in 1 drop of solution delivered from the teat pipette.
   Remember that 1000 cm^3 of this solution contains 0.05 cm^3 of oleic acid.

$$\text{Volume of oleic acid in 1 drop} = \underline{\quad\quad} \text{ cm}^3$$

3. Calculate the volume of oleic acid delivered to make the monomolecular layer; i.e. the volume of oleic acid in 1 drop × the number of drops required.

$$\text{Volume of oleic acid in monolayer} = \underline{\quad\quad} \text{ cm}^3$$

4. Calculate the surface area of the oleic acid layer.

$$\text{Area} = \pi d^2/4 = \underline{\quad\quad} \text{ cm}^2$$

5. You know the volume of oleic acid (from 3) and the surface area it covers (from 4). It is a simple matter to calculate the thickness of the layer because volume = area × thickness.

Thickness = ____ cm

Figure 1.4

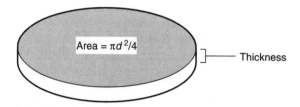

Area = $\pi d^2/4$

Thickness

6. Calculate the volume of one molecule of oleic acid by assuming that it is a cube, with sides equal to the thickness of the layer.

Volume of one molecule = ____ cm^3

7. Calculate the volume of a mole of oleic acid given that its density is 0.890 g cm^{-3} and its molar mass is 282 g mol^{-1}.

Volume per mole of oleic acid = ____ cm^3 mol^{-1}

8. Divide the volume per mole by the volume of one molecule to determine the Avogadro constant.

$$L = \_\_\_\_\ \text{mol}^{-1}$$

Questions
1. Suggest some sources of error in this experiment which account for the discrepancy between the value of L that you obtained and the accepted value of $L = 6.02 \times 10^{23}$ mol^{-1}.
2. Which of the values that you used in your calculations is subject to the greatest error?
3. Pentane is not the only liquid that can be used in this experiment. Suggest four properties which a suitable substitute must have.

EXPERIMENT 1.2 Preparing a standard solution

Aim The purpose of this experiment is to prepare a standard solution of potassium hydrogenphthalate.

Introduction Potassium hydrogenphthalate, $C_8H_5O_4K$, is a primary standard because it meets certain requirements.
■ It must be available in a highly pure state.
■ It must be stable in air.
■ It must be easily soluble in water.
■ It should have a high molar mass.
■ In solution, when used in volumetric analysis, it must undergo complete and rapid reaction.

Weigh accurately a sample of potassium hydrogenphthalate and use it to make a solution of concentration close to 0.10 mol dm^{-3}. In Experiment 1.3 you use this solution to determine the concentration of a solution of sodium hydroxide.

Requirements
- safety spectacles
- weighing bottle
- spatula
- potassium hydrogenphthalate, $C_8H_5O_4K$
- access to a balance capable of weighing to within 0.01 g
- beaker, 250 cm^3
- wash-bottle of distilled water
- stirring rod with rubber end
- volumetric flask, 250 cm^3, with label
- filter funnel
- dropping pipette

Procedure

1. Transfer between 4.8 g and 5.4 g of potassium hydrogenphthalate into a weighing bottle and weigh it to the nearest 0.01 g.
2. Put about 100 cm^3 of distilled water into a 250 cm^3 beaker. Carefully transfer the bulk of the potassium hydrogenphthalate from the weighing bottle into the beaker.
3. Reweigh the bottle with any remaining potassium hydrogenphthalate to the nearest 0.01 g.
4. Stir to dissolve the solid, using a glass rod with a flattened end. The solid will dissolve faster if you use the flattened end of the rod to grind the crystals to a smaller size. Press the rod down on the crystals and twist. Do **not** 'hammer' the crystals as this may crack the beaker! Stir rapidly and then wait for a few seconds; the undissolved crystals will collect in the centre and you can then repeat the process until all the solid has dissolved. Add some more distilled water if necessary. Rinse any remaining solution on the rod back into the beaker with a little water.
5. Transfer the solution to the volumetric flask through the filter funnel. Rinse the beaker well, making sure all the liquid goes into the volumetric flask.
6. Add distilled water, swirling at intervals to mix the contents but **not** inverting, until the level is within about 1 cm of the mark on the neck of the flask.
7. Using the dropping pipette, add enough water to bring the bottom of the meniscus to the mark as in Fig. 1.5. Insert the stopper and shake thoroughly ten times to ensure complete mixing. Simply inverting the flask once or twice does **not** mix the contents properly and is a very common fault.

Figure 1.5

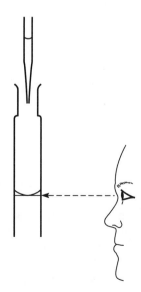

8. Label the flask with the contents, your name and the date. Leave a space for the concentration to be filled in after you have calculated it. Set aside the flask for Experiment 1.3.

Results and calculations

Using your data, you can fill in a copy of Results Table 1.2.

Results Table 1.2

Molar mass of potassium hydrogenphthalate, M	g mol^{-1}
Mass of bottle and contents before transfer, m_1	g
Mass of bottle and contents after transfer, m_2	g
Mass of potassium hydrogenphthalate, $m = (m_1 - m_2)$	g
Amount of potassium hydrogenphthalate, $n = m/M$	mol
Volume of solution, V	dm^3
Concentration of potassium hydrogenphthalate, $c = n/V$	mol dm^{-3}

Question

What effect would each of the errors described below have on the concentration of potassium hydrogenphthalate?

a Some of the solid potassium hydrogenphthalate was spilled in making the transfer.

b Not enough water was added to bring the volume up to the mark.

EXPERIMENT 1.3 An acid–base titration

Aim

The purpose of this experiment is to determine the concentration of a solution of sodium hydroxide by titration against a standard solution of potassium hydrogenphthalate.

Introduction

You have already made a standard solution of potassium hydrogenphthalate, a primary standard. The substance has the formula $C_8H_5O_4K$, but because it behaves as a monoprotic (monobasic) acid in producing one mole of hydrogen ions per mole of compound, we can simplify the formula to HA. This simple formula is often used to represent an acid with a complicated structure.

Sodium hydroxide reacts with potassium hydrogenphthalate according to the equation:

or

$$HA(aq) + Na^+OH^-(aq) \rightarrow Na^+A^-(aq) + H_2O(l)$$

To show you when the reaction is complete – the stoichiometric point or equivalence point – you use an indicator called phenolphthalein, which is colourless in acid and pink in alkaline solution. The point at which the addition of one drop (or even less) of alkali changes the solution from colourless to just faintly pink is called the end-point and, in this case, shows that the reaction is just complete.

Requirements
- safety spectacles
- filter funnel, small
- burette, 50 cm^3, and stand
- two beakers, 100 cm^3
- sodium hydroxide solution (approx. 0.1 M NaOH)
- pipette, 25 cm^3
- pipette filler
- standard potassium hydrogenphthalate solution (prepared in Experiment 1.2)
- four conical flasks, 250 cm^3
- phenolphthalein indicator solution
- white tile
- wash-bottle of distilled water

HAZARD WARNING

Sodium hydroxide solution is very corrosive. Even when dilute it can damage your eyes. Therefore you **must**:
- **wear safety spectacles throughout the experiment.**

Procedure

1. Using the funnel, rinse the burette with the sodium hydroxide solution and fill it with the same solution. Do not forget to rinse and fill the tip. Record the initial burette reading in the 'Trial' column of Results Table 1.3.
2. Using a pipette filler, rinse the pipette with some of the potassium hydrogenphthalate solution and carefully transfer 25.0 cm^3 of the solution to a clean 250 cm^3 conical flask.
3. Add two to three drops of the phenolphthalein indicator solution.
4. Run sodium hydroxide solution from the burette into the flask, with swirling, until the solution just turns pink. This first flask may be used as a trial run, because you will probably overshoot the end-point. Record the final burette reading.
5. Refill the burette with the sodium hydroxide solution, and again record the initial burette reading to the nearest 0.05 cm^3 (one drop).
6. Using the pipette, transfer 25.0 cm^3 of the potassium hydrogenphthalate solution to another clean conical flask. Add two to three drops of the phenolphthalein solution.
7. Carefully titrate this solution to the end-point, adding the alkali drop-by-drop when you think the colour is about to change.
8. Repeat steps 5, 6 and 7 at least twice more.
9. Empty the burette and wash it carefully immediately after the titration, especially if it has a ground glass tap.

Accuracy You should record burette readings to the nearest 0.05 cm^3 (approximately one drop). Consecutive titrations should agree to within 0.10 cm^3 and, strictly, you should repeat the titration until this is achieved. However, you may have neither the time nor the materials to do this. With practice, your technique will improve so that it is not necessary to do more than four titrations. Calculate the mean of the two (or preferably three) closest consecutive readings and quote this also to the nearest 0.05 cm^3. This does not introduce a fourth significant figure; it merely makes the third figure more reliable.

Results Table 1.3

Pipette solution						mol dm^{-3}		cm^3
Burette solution						mol dm^{-3}		
Indicator								
		Trial	1	2	3	(4)		
Burette readings	Final							
	Initial							
Volume used (titre)/cm^3								
Mean titre/cm^3								

Calculation Calculate the concentration of the sodium hydroxide solution.

Questions 1. What effect would each of the errors described below have on the calculated value of the concentration of sodium hydroxide?
  a The burette is not rinsed with the sodium hydroxide solution.
  b The pipette is not rinsed with the potassium hydrogenphthalate solution.
  c The tip of the burette is not filled before titration begins.
  d The conical flask contains some distilled water before the addition of potassium hydrogenphthalate.
2. In using phenolphthalein as an indicator, we prefer to titrate from a colourless to pink solution rather than from pink to colourless. Suggest a reason for this.
3. Why is it advisable to remove sodium hydroxide from the burette as soon as possible after the titration?

EXPERIMENT 1.4 A redox titration

Aim The purpose of this experiment is to balance the equation for the reaction between sodium thiosulphate and iodine.

$$a\, Na_2S_2O_3(aq) + b\, I_2(aq) \rightarrow \text{Products}$$

Introduction You are to determine the ratio of a to b and so determine the stoichiometry of the reaction. You do this by taking a known amount of iodine and titrating it with standard sodium thiosulphate.

  The indicator that you use in this titration is starch solution, which is deep blue in the presence of iodine; it is added near the end of the titration when the solution is straw-coloured. If you add starch too soon, you may get a blue–black precipitate which does not dissolve again easily even though there is an excess of thiosulphate. The end-point in this titration is the point at which the addition of one drop of sodium thiosulphate causes the disappearance of the deep blue colour.

Requirements ■ safety spectacles
■ filter funnel
■ burette, 50 cm^3, and stand
■ two beakers, 100 cm^3
■ sodium thiosulphate solution, standardised
■ pipette, 10 cm^3
■ pipette filler
■ iodine solution, standardised
■ four conical flasks, 250 cm^3

■ starch indicator solution
■ white tile
■ wash-bottle of distilled water

Procedure
1. Using the funnel, rinse the burette and tip with the sodium thiosulphate solution. Fill it with the same solution. Don't forget to fill the tip. Record the initial burette reading in Results Table 1.4.
2. Rinse the pipette with some of the iodine solution and carefully transfer 10.0 cm³ of the solution to one of the conical flasks.
3. Titrate this solution until the colour of the iodine has **almost** gone (as indicated by a pale straw colour).
4. Add 1–2 cm³ of starch solution and continue the titration, adding sodium thiosulphate dropwise until the end-point. Use the first flask for a trial run. Record the final burette reading.
5. Repeat the titration three more times. Enter your results into a copy of Results Table 1.4. These titrations should agree to within 0.10 cm³.

Results Table 1.4

Pipette solution						mol dm⁻³	cm³
Burette solution						mol dm⁻³	
Indicator							
		Trial	1	2	3	(4)	
Burette readings	Final						
	Initial						
Volume used (titre)/cm³							
Mean titre/cm³							

Calculation
1. Use your results to determine the stoichiometric coefficients, a and b, in the equation:

$$a\, Na_2S_2O_3(aq) + b\, I_2(aq) \rightarrow Products$$

2. All the iodine forms sodium iodide, NaI. There is one other product – work out its formula.

EXPERIMENT 1.5 A precipitation titration

Aim
The purpose of this experiment is to determine the number of molecules of water of hydration in hydrated barium chloride, i.e. to calculate the value of x in the formula $BaCl_2 \cdot xH_2O$.

Introduction
You titrate chloride ions with silver ions, according to the equation:

$$Ag^+(aq) + Cl^-(aq) \rightarrow AgCl(s)$$

This provides you with the data necessary to do the calculations. The indicator for the titration is potassium chromate(VI). When all the chloride ions have reacted, any more silver ions react with the indicator producing a red precipitate of silver chromate(VI). This is because silver chloride is less soluble than silver chromate(VI).

$$2Ag^+(aq) + CrO_4^{2-}(aq) \rightarrow Ag_2CrO_4(s)$$

The end-point in this reaction is when one drop of silver ion solution produces a red tinge on the precipitate of silver chloride.

Barium ions also react with chromate ions so the barium must be removed by adding sulphate ions:

$$Ba^{2+}(aq) + SO_4^{2-}(aq) \rightarrow BaSO_4(s)$$

This does not affect the concentration of chloride ions.

Requirements
- safety spectacles
- weighing bottle
- spatula
- barium chloride crystals
- access to balance capable of weighing to 0.01 g
- beaker, 250 cm^3
- wash-bottle of distilled water
- stirring rod with rubber end
- volumetric flask, 250 cm^3, with label
- filter funnel
- dropping pipette
- burette, 50 cm^3, and stand
- two beakers, 100 cm^3
- silver nitrate solution, standardised
- pipette, 10 cm^3
- pipette filler
- four conical flasks, 250 cm^3
- sodium sulphate
- potassium chromate solution
- 'silver residues' bottle

HAZARD WARNING

Barium chloride is harmful if swallowed. Silver nitrate is corrosive and can stain the skin. Therefore you **must**:
- **use the pipette filler provided;**
- **wash your hands after use.**

Procedure

1. Prepare a standard solution of hydrated barium chloride by accurately weighing out between 1.4 g and 1.6 g of the salt. Dissolve this and make up to 250 cm^3 in a volumetric flask. Fill in a copy of Results Table 1.5.
2. Rinse the burette with some silver nitrate solution and fill. Don't forget the tip.
3. Rinse the 10.0 cm^3 pipette with barium chloride solution, and transfer 10.0 cm^3 to a conical flask.
4. Add about 1 g of sodium sulphate crystals to the flask and swirl it.
5. Add two to three drops of potassium chromate(VI) indicator. Titrate the solution to the end-point, as shown by the first appearance of a permanent but faint reddish precipitate of silver chromate(VI). Use the first flask for a trial run. Enter your results in a copy of Results Table 1.6.
6. Repeat steps 2–5 three times. Don't wash the contents of the titration flasks down the sink – pour them into a 'silver residue' bottle.

Results and calculations

Results Table 1.5

Mass of bottle and contents before transfer, m_1	g
Mass of bottle and contents after transfer, m_2	g
Mass of sample, $m = (m_1 - m_2)$	g
Mass of $BaCl_2 \cdot xH_2O$ in 10.0 cm³ of solution	g

Results Table 1.6

Pipette solution						mol dm⁻³	cm³
Burette solution						mol dm⁻³	
Indicator							
		Trial	1	2	3	(4)	
Burette readings	Final						
	Initial						
Volume used (titre)/cm³							
Mean titre/cm³							

Calculation

1. From the mean titre and concentration of silver nitrate, calculate the amount of chloride ions present in a 10.0 cm³ sample.
2. Calculate the mass of anhydrous barium chloride, $BaCl_2$, present in a sample.
3. Calculate the mass of water present by subtracting the mass of $BaCl_2$ from the mass of $BaCl_2 \cdot xH_2O$.
4. Determine the ratio of amount of $BaCl_2$ to amount of H_2O and thus the value of x.

A flow-chart for this multi-step calculation is as follows:

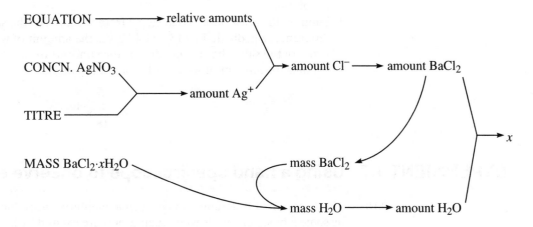

EXPERIMENT 1.6 A titration exercise

Aim

The purpose of this experiment is to determine x in the formula $Fe(NH_4)_2(SO_4)_2 \cdot xH_2O$ by titration against a standard solution of potassium manganate(VII) (permanganate).

Introduction

A is a solution of ammonium iron(II) sulphate, $Fe(NH_4)_2(SO_4)_2 \cdot xH_2O$, the precise concentration of which (in g dm⁻³) is given by the teacher.

B is a solution of potassium manganate(VII), $KMnO_4$ (permanganate), the precise concentration of which (in mol dm⁻³) is given by the teacher.

Results Table 1.7

Pipette solution						mol dm^{-3}	cm^3
Burette solution						mol dm^{-3}	
Indicator							
		Trial	1	2	3	(4)	
Burette readings	Final						
	Initial						
Volume used (titre)/cm^3							
Mean titre/cm^3							

Procedure

Pipette 25 cm^3 of the ammonium iron(II) sulphate solution, A, into a conical flask and add an equal volume of dilute sulphuric acid. Titrate with potassium manganate(VII) solution, B, until a permanent faint pink colour appears. Repeat the titration twice and enter your results in a copy of Results Table 1.7.

The overall equation for the reaction is

$$MnO_4^-(aq) + 5Fe^{2+}(aq) + 8H^+(aq) \rightarrow Mn^{2+}(aq) + 5Fe^{3+}(aq) + 4H_2O(l)$$

Calculation

Use your results to determine x in the formula $Fe(NH_4)_2(SO_4)_2 \cdot xH_2O$. You should set out your calculations so that every step in your working is clearly shown. If you cannot work out a method of calculation, use the suggestions below.

Calculation steps

1. From the titre and the equation for the reaction calculate the concentration of Fe^{2+} ions.
2. From the concentration calculate the mass of anhydrous $Fe(NH_4)_2(SO_4)_2$ in one litre of solution.
3. Subtract the mass obtained in step 2 from the mass of the salt in one litre. This difference, z g, divided by 18 g mol^{-1} gives the amount of water of crystallisation in y mol of the salt, where y mol dm^{-3} is the concentration calculated in step 1.
4. x mol is the amount of water in 1 mol of the salt, i.e.

$$x = \frac{z}{18} \times \frac{1}{y}$$

EXPERIMENT 1.7 Using a hand spectroscope to observe emission spectra

Aim

This experiment is designed to give you a qualitative introduction to the spectra emitted by some s-block elements when their atoms are excited by heating samples in a Bunsen flame.

Introduction

You use a hand spectroscope to observe the continuous spectrum emitted by the tungsten filament of a light bulb. Using a flame test wire, you then obtain coloured emissions from some s-block elements, view these in turn through the spectroscope and compare them with the continuous spectrum from the tungsten filament.

We recommend that you work in pairs in this experiment. All three operations – preparing the flame test wire, obtaining a brightly coloured flame and having the spectroscope ready to look at the flame for the few moments that it lasts – are fairly tricky and require practice and concentration. We suggest that one person prepares the flame while the other stands ready with the spectroscope. You can then change roles so that you both have a chance to observe each spectrum.

Requirements
- safety spectacles
- fume cupboard with gentle fan
- electric lamp with tungsten filament pearl light bulb
- hand spectroscope
- colour plate of spectra
- Bunsen burner and bench protection sheet
- flame test wire (or tongs and supply of filter paper)
- hydrochloric acid, HCl, concentrated
- boiling-tube or other glass container for hydrochloric acid
- small pestle and mortar
- spatulas
- watch glasses

at least three of the following:
- barium chloride, $BaCl_2(s)$
- calcium chloride, $CaCl_2(s)$
- lithium chloride, $LiCl(s)$
- potassium chloride, $KCl(s)$
- sodium chloride, $NaCl(s)$
- strontium chloride, $SrCl_2(s)$

HAZARD WARNING

- **Hydrochloric acid** has a corrosive vapour which irritates and can damage your eyes. Wear safety spectacles and work in the fume cupboard for this experiment.
- **Spectroscope.** *Under no circumstances* must you look through this at the sun. If you do so, your eyes may be permanently damaged.

Procedure

1. Switch on the lamp and look at the bulb through the spectroscope. Look for a series of colours, one running into the next. This is a continuous spectrum. Compare what you see with the coloured plate showing the emission spectrum from a tungsten filament.
2. Hold the spectroscope up to a window which does not face the sun. You must **never** point the spectroscope directly at the sun. This could result in permanent damage to your eyes.
    You should see the continuous spectrum of visible light.
3. Light the Bunsen burner – adjust it to get a roaring flame.
4. Dip the flame test wire into concentrated hydrochloric acid, then hold it in the hottest part of the flame. Repeat the process until there is little or no colour from the flame test wire in the flame. You may have to repeat this step several times, especially towards the end of the experiment, but certainly no more than 12 times.
5. Crush a little of the salt to be tested finely with a pestle and mortar and mix with a little concentrated hydrochloric acid on a watch glass. Be careful here – use just enough of the acid to give you a semi-solid 'mush' of crystals.
6. Dip the cleaned flame test wire into the mush of the salt to be tested. Adjust the flame until it is pale blue and hold the wire in it. Your partner should be standing by with the spectroscope and should now look through it at the flame. Look for brightly coloured lines. (*Alternatively*, hold with tongs a piece of filter paper soaked in a solution of the chloride in the Bunsen flame.)
    There are several lines for each element and it will probably not be possible to get them all into view at once. The yellow line in the sodium spectrum is easy to see and will probably persist through the spectra of all the elements you try. You can use this line to help you locate lines on the spectra of the other elements, by looking either to the right or to the left of it. Checking with the coloured plate of spectra will give you an idea of where to look for lines from a particular element.

7. Repeat steps 3–6 with the salts of at least two other elements. Also use the spectroscope on any other vapour lamps which may be available, including street lamps, if there is one in view from the laboratory.

Question What is the difference between a continuous spectrum and a line emission spectrum?

ILPAC

2

CHEMICAL ENERGETICS

EXPERIMENT 2.1 Determining an enthalpy change of reaction

Aim The purpose of this experiment is to determine the enthalpy change for the displacement reaction:

$$Zn(s) + Cu^{2+}(aq) \rightarrow Cu(s) + Zn^{2+}(aq)$$

Introduction By adding an excess of zinc powder to a measured amount of aqueous copper(II) sulphate, and measuring the temperature change over a period of time, you can then calculate the enthalpy change for the reaction.

Requirements

■ safety spectacles
■ pipette, 25 cm^3
■ pipette filler
■ polystyrene cup with lid
■ copper(II) sulphate solution, 1.00 M CuSO$_4$ (harmful if swallowed)
■ weighing bottle
■ spatula
■ zinc powder
■ balance
■ thermometer, 0–100 °C (0.1° graduations)
■ watch or clock with second hand

Procedure
1. Pipette 25.0 cm^3 of the copper(II) sulphate solution into a polystyrene cup.
2. Weigh about 6 g of zinc powder in the weighing bottle. Since this is an excess, there is no need to be accurate.
3. Put the thermometer through the hole in the lid, stir and record the temperature to the nearest 0.1 °C every half minute for 2½ minutes.
4. At precisely 3 minutes, add the zinc powder to the cup.
5. Continue stirring and record the temperature for an additional 6 minutes to complete a copy of Results Table 2.1.

Results Table 2.1

Time/min	0.0	0.5	1.0	1.5	2.0	2.5	3.0	3.5	4.0	4.5
Temperature/°C							–			
Time/min	5.0	5.5	6.0	6.5	7.0	7.5	8.0	8.5	9.0	9.5
Temperature/°C										

Calculations
1. Plot the temperature (y-axis) against time (x-axis).
2. Extrapolate the curve to 3.0 minutes to establish the maximum temperature rise as shown in Fig. 2.1.

Figure 2.1

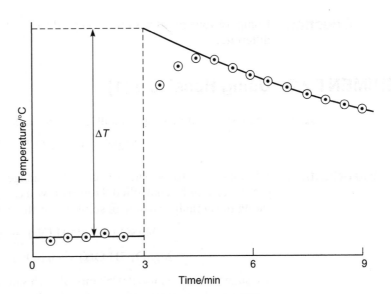

3. Calculate the enthalpy change for the quantities used, making appropriate assumptions.
4. Calculate the enthalpy change for one mole of Zn and $CuSO_4$(aq), and write the thermochemical equation for the reaction.

Questions   1. Compare your result with the accepted value of -217 kJ mol^{-1} by calculating the percentage error in your answer:

$$error = \frac{\text{experimental value} - \text{accepted value}}{\text{accepted value}} \times 100\%$$

2. List possible reasons for any difference between your value and the accepted value.
3. Why do you think the temperature increases for a few readings after adding the zinc? (Hint: it does **not** increase if a large excess of zinc is used or if the powder is very finely divided.)

EXPERIMENT 2.2   Determining an enthalpy change of solution

Aim   The purpose of this experiment is to determine the enthalpy change for the process

$$NH_4Cl(s) + 100H_2O(l) \rightarrow NH_4Cl(aq, 100H_2O)$$

Introduction   Because this is a planning experiment, we give fewer details and instructions than you have been used to. It is, of course, very similar to Experiment 2.1, but you need not plot a temperature/time graph because the maximum temperature change occurs rapidly and is, in any case, much smaller.

Requirements   Make a list of requirements including the masses and amounts needed; show the list to your teacher with your planned procedure.

Procedure   Work this out for yourself and keep an accurate record. Note that ammonium chloride is harmful if swallowed.

Results   1. Tabulate your results in an appropriate form.
2. Calculate the enthalpy change of solution for the thermochemical equation in the aim.

Question Compare your result with the accepted value of $+16.4$ kJ mol^{-1}. Suggest reasons for any difference.

EXPERIMENT 2.3 Using Hess' law (1)

Aim The purpose of this experiment is to determine the enthalpy change for the reaction

$$MgSO_4(s) + 7H_2O(l) \rightarrow MgSO_4 \cdot 7H_2O(s)$$

Introduction It is impossible to measure the enthalpy change for this reaction directly because the process cannot be controlled. However, you can calculate this enthalpy change by measuring the enthalpy change of solution for the two solids:

$$MgSO_4(s) + 100H_2O(l) \rightarrow MgSO_4(aq, 100H_2O)$$

$$MgSO_4 \cdot 7H_2O(s) + 93H_2O(l) \rightarrow MgSO_4(aq, 100H_2O)$$

We suggest that you use 0.0250 mol of each salt, so we have calculated, from the equations, the required masses of each salt and water.

Requirements
- safety spectacles
- 2 weighing bottles
- spatula
- magnesium sulphate (anhydrous), $MgSO_4$
- access to balance
- 2 polystyrene cups and lids
- distilled water
- teat pipette
- thermometer (0–50 °C)
- magnesium sulphate-7-water, $MgSO_4 \cdot 7H_2O$

Procedure – Part A **Heat of solution of $MgSO_4(s)$**
1. Weigh 3.01 g of $MgSO_4$ to the nearest 0.01 g into a clean, dry weighing bottle. Record, in a copy of Results Table 2.2, the masses of weighing bottle empty and with contents, unless your balance has a reliable taring device.
2. Similarly, weigh 45.00 g of H_2O to the nearest 0.01 g into a polystyrene cup.
3. Put the thermometer through the hole in the lid and measure the temperature of the water. Record this in Results Table 2.2.
4. Carefully transfer the $MgSO_4$ into the water, stir gently with the thermometer, and record the maximum temperature.

Procedure – Part B **Heat of solution of $MgSO_4 \cdot 7H_2O(s)$**
5. Weigh 6.16 g of $MgSO_4 \cdot 7H_2O$ to the nearest 0.01 g into a clean, dry weighing bottle.
6. Weigh 41.85 g of H_2O to the nearest 0.01 g into a polystyrene cup.
7. Measure and record the temperature change associated with dissolving the $MgSO_4 \cdot 7H_2O$.

Results Table 2.2

	MgSO$_4$	MgSO$_4$·7H$_2$O
Mass of weighing bottle		
Mass of weighing bottle + salt		
Mass of salt	3.01 g	6.16 g
Mass of polystyrene cup		
Mass of polystyrene cup + water		
Mass of water	45.00 g	41.85 g
Initial temperature		
Final temperature		

Calculations

1. From the data in Results Table 2.2, calculate the enthalpy change of solution for one mole of MgSO$_4$. Assume $c_p = 4.18$ kJ kg^{-1} K^{-1}.
2. Similarly, calculate the enthalpy change of solution for one mole of MgSO$_4$·7H$_2$O.
3. By means of an energy cycle, calculate the enthalpy change for the reaction:

$$MgSO_4(s) + 7H_2O(l) \rightarrow MgSO_4 \cdot 7H_2O(s)$$

Questions

1. Plot the results on an energy-level diagram.
2. Why is it not necessary to plot a temperature/time graph as you did in Experiment 2.1?
3. Compare your result with the accepted value of -104 kJ mol^{-1}. Suggest reasons for any difference.

EXPERIMENT 2.4   Determining enthalpies of combustion

Aim

The purpose of this experiment is to determine the heats of combustion of a series of similar alcohols from butan-1-ol to octan-1-ol.

Introduction

In this experiment, you burn a measured mass of an alcohol in a spirit lamp and transfer the heat energy released to a calorimeter containing water. From the resulting temperature rise you can calculate the heat of combustion.

In your earlier calorimetric experiments, you assumed that **all** the heat energy released in a chemical reaction was absorbed by the contents of the calorimeter. You cannot make that assumption in this experiment for two reasons.

1. The heat energy is released in a flame, and although the apparatus is designed to transfer most of the energy to the calorimeter, a significant quantity is lost to the surrounding air.
2. The heat capacity of the calorimeter itself is **not** so small as to be insignificant compared with the heat capacity of its contents.

You can take account of both these factors by calibrating the apparatus using an alcohol with known heat of combustion.

Requirements

- safety spectacles
- heat of combustion apparatus
- spirit lamp
- wood block
- retort stand (with 2 clamps and bosses)
- Drechsel bottle

- filter pump
- rubber tubing (for connections to filter pump)
- water (at room temperature)
- adhesive labels
- propan-1-ol, C_3H_7OH
- butan-1-ol, C_4H_9OH
- pentan-1-ol, $C_5H_{11}OH$
- hexan-1-ol, $C_6H_{13}OH$
- heptan-1-ol, $C_7H_{15}OH$
- octan-1-ol, $C_8H_{17}OH$

(If these alcohols are supplied in separate spirit lamps, you will not need the next two items.)

- 6 beakers, 50 cm^3
- 6 teat pipette droppers
- Bunsen burner and protective mat
- wood splints
- tweezers (not plastic-tipped)
- balance (preferably capable of weighing to 0.001 g, but 0.01 g will do)
- thermometer −5 to −50 °C (in 0.1°C)

HAZARD WARNING

The alcohols you will be using are highly flammable and are harmful by absorption through the skin and lungs. Therefore you **must**:
- **keep the stoppers on the bottles when not in use;**
- **keep the bottles away from flames;**
- **wash your hands after use (or wear gloves);**
- **wear safety spectacles.**

Procedure

Determination of the heat capacity of the apparatus

1. Arrange the heat of combustion apparatus (i.e. the calorimeter), the Drechsel bottle, etc., as shown in Fig. 2.2. Don't use the calorimeter base supplied by the manufacturer but stand the burner on a small block of wood to ensure a good flow of air. Adjust the height of the calorimeter (or the size of the block) so that the top of the spirit lamp is level with the bottom of the calorimeter.

Figure 2.2
Heat of combustion apparatus.

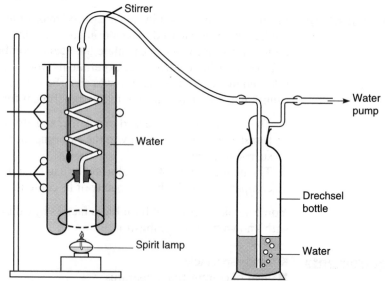

2. Use water at room temperature (not direct from the tap) to fill the calorimeter to about 1.5 cm below the rim. Mark this level with a label.
3. Pour a little propan-1-ol into a small beaker and use a teat pipette to half-fill the spirit lamp. (This may have been done for you already.) Replace the wick and cap,

return any excess alcohol to the bottle, and remove both bottle and beaker to a safe distance from any flame.

4. Turn on the filter pump and adjust the flow of air through the Drechsel bottle to about 3–4 bubbles per second.

5. Stand the spirit lamp away from the calorimeter, and use a wood splint to light it. Adjust the height of the wick, using metal tweezers, to obtain a flame about 1 cm high.

6. Check that the lamp burns satisfactorily for about 15 seconds in position under the calorimeter. If it goes out, either increase the flow of air or adjust the height of the lamp relative to the calorimeter. Once these adjustments have been made, **they should not be changed** for the rest of the experiment. Extinguish the flame and put on the cap.

7. Weigh the spirit lamp, including the cap, as accurately as possible and record the mass in Results Table 2.3.

8. Stir the water in the calorimeter and record its temperature, to the nearest 0.1°C.

9. Put the lamp under the calorimeter and light it.

10. Slowly and continuously stir the water in the calorimeter and watch the thermometer. When the temperature has risen by about 10°C, extinguish the flame and immediately replace the cap. Keep stirring and record the maximum temperature of the water.

11. Re-weigh the spirit lamp and cap and record the mass.

12. Without removing the calorimeter from the stand, and holding **both together carefully**, pour away the water.

13. If you have time, repeat the experiment to increase the accuracy of your calibration. This second run should be much quicker because you should not need to make any adjustments (i.e. omit steps 1 and 3–6).

14. Before doing any calculations, repeat the experiment using as many of the other alcohols as you have time for and complete Results Table 2.4. If you have to use the same spirit lamp, you will have to empty it, rinse it with the new alcohol, and fit a new wick (or dry the old wick). If time is limited, your teacher may suggest that you share your results with other students, or may give you some pre-determined results.

Results Table 2.3

	1st run	2nd run	
Molar mass of propan-1-ol, M			g mol^{-1}
Initial mass of spirit lamp + alcohol, m_1			g
Final mass of spirit lamp + alcohol, m_2			g
Mass of alcohol burned, $m_1 - m_2$			g
Amount of alcohol burned, $n = (m_1 - m_2)/M$			mol
Initial temperature of calorimeter			°C
Final temperature of calorimeter			°C
Temperature change, ΔT			K
ΔH_c°[propan-1-ol] (given)		–2017	kJ mol^{-1}
Heat released during the experiment, ΔH $\quad = \Delta H_c^{\circ}$[propan-1-ol] × amount burned $\quad = -2017$ kJ mol$^{-1} \times n$			kJ
Heat required for a rise in temperature of 1 K $= \dfrac{\Delta H}{\Delta T} = C$, the calorimeter calibration factor			kJ K^{-1}
Average value of C			kJ K^{-1}

Results Table 2.4

	C_4H_9OH	$C_5H_{11}OH$	$C_6H_{13}OH$	$C_7H_{15}OH$	$C_8H_{17}OH$
Molar mass, M/g mol^{-1}					
Initial mass of lamp/g					
Final mass of lamp/g					
Mass of alcohol burned/g					
Amount burned, n/mol					
Initial temperature/°C					
Final temperature/°C					
Temperature change, ΔT/K					
$\Delta H_c = \dfrac{C \times \Delta T}{n}$/kJ mol^{-1}					

EXPERIMENT 2.5 A thermometric titration

Aim

The purpose of this experiment is to determine the concentrations of two acids, hydrochloric acid, HCl, and ethanoic acid, CH_3CO_2H, by thermometric titration; and having done that, to calculate the enthalpy change for each reaction – the enthalpy change of neutralisation.

Introduction

You titrate both hydrochloric acid and ethanoic acid in turn with a standardised solution of sodium hydroxide and record the temperature of the mixtures during the course of the titrations. In each case a plot of temperature against time will enable you to determine the maximum temperature rise, from which you calculate both the concentration of the acid and the enthalpy change of neutralisation.

Requirements

■ safety spectacles
■ pipette, 50.0 cm^3
■ pipette filler
■ expanded polystyrene cup
■ sodium hydroxide solution, 1 M NaOH (standardised)
■ thermometer, 0–50 °C (in 0.1 °C)
■ burette, 50.0 cm^3, and stand
■ filter funnel, small
■ hydrochloric acid, ~ 2.0 M HCl
■ ethanoic acid, ~ 2.0 M CH_3CO_2H

HAZARD WARNING

Sodium hydroxide solution is corrosive. Ethanoic acid and hydrochloric acid solutions are irritants. Therefore you **must**:
■ **use the pipette filler supplied;**
■ **wear safety spectacles.**

Procedure – Part A

Titration of hydrochloric acid with standard sodium hydroxide solution

1. Using a pipette and filler, transfer 50.0 cm^3 of NaOH solution into the polystyrene cup. Allow to stand for a few minutes.
2. Record the temperature of the solution.

3. From a burette, add 5.0 cm³ of HCl solution to the cup.
4. Stir the mixture with the thermometer and record its temperature. Work quickly to minimise heat loss to the surroundings.
5. Add successive 5.0 cm³ portions of HCl solution, stirring the mixture and recording its temperature after each addition.
6. Record your results in a copy of Results Table 2.5. Stop after the addition of 50.0 cm³ of acid.

Procedure – Part B

Titration of ethanoic acid with standard sodium hydroxide solution
7. Follow the same procedure as you did for the titration of HCl, except that you use ethanoic acid in the burette. When filling the burette, remember to use correct rinsing procedures. If in doubt, ask your teacher.
8. Record your results in a copy of Results Table 2.6.

Results Table 2.5
Titration of hydrochloric acid

Volume added/cm³	0.0	5.0	10.0	15.0	20.0	25.0	30.0	35.0	40.0	45.0	50.0
Temperature/°C											

Results Table 2.6
Titration of ethanoic acid

Volume added/cm³	0.0	5.0	10.0	15.0	20.0	25.0	30.0	35.0	40.0	45.0	50.0
Temperature/°C											

Calculation

1. Plot temperature (y-axis) against volume of acid added (x-axis) for each acid on the same graph.
2. Extrapolate the curves as shown in Fig. 2.3. The point at which they meet corresponds to both the volume of acid required for neutralisation and to the maximum temperature.
3. Calculate the concentration of each of the acids.

Figure 2.3

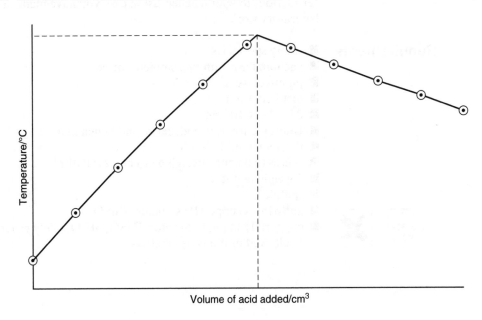

Volume of acid added/cm³

4. From the maximum temperature rise, determine the quantity of energy released in each titration. Assume that the specific heat capacity of the solutions is the same as that for water, $4.18 \text{ kJ kg}^{-1}\text{K}^{-1}$ and that the heat capacity of the cup is zero.

5. Calculate the standard enthalpy change of neutralisation for each reaction.

Questions

1. The enthalpy change of neutralisation for a very dilute strong acid (i.e. an acid which is completely ionised in solution) reacting with a very dilute strong base is constant at $-57.6 \text{ kJ mol}^{-1}$, where mol^{-1} refers to one mole of water produced. Why is the value constant?

2. Experimental results for hydrochloric acid are usually a little less negative than $-57.6 \text{ kJ mol}^{-1}$. Suggest two reasons for this.

3. Ethanoic acid is a weak acid, i.e. it is not completely ionised in solution. Suggest a reason why the enthalpies of neutralisation for reactions involving weak acids and/or weak bases are always less negative than for strong acids and bases.

EXPERIMENT 2.6 Using Hess' law (2)

Aim

The purpose of this experiment is to determine the enthalpy change for the reaction

$$CuSO_4(s) + 5H_2O(l) \rightarrow CuSO_4 \cdot 5H_2O(s)$$

Introduction

Because $CuSO_4(s)$ is slow to dissolve, and $\Delta H°$ is small, it is best to do this experiment in a vacuum flask. However, the flask has a measurable heat capacity which you must determine before you proceed with the experiment.

To calculate the required enthalpy change, you perform two 'heat of solution' determinations. You should calculate the masses of the salts and water required. Base your calculations on the following equations

$$CuSO_4(s) + 100H_2O(l) \rightarrow CuSO_4(aq, 100H_2O)$$

$$CuSO_4 \cdot 5H_2O(s) + 95H_2O(l) \rightarrow CuSO_4(aq, 100H_2O)$$

and use 0.025 mol of the appropriate salt in each of the determinations. Show your calculations to your teacher just in case you have made an error which would spoil your laboratory work.

Requirements

- safety spectacles
- vacuum flask with thermometer fitted
- pipette, 50 cm^3
- distilled water
- 2 beakers, 100 cm^3
- Bunsen burner, tripod, gauze and bench mat
- thermometer, 0–100 °C
- access to balance (weighing to nearest 0.01 g)
- 2 weighing bottles
- spatula
- anhydrous copper(II) sulphate, $CuSO_4$

- copper(II) sulphate-5-water, $CuSO_4 \cdot 5H_2O$, finely ground beforehand (harmful if swallowed or if dust is inhaled)

Figure 2.4

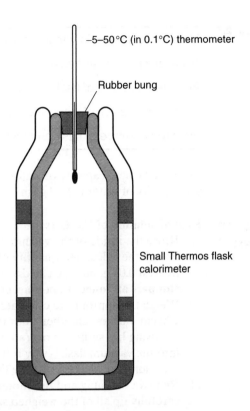

−5–50 °C (in 0.1°C) thermometer

Rubber bung

Small Thermos flask
calorimeter

**Procedure
– Part A**

Determination of the heat capacity of the vacuum flask

1. Check that the inside of the vacuum flask is reasonably dry and pipette into it 50 cm³ of distilled water at room temperature.
2. Place the thermometer-fitted bung in position and shake gently. Make sure that the entire inside surface of the flask is wet. To read the steady temperature, hold the bung firmly in and turn the flask on its side so that the water covers the mercury reservoir of the thermometer. Read the steady temperature to the nearest 0.1°C. Leave the bung and thermometer in position.
3. Pipette 50 cm³ of distilled water into a clean, dry 100 cm³ beaker and heat it gently until its temperature reaches about 40 °C – use a small 0–100 °C thermometer. Remove from heat.
4. Use the thermometer from the vacuum flask (with bung still fitted) to gently stir the water in the beaker to ensure its temperature is uniform throughout. Record this temperature to the nearest 0.1 °C.
5. **Immediately** pour all of the warmed distilled water into the vacuum flask, close with bung and thermometer, shake gently and note the steady temperature to the nearest 0.1 °C. Remember to wet the inside surface and tilt the flask to read the temperature as before.
6. Complete Results Table 2.7 and then, if you have time, repeat the procedure. It is good practice to do the determination twice and average the results. Furthermore, because this is the first time you have done such an experiment, the second determination should improve your technique.
7. To make best use of laboratory time, we suggest that you complete parts B and C of the experiment before calculating the heat capacity of the flask.

Results Table 2.7

Mass of cold water in vacuum flask	g	g
Mass of warm water added	g	g
Initial temperature of flask and cold water	°C	°C
Initial temperature of warm water	°C	°C
Final temperature of flask and mixture	°C	°C

The specific heat capacity of water is $4.18 \, \text{kJ kg}^{-1} \text{K}^{-1}$.
The density of water is $1.00 \, \text{g cm}^{-3}$.

Procedure – Part B

Heat of solution of $CuSO_4(s)$

8. Rinse the inside of the vacuum flask with distilled water **and drain well**.
9. Weigh the calculated quantity of anhydrous copper(II) sulphate ($CuSO_4$), to the nearest 0.01 g, into a clean dry weighing bottle. (**Do not keep bottle lids and/or stoppers off longer than is necessary**. Why not?)
10. Weigh the appropriate calculated quantity of water, to the nearest 0.1 g, into a dry $100 \, \text{cm}^3$ beaker, and then pour this water into the vacuum flask. (If the balance you are using has sufficient overall weighing capacity, you may weigh the water directly into the vacuum flask – why is it better to do this?) Close with bung and thermometer, shake, and note the steady temperature, tilting the flask as before.
11. Remove the bung and thermometer from the vacuum flask and quickly and carefully tip **all** of the weighed sample of anhydrous copper(II) sulphate into the water. Replace the bung and thermometer, shake to dissolve the salt, and note the temperature once it has become steady. **This last step may take up to 15 min** (shaking periodically) because the anhydrous salt is often very slow to dissolve.
12. Return the copper sulphate solution to the technician. It could be used for other experiments. If it is not required it must be diluted with a large volume of water before being poured away.
13. Complete Results Table 2.8 and then move on to part C.

Results Table 2.8

Mass of anhydrous copper(II) sulphate	g
Mass of water	g
Initial temperature of vacuum flask and water	°C
Maximum temperature of vacuum flask and solution	°C

Procedure – Part C

Heat of solution of $CuSO_4 \cdot 5H_2O$ (s)

Wash out your apparatus and then repeat the procedure in part B using the hydrated salt ($CuSO_4 \cdot 5H_2O$). In this second determination the salt dissolves quickly in step 11 and the final steady temperature will be obtained within half a minute. Complete Results Table 2.9.

Results Table 2.9

Mass of anhydrous copper(II) sulphate-5-water	g
Mass of water	g
Initial temperature of vacuum flask and water	°C
Maximum temperature of vacuum flask and solution	°C

Calculation – Part A

Heat capacity of flask

1. Since the flask is insulated, no heat energy is transferred between system and surroundings (in this case, the flask is part of the system). Therefore you can write:

$$\left[\begin{array}{c}\text{Change in heat} \\ \text{energy of flask}\end{array}\right] + \left[\begin{array}{c}\text{Change in heat} \\ \text{energy of cold water}\end{array}\right] + \left[\begin{array}{c}\text{Change in heat} \\ \text{energy of warm water}\end{array}\right] = 0$$

2. In each case, the change in heat energy = heat capacity $\times \Delta T$
   and for the water, heat capacity = mass $\times$ specific heat capacity
   $$= \text{mass} \times 4.18 \text{ kJ kg}^{-1} \text{ K}^{-1}$$

3. Substitute values from Results Table 2.7 into these expressions and so obtain a value for the heat capacity, C, of the flask. Remember that ΔT is positive for the flask and the cold water but negative for the hot water, and also that the mass must be in kg.

Calculation – Parts B and C

Enthalpy changes

1. Again, there is no heat energy transfer between system and surroundings so that:

$$\left[\begin{array}{c}\text{Change in heat} \\ \text{energy of flask}\end{array}\right] + \left[\begin{array}{c}\text{Change in heat} \\ \text{energy of contents}\end{array}\right] + \left[\begin{array}{c}\text{Enthalpy change} \\ \text{of solution}\end{array}\right] = 0$$

2. Use this expression and values from Results Tables 2.8 and 2.9 to obtain the enthalpy changes for dissolving the weighed amounts of the two salts. Ignore the very small heat capacities of the salts, i.e. use the mass and specific heat capacity of the **water** in your calculations.

3. Scale up to the amounts shown in the equations.

4. Use Hess' law to calculate the required standard enthalpy change.

Questions

1. Suggest a reason why it would be difficult to determine, by **direct** experiment, ΔH° for the reaction

$$CuSO_4(s) + 5H_2O(l) \rightarrow CuSO_4 \cdot 5H_2O(s)$$

2. Why is it good practice to replace the stoppers/lids of chemical bottles as soon as possible?

3. Why, in step 10 of part B of the experiment, would it be better to weigh the water directly into the vacuum flask rather than in a beaker?

ILPAC

3

BONDING AND STRUCTURE

EXPERIMENT 3.1 Making models of two metallic structures

Aim The aim of the experiment is to make and compare models of two structures commonly found in metals – cubic close-packing and hexagonal close-packing. In the course of the construction, the concepts of close-packing, co-ordination number, and unit cell are illustrated and clarified.

Introduction The model-building experiment is in the form of a Revealing Exercise. You should cover with a sheet of paper that part of the page below the next ruled line until you have followed the instruction and answered the question above the line.

  You will use expanded polystyrene spheres to represent atoms of metals and stick them together with small blobs of Blu-tak or a similar demountable adhesive. To get maximum rigidity, you should use adhesive on **every** contact (except where you are told not to do so!) and press the spheres firmly together so that they are as close as possible.

  Do not dismantle any structure until the end except where you are told.

Requirements ■ 31 expanded polystyrene spheres
■ Blu-tak or similar adhesive

Procedure 1. Put one sphere on a flat surface and surround it with as many others as you can fit in the same plane, i.e. all must touch both the flat surface and the central sphere. Stick the surrounding spheres together but not to the central sphere (you will need to remove it later).

Q1 How many spheres touch the central sphere, and what shape would be outlined by joining their centres?

A1 Six spheres touch the central sphere, outlining a regular hexagon.

2. You have just constructed part of a close-packed layer or plane. Satisfy yourself that this arrangement can be continued to infinity in any direction by adding more spheres (without sticking) around any of the outer ones.

Q2 What is the co-ordination number of any sphere in an infinite close-packed layer?

A2 Six. Note that this refers only to a two-dimensional structure. You will work out the co-ordination number for a three-dimensional structure later.

3. Stick three more spheres to your hexagon to make a triangular layer. Now you will extend close-packing to three dimensions. Try a single sphere, without adhesive, in different positions as part of a second layer to help you answer Q3 and Q4.

Q3 What is the maximum number of spheres in the first layer that can be touched by a single sphere in the second layer?

A3 Three.

Q4 How many sites are there where you can add a single sphere in the second layer so that it touches three others in the first layer?

A4 Nine. These are shown by crosses in Fig. 3.1.

4. Add more spheres to make a close-packed second layer – do not stick them together yet.

Figure 3.1

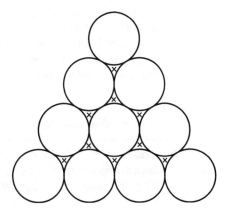

Q5 How many of the nine sites can you actually use to make a close-packed layer?

A5 Either six or three. In an infinite layer, half the sites can be used, corresponding to alternate crosses in Fig. 3.1.

5. Consider both ways of adding the second layer – adding three spheres or six spheres – and answer the questions for each of the ways.

Q6 a Is the second layer close-packed?
 b Is it close-packed with respect to the first layer?
 c If the layers were extended in all directions, could you distinguish between the two ways of adding the second layer?

A6 a Yes, for both ways.
 b Yes, for both ways.
 c No, the two ways of adding the second layer are indistinguishable. It is only the fact that you are looking at a small part of the structure that makes them **seem** different.

6. Arrange your second layer to have six close-packed spheres and stick them together as a triangle. This is best done on a flat surface – then lift the complete layer back into position. Do not stick the layers together.
 Now consider the different ways of adding a third layer.

Q7 How many close-packing sites are there? Can you use them all?

A7 There are four sites. You can use three or one. In an extended layer, **half** the sites can be used.

7. Look carefully at the four sites from a position vertically above each one, so that you look through to the first layer.

Q8 Is there any difference between the sites? If so, what difference can you see?

A8 The central site is directly above a sphere in the first layer. The other three sites are directly above holes in the first layer.

8. Use the three outer sites to make a third layer. Stick the spheres together but not to the second layer.

Now stick another sphere in position to make a fourth layer. You have now constructed a model of part of the structure adopted by many metals, e.g. copper, silver and gold. This structure is known by two names – *abc* close-packing or cubic close-packing. It is sometimes called a face-centred cubic structure, which is correct but not precise because there are other face-centred cubic structures.

Q9 Why do you think the structure is known as *abc* close-packing? (You have answered this in a different way in Q8.)

A9 The third layer is not directly above the first, but the fourth layer is. The first three layers are referred to as *a*, *b* and *c*, while the fourth is regarded as another *a* layer. The sequence continues *abcabcabcabc* ... .

9. It is not so easy to see why the structure is called cubic, although you may perhaps know that the shape of your pyramid is a regular tetrahedron which fits into a cube with its points at four of the eight corners, as shown in Fig. 3.2.

Figure 3.2

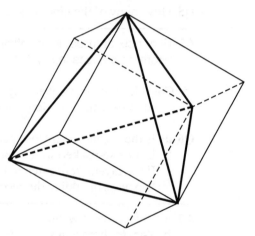

To show the cubic nature of the structure more clearly, take the second layer of your tetrahedron, six spheres still firmly stuck together, and place it on a flat surface. Stick one more sphere in the central site so that you have a two-layer structure of seven spheres.

Make another identical seven-sphere structure by adding three spheres to the third and fourth layers removed from the tetrahedron.

Hold one structure in each hand by means of the single sphere and bring the two six-sphere triangles together. Then rotate one triangle until it fits into the other, using three close-packing sites in each triangle.

Q10 Describe the structure you now have in a few words – what is its overall shape and how do the spheres fit into it?

A10 It is a cube, each face of which has a sphere at each corner and one at the centre touching the other four – hence the name 'face-centred cubic'.

Q11 Do the faces of your cube represent close-packed layers?

A11 No. The co-ordination number is 4 and not 6.

Q12 Where are the close-packed layers in the cube?

A12 Along planes joining any diagonal of a face with **one** other corner. The shaded spheres in Fig. 3.3 make one such layer.

Figure 3.3

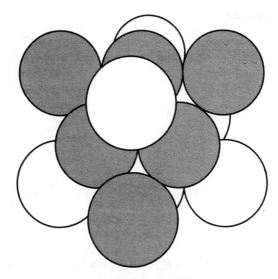

Q13   What is the co-ordination number of any sphere in the extended structure?

A13   Twelve. Six touch it in one close-packed layer, three in the layer above, and three in the layer below.

10. Turn the cube and stand it on one corner so that the close-packed planes are horizontal. There are four such planes, containing 1, 6, 6 and 1 sphere. Check that the sequence is *abca* as in A9.

   Another way of seeing that the face-centred cube you have made has the same structure as the pyramid you built at first is to remove the central sphere from the original first layer and stand the cube with a corner sphere in the hole in such a way that the original pyramid shape can be seen, but with an extra sphere projecting from three of its faces.

   Draw an outline cube and draw small blobs (ideally they should be just points) in positions corresponding to the centres of the spheres in your model structure. Compare your drawing with drawings in your textbook. The drawing represents the unit cell of the cubic close-packed structure since the whole structure can be built up by repeating it.

Q14   However, the face-centred cube you have made from spheres is not, strictly speaking, a unit cell. Can you see why not?

A14   The stacking of identical cubes side-by-side would **not** repeat the structure, unless the spheres are regarded as being **shared** between neighbouring cubes, as in Fig. 3.4 (see page 34). You will do an exercise later which will make clearer the sharing of spheres between neighbouring unit cells.

Figure 3.4

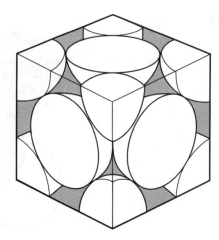

11. Now you will investigate the structure made by using the second way of arranging the third layer.

    Return half of your face-centred cube to the hole in the first layer so that you have two triangular layers just as you did at the beginning. You recall that to make the cubic close-packed structure, the third layer spheres used the outer three close-packing sites. This time, place a sphere in the central site and stick six more spheres to it to make a third layer.

Q15 How do the positions of the third layer spheres relate to those in the first layer?

A15 Each sphere is vertically above a sphere in the first layer.

12. You have now made a model of part of the structure adopted by a number of other metals, e.g. magnesium and calcium. This structure is also known by two names – *aba* close-packing or hexagonal close-packing.

Q16 Why is it called *aba* close-packing?

A16 The third layer is directly above the first. Compare this with cubic close-packing where the fourth layer is directly above the first.

13. The hexagonal nature of the structure is best seen by removing the three corner spheres from the first layer and making these three the second layer (first filling the hole in the first layer). Finally, replace the third layer directly above the first, so that the overall hexagonal shape is apparent.

    Compare your model with drawings in your textbooks and with a permanent model if one is available. You should be able to draw an outline of the hexagonal close-packed unit cell using only dots and lines as you did for cubic close-packing. Remember that your model is not strictly a unit cell unless spheres are shared with neighbouring cells.

14. Before you dismantle your models, look at them again, side by side, and make sure that you can:
    a pick out the close-packed layers,
    b see that the overall co-ordination number is 12 in both cases,
    c draw unit cells, representing the centres of spheres by dots.

EXPERIMENT 3.2   Recognising ionic, covalent and metallic structures

Aim   The aim of this experiment is to examine some unknown substances and to determine their structures (as far as possible) using the minimum number of tests.

Introduction   Several tests are suggested, as shown in Results Table 3.1. You should devise your own simple procedures, using only the apparatus provided, but we recommend that you complete work on one substance before examining another.

Do not necessarily perform every test on each substance, but aim at getting the maximum information from the minimum number of tests. The result of one test may suggest which test to do next. In some cases, it may not be possible to come to a definite conclusion. In estimating melting points to the nearest 100°C, you should note that the maximum temperature of an ordinary Bunsen burner flame is about 800°C.

Requirements
- safety spectacles
- 6 test-tubes in rack
- 6 ignition tubes
- test-tube holder
- Bunsen burner and protective mat
- beaker, 100 cm^3
- battery and lamp in holder
- 2 carbon electrodes
- 3 connecting leads with crocodile clips
- unknown substances, in bottles labelled A–G

Results Table 3.1

	A	B	C	D	E	F	G
Appearance							
Estimate of melting point							
Solubility in water							
Conductivity of solution							
Conductivity of solid							
Action of dilute HCl							
Structure							

Questions   1. What further tests would probably help to identify the structures which you could not identify in the experiment?
2. Why is it more difficult to recognise a powdered metal than a solid lump?

EXPERIMENT 3.3 Testing liquids for polarity

Aim The purpose of this experiment is to test a number of liquids in order to find out if their molecules are polar.

Introduction In this experiment you study the effect of a charged rod on a stream of liquid from a burette. A deflection of the stream indicates that the liquid consists of polar molecules.

Figure 3.5

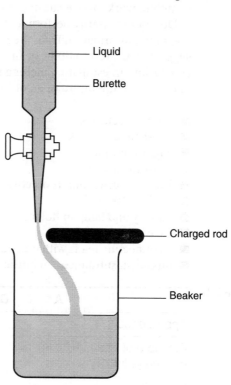

The extent of the deflection, under standard conditions, shows how polar the molecules are.

Requirements
■ 6 dry beakers, with labels
■ 6 labelled burettes in stands, each corked and containing one of the following liquids:
    cyclohexane, C_6H_{12}
    cyclohexene, C_6H_{10}
    distilled water, H_2O
    hexan-1-ol, $C_6H_{13}OH$
    methyl ethanoate, $CH_3CO_2CH_3$
    propanone, CH_3COCH_3
■ 6 small funnels
■ polythene rod
■ piece of fur or suitable cloth

Procedure   1. Rub the polythene rod with the fur. This will give it a negative charge.
2. Position a beaker beneath the jet of one of the burettes as shown in Fig. 3.5. Remove the cork and allow a stream of the liquid to run from the burette with the tap fully open.
3. Bring the charged rod close to the stream of liquid and note any deflection that occurs. Also note the extent of deflection on an arbitrary scale from 0 to 3 (0 = no deflection; 3 = greatest deflection). Record your results in a copy of Results Table 3.2.
4. Pour the liquid from the beaker back into the labelled burette to avoid waste. Leave this set up in a fume cupboard with the cork replaced in the top of the burette. This is then ready for other students to use.
5. Repeat the above procedure with each liquid in turn. Try to standardise the conditions, otherwise your rating of the deflection will be worthless. The liquid level in the burettes, the tap aperture, the position of the rod, and the extent to which the rod is charged should always be the same.

Results Table 3.2

Compound	Formula	Structural formula	Deflection
Cyclohexane			
Cyclohexene			
Hexane*	C_6H_{14}	(see structure below)	0
Hexan-1-ol			
Methyl ethanoate			
Propanone			
Tetrachloromethane*	CCl_4	(see structure below)	0
Trichloromethane*	$CHCl_3$	(see structure below)	3
Water			

Hexane structural formula:

```
    H   H   H   H   H   H
    |   |   |   |   |   |
H — C — C — C — C — C — C — H
    |   |   |   |   |   |
    H   H   H   H   H   H
```

Tetrachloromethane structural formula:

```
      Cl
      |
Cl — C — Cl
      |
      Cl
```

Trichloromethane structural formula:

```
      Cl
      |
Cl — C — Cl
      |
      H
```

*You should not test these three liquids yourself but they are included in the results table and specimen results for discussion purposes.

Questions   1. Explain the effect of the charged rod on a jet of water.
2. What do you think would happen with a rod of opposite charge? Explain your answer.
3. Place the liquids in an approximate order of decreasing polarity. Interpret this order in terms of the structure of each molecule and comment particularly on the different results in the following pairs of liquids:
   a trichloromethane, $CHCl_3$, and tetrachloromethane, CCl_4;
   b cyclohexane, C_6H_{12}, and cyclohexene, C_6H_{10}.
4. How would the different densities of the liquids affect the results?

EXPERIMENT 3.4   The effect of hydrogen bonding on liquid flow

Aim   The purpose of this experiment is to compare the viscosities of four different liquids and to interpret the results in terms of hydrogen bonding.

Introduction   You are supplied with sealed tubes containing four different liquids. Each tube has a small air bubble trapped at one end. If the tubes are inverted in turn, the time it takes for the air bubble to travel through the length of the tube can be taken as a measure of the intermolecular forces in the liquid.

Requirements   ■ 4 sealed tubes containing:
      propan-1-ol
      propane-1,2-diol
      propane-1,2,3-triol
      propane-1,2,3-triyl triethanoate
  ■ stopclock or stopwatch

Procedure   Invert each tube in turn and measure the time it takes for the air bubble to travel through the length of the tube. Record your results in a copy of Results Table 3.3.

Results Table 3.3

Liquid	Formula	Time/s
Propan-1-ol	$CH_3CH_2CH_2OH$	
Propane-1,2-diol	$CH_3CH(OH)CH_2OH$	
Propane-1,2,3-triol	$CH_2(OH)CH(OH)CH_2OH$	
Propane-1,2,3-triyl triethanoate	$CH_2(OCOCH_3)CH(OCOCH_3)CH_2OCOCH_3$	

Questions   1. Account for the differences in viscosity between the three alcohols you have investigated.
     2. Propane-1,2,3-triyl triethanoate has much larger molecules than propane-1,2,3-triol, and yet it is much less viscous. Why is this?

EXPERIMENT 3.5   Variation of boiling point with composition of a mixture

Aim   The purpose of this experiment is to construct boiling point/composition curves for mixtures of two different liquids.

Introduction   In this experiment you study one or both of the following systems:
  1. ethanol and cyclohexane,
  2. propan-1-ol and propan-2-ol.
Specimen results are given for a third system as well for discussion of theoretical points.

    You measure the boiling points of these mixtures at various compositions and construct boiling point/composition curves from your results. Inversion of these curves into vapour pressure/composition curves will then enable you to describe the deviation from ideality (if any) for each mixture. For simplicity, you plot volume composition rather than mole fraction – the curves have the same general shape.

Requirements   ■ safety spectacles
  ■ ground-glass-joint apparatus in Fig. 3.6a or 3.6b
  ■ thermometer, 0–100 °C, ± 0.1°C
  ■ anti-bumping granules

- 2 burettes and stands
- 2 small funnels
- test-tube
- Bunsen burner, gauze and tripod
- ethanol, C_2H_5OH
- cyclohexane, C_6H_{12}
- propan-1-ol, $CH_3CH_2CH_2OH$
- propan-2-ol, $CH_3CH(OH)CH_3$

HAZARD WARNING

Ethanol, cyclohexane, propan-1-ol and propan-2-ol are highly flammable.
Therefore you **must:**
- **keep the stoppers on the bottles as much as possible;**
- **keep the bottles away from flames;**
- **wear safety spectacles.**

Figure 3.6a

**Figure 3.6b
(right)**

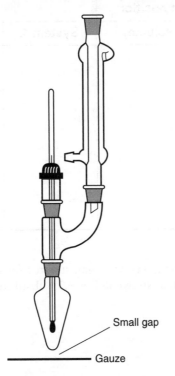

Small gap

Gauze

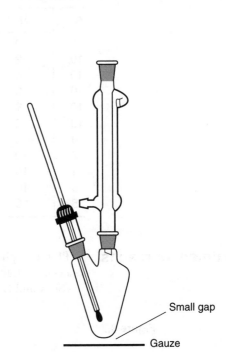

Small gap

Gauze

Procedure

1. Set up a suitable assembly for reflux, either Fig. 3.6a or Fig. 3.6b, with the flask positioned over a tripod and gauze. It is important that the thermometer is positioned so that it will dip into the liquid mixture but it must not touch the walls of the flask.

2. Choose one of the first two systems shown in Table 3.1 and, if possible, ensure that other students in your class investigate the other system. In the remaining procedure steps we refer to the components of each system as A or B, as shown in Table 3.1. You should not test system 3 yourself.

Table 3.1

System	Component A	Component B
1	ethanol, C_2H_5OH	cyclohexane, C_6H_{12}
2	propan-1-ol, $CH_3(CH_2)_2OH$	propan-2-ol, $CH_3CH(OH)CH_3$
3	trichloromethane, $CHCl_3$	methyl ethanoate, $CH_3CO_2CH_3$

3. Pour 20 cm^3 of A and 20 cm^3 of B into separate labelled burettes.
4. Transfer 10.0 cm^3 of A from the burette to the pear-shaped flask containing a few anti-bumping granules. Heat the flask **gently** until the liquid just begins to boil.
5. Record the boiling point of A in a copy of Results Table 3.4.
6. Turn off the Bunsen burner and allow the apparatus to cool for about two minutes.
7. Measure 2.0 cm^3 of liquid B from the burette into a test-tube and pour the liquid down the condenser into the pear-shaped flask.
8. Reheat the flask gently until the liquid mixture just boils and record its boiling point.
9. Repeat stages 6, 7 and 8 with further additions of 2 cm^3 portions of component B until a total of 10 cm^3 of B has been added.
10. Allow the apparatus to cool and ask your teacher how you can safely dispose of the mixture.
11. Repeat the experiment from step 4, this time starting with 10 cm^3 of liquid B in the flask and adding 2 cm^3 of component A after each boiling point determination until a total of 10 cm^3 of A has been added.

Results Table 3.4

Volume/cm^3		% composition	Boiling point/°C		
A	**B**	**A (by volume)**	**System 1**	**System 2**	**System 3**
10	0	100			61.2
10	2	83.3			64.0
10	4				65.2
10	6				64.8
10	8				64.6
10	10				64.4
0	10				58.0
2	10				60.0
4	10				62.0
6	10				64.0
8	10				64.2

Treatment of results

1. Plot a graph of boiling point (*y*-axis) against percentage composition by volume (*x*-axis). Label the graph as shown in Fig. 3.7, substituting the names of your liquids for A and B.

Figure 3.7

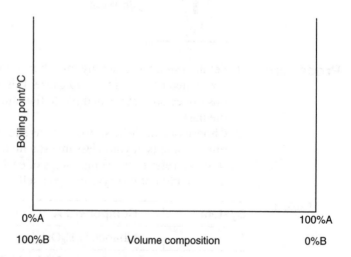

2. Collect the results for the other two systems from other students or from the specimen results and plot the results in exactly the same way.

Questions
1. For each boiling point/composition curve, deduce an approximate vapour pressure/composition curve. Insert dotted lines to represent the vapour pressures you would expect for 'ideal' mixtures.
2. Study the vapour pressure curves and classify each mixture as ideal or as showing positive or negative deviations from ideality.

EXPERIMENT 3.6   Measuring the temperature change on forming solutions

Aim
The purpose of this experiment is to measure the change in temperature which occurs on mixing two components of a non-ideal mixture and to see how it correlates with the vapour pressure/composition curves obtained in Experiment 3.5.

Introduction
The enthalpy change on mixing two miscible liquids A and B, $\Delta H^{\ominus}_{mix}$, can be defined as the heat change which occurs when 1 mole of liquid A is mixed with 1 mole of liquid B under standard conditions. However, we are not particularly concerned with the numerical value of $\Delta H^{\ominus}_{mix}$ but mainly with its sign. This is easy to establish from the temperature change on mixing liquids A and B. An increase in temperature indicates that the sign is negative whereas a decrease in temperature indicates that the sign is positive. Using the same systems as in Experiment 3.5 you determine the sign of $\Delta H^{\ominus}_{mix}$ for each pair of liquids. This gives information about the intermolecular forces acting between A ···· A, B ···· B and A ···· B.

Requirements
■ safety spectacles
■ boiling-tube
■ cotton wool
■ beaker, tall form, 250 cm^3
■ 2 measuring cylinders, 10 cm^3
■ 2 small funnels
■ thermometer, −5–50°C, ± 0.1°C
■ ethanol, C_2H_5OH
■ cyclohexane, C_6H_{12}
■ propan-1-ol, $CH_3CH_2CH_2OH$
■ propan-2-ol, $CH_3CH(OH)CH_3$

HAZARD WARNING

Ethanol, cyclohexane, propan-1-ol and propan-2-ol are highly flammable.
Therefore you **must:**
■ **keep the stoppers on the bottles as much as possible;**
■ **keep the bottles away from flames;**
■ **wear safety spectacles.**

Procedure
1. You should have time to test the first two mixtures. Specimen results are given for the third mixture as in the last experiment.
2. Place a boiling-tube into a beaker and surround the tube with cotton wool, as shown in Fig. 3.8.
3. Pour 10 cm^3 of one of the components (liquid A) from a measuring cylinder into the insulated boiling-tube.
4. Measure 10 cm^3 of liquid B in a clean measuring cylinder.
5. Record the temperature of liquid A, T_A, and liquid B, T_B. Record the average value as T_1 in a copy of Results Table 3.5.
6. Pour the liquid from the measuring cylinder into the liquid in the insulated tube and stir carefully with the thermometer. Record the new temperature, T_2, and the temperature difference, ΔT.

Figure 3.8

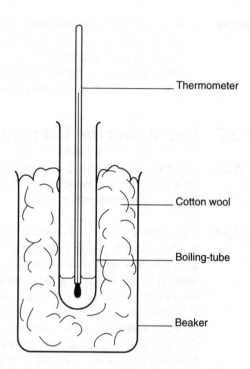

Thermometer

Cotton wool

Boiling-tube

Beaker

7. Dispose of the mixture according to your teacher's instructions.

Results Table 3.5

Mixture	$T_A/°C$	$T_B/°C$	$T_1/°C$	$T_2/°C$	$\Delta T/°C$
1. Ethanol and cyclohexane					
2. Propan-1-ol and propan-2-ol					
3. Trichloromethane and methyl ethanoate	23.0	23.0	23.0	32.0	+9.0

Questions

1. State the sign of ΔH°_{mix} for each mixture.
2. Which of the three mixtures most closely approaches ideal behaviour? Explain your answer.
3. Explain the temperature change on mixing trichloromethane and methyl ethanoate in terms of the interactions between the molecules.
4. Explain the shape of the vapour pressure curve for this system as determined in Experiment 3.5, based on your answer to 3.
5. Correlate the vapour pressure/composition curve with the sign of ΔH°_{mix} for the ethanol/cyclohexane system.

ILPAC

4

s-BLOCK ELEMENTS

THE HALOGENS

THE PERIODIC TABLE

EXPERIMENT 4.1   Reaction between sodium peroxide and water

Aim The purpose of this experiment is to identify the products formed when sodium peroxide, Na_2O_2, reacts with water.

Introduction When the s-block monoxides dissolve in water, they produce hydroxide ions which make the resulting solutions alkaline. For example,

$$CaO(s) + H_2O(l) \rightarrow Ca(OH)_2(aq)$$

In this experiment, you will note the pH of the resulting solution when sodium peroxide, Na_2O_2, reacts with water, and identify other products which are also formed.

One of the products you will be asked to test for is hydrogen peroxide, H_2O_2. A very sensitive test for this is one which involves shaking it with orange potassium dichromate(VI) solution, $K_2Cr_2O_7$, dilute sulphuric acid and 2-methylbutan-1-ol, $C_5H_{11}OH$. If a blue colour develops in the organic layer, then hydrogen peroxide is present.

(The blue colour is thought to be due to CrO_5, which contains O–O bonds and is stable in 2-methylbutan-1-ol but not in water.)

Requirements
- safety spectacles
- 4 test-tubes in rack
- Bunsen burner and bench mat
- spatula
- sodium peroxide, Na_2O_2
- distilled water
- wood splints
- 3 dropping pipettes
- universal indicator
- potassium dichromate(VI) solution, 0.02 M $K_2Cr_2O_7$
- dilute sulphuric acid, 2 M H_2SO_4
- 2-methylbutan-1-ol (amyl alcohol), $C_5H_{11}OH$

HAZARD WARNING

2-Methylbutan-1-ol is highly flammable. Therefore you **must:**
- **keep the stopper on the bottle when not in use;**
- **keep the liquid away from flames.**

Sodium peroxide is corrosive and a powerful oxidant. Therefore you **must:**
- **wear safety spectacles;**
- **avoid contact with skin**

Procedure
1. Cautiously add about 0.1 g of sodium peroxide to about 3 cm^3 of distilled water in a test-tube, and immediately test the gas evolved. (What are the possibilities?)
2. To the resulting solution add a few drops of universal indicator.
3. Put a few grains (less than 0.1 g) of sodium peroxide in a test-tube and add the following reagents, in order: 3 cm^3 of distilled water, 3 drops of potassium dichromate solution, 1 cm^3 of 2-methylbutan-1-ol and 3 cm^3 of dilute sulphuric acid. Shake gently and let the two layers separate.
4. Record your observations and conclusions in a copy of Results Table 4.1.

Results Table 4.1

Experiment	Observation	Conclusion
Sodium peroxide added to water and universal indicator	Colour of gas . . . . Effect on glowing splint . . . . pH of solution . . .	The gas is . . . . .
Sodium peroxide plus water, added to acidified dichromate solution plus 2-methylbutan-1-ol	Colour of organic (top) layer . . . . Colour of aqueous layer	The colour of the organic layer shows . . . .

Questions

1. At $0\,°C$, sodium peroxide reacts with water without the evolution of oxygen. Hydrogen peroxide is detected at this temperature.
   a Write an equation for this reaction.
   b The evolution of oxygen at higher temperatures is believed to be due to a secondary reaction. Write an equation for this secondary reaction.
   c What products are likely to be obtained if sodium peroxide is added to very hot water? Give a balanced equation.
2. a Predict the reaction between barium peroxide and ice-cold water. Give a balanced equation in your answer.
   b Hydrogen peroxide can be prepared in the laboratory by adding barium peroxide to ice-cold dilute sulphuric acid.
      i) Write an equation for this reaction.
      ii) Why do you think dilute sulphuric acid is used in place of water?
3. All s-block oxides (apart from BeO) are basic oxides and thus react with water to form hydroxides, and with acidic substances to form salts. How would you expect the following oxides to react with carbon dioxide?
   a Na_2O,   b Na_2O_2,   c KO_2.

EXPERIMENT 4.2 Heating the nitrates and carbonates of s-block elements

Aim

The aim of this experiment is two-fold: to identify the products of thermal decomposition and to estimate the order of thermal stability of these compounds.

Introduction

In this experiment you heat small samples of the nitrate and carbonate of each element, using the same size flame. You then note the time taken to detect the products of decomposition. Your pre-A-level experience should enable you to recognise nitrogen dioxide, NO_2 (brown gas), produced from nitrates, and carbon dioxide, CO_2, from carbonates. In order to save time, we suggest that you work in pairs, one student on each part of the experiment.

Requirements

- safety spectacles
- 30 test-tubes
- 2 test-tube racks
- labels for test-tubes
- solid nitrates and carbonates (anhydrous if possible) of Groups I and II
- 2 spatulas
- retort stand, clamp and boss
- bent delivery tube to fit test-tubes
- lime-water
- 2 Bunsen burners and mats
- 2 stopclocks (or watches)

- 2 test-tube holders
- wood splints
- hydrochloric acid, dilute, 2 M HCl

HAZARD WARNING

Barium compounds are **toxic** if swallowed or absorbed through the skin.
- **Avoid contact with skin.**

Nitrogen dioxide is a **toxic** gas.
- **Heat nitrates in a fume cupboard.**

Nitrates are strong oxidising agents.
- **Do not allow pieces of glowing splint to drop onto hot nitrates.**

Procedure – Part A

Effect of heat on carbonates.

1. Set up two rows of four or five test-tubes each.
2. Label the test-tubes in the first row with the names of the Group I carbonates, and the second row with the names of the Group II carbonates.
3. To each test-tube add a spatula-measure of the appropriate carbonate.
4. For the first carbonate, set up the apparatus as shown in Fig. 4.1.

Figure 4.1

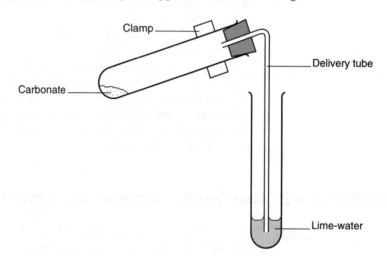

5. Start the clock at the moment you begin heating the carbonate by holding the end of the tube just above the inner blue cone of a roaring Bunsen flame. It is important that you can reproduce this method of heating so that your comparisons with other carbonates will be valid.
6. Note the time for the lime-water to just turn milky (if it does at all) and, before removing the flame, prevent 'suckback' by lifting the delivery tube out of the lime-water. This is simply done by lifting the clamp and stand.
7. Repeat the heating procedure for each carbonate in turn, making sure that the tube height and the flame size are the same for each one.
8. Record your results in a copy of Results Table 4.2.

Results Table 4.2
Effect of heat on the s-block carbonates

Carbonate	Time to detect CO$_2$	Observations
Li$_2$CO$_3$		
Na$_2$CO$_3$		
K$_2$CO$_3$		
Rb$_2$CO$_3$*		
Cs$_2$CO$_3$*		
MgCO$_3$		
CaCO$_3$		
SrCO$_3$		
BaCO$_3$		

*If available.

Procedure – Part B

Effect of heat on nitrates. (To be done in a fume cupboard.)

9. Heat small quantities of sodium nitrate and magnesium nitrate separately, in clean test-tubes. In each case, test for oxygen and note the appearance of any brown fumes. (This will give you an idea of the products you can expect when Groups I and II nitrates are heated.)

10. Set up two rows of four test-tubes each containing the appropriate nitrates, as you did for the carbonates.

11. Start the clock at the moment you begin heating the first nitrate by holding the end of the test-tube just above the blue cone of a roaring Bunsen flame.

12. Test for oxygen at short regular intervals (place the glowing splint in the same part of the test-tube) and also look for the first signs of a brown gas. (A white background is helpful.)

13. In a copy of Results Table 4.3, record the time for the first appearance of brown fumes or when oxygen is detected. (Whichever method of detection you choose for one member of a group you must also apply to the other members of the same group.) Continue heating for another minute.

Results Table 4.3
Effect of heat on the s-block nitrates

Nitrate	Time to detect O$_2$ or NO$_2$	Observations	Effect of adding dilute HCl to cold residue
LiNO$_3$			
NaNO$_3$			
KNO$_3$			
RbNO$_3$*			
CsNO$_3$*			
Mg(NO$_3$)$_2$			
Ca(NO$_3$)$_2$			
Sr(NO$_3$)$_2$			
Ba(NO$_3$)$_2$			

*If available.

14. Repeat steps 11, 12 and 13 for the other nitrates in turn.
15. To the **cold** solid residue remaining after each nitrate is heated add a few drops of dilute hydrochloric acid and warm.

Questions

1. Explain why many of these nitrates rapidly turn into colourless liquids on first heating, but on further heating become white solids again, before they decompose. (Hint: look at the formulae of the nitrates on the reagent bottles.)
2. Which of the nitrates and carbonates of Group I most resemble those of Group II in their reaction to heat?
3. Describe the trend in thermal stability of the nitrates and carbonates as each group is descended.
4. How do Group I nitrates and carbonates compare with their Group II counterparts in terms of thermal stability?
5. Write balanced equations, where applicable, for the thermal decompositions of:
   a lithium nitrate and lithium carbonate,
   b potassium nitrate and potassium carbonate,
   c magnesium nitrate and magnesium carbonate.
6. Why are brown fumes produced when dilute HCl is added to the cold residue obtained when many of the Group I nitrates are heated?

EXPERIMENT 4.3   The solubility of some salts of Group II elements

Aim

The aim of this experiment is to demonstrate the trends in solubility of the Group II carbonates, sulphates, sulphites and hydroxides.

Introduction

In this experiment, you add each of the anion solutions to 1 cm^3 of each cation solution provided, drop-by-drop, until the first sign of a precipitate appears. For each salt, the solubility is proportional to the number of drops of anion solution added.

Requirements

■ 16 test-tubes
■ 4 test-tube racks
■ labels for test-tubes
■ 5 teat pipettes (marked off at 1 cm^3)
■ 0.1 M solutions of the following cations: Mg^{2+}, Ca^{2+}, Sr^{2+}, Ba^{2+}
■ 1.0 M solution of OH^- ions
■ 0.5 M solution of SO_4^{2-} and SO_3^{2-} ions
■ 0.05 M solution of CO_3^{2-} ions
■ distilled water

HAZARD WARNING

■ 1.0 M solutions of OH^- ions are corrosive. Therefore you **must wear safety spectacles**;
■ Solutions of sulphite ions, SO_3^{2-}, release a **toxic** gas, sulphur dioxide, if acid is added. **Take care with disposal of sulphite solutions, especially if you suffer from asthma.**

Procedure

1. Set up four rows of four test-tubes each.
2. For each row, label the first test-tube Mg^{2+}, the second test-tube Ca^{2+}, the third test-tube Sr^{2+} and the fourth test-tube Ba^{2+}.
3. Add 1 cm^3 of the appropriate cation solution to each test-tube, using a teat pipette with a 1 cm^3 mark.
4. Label the first row of test-tubes OH^-, the second row SO_4^{2-}, the third row SO_3^{2-} and the fourth row CO_3^{2-}.

5. Add the solution of OH⁻, drop-by-drop, with shaking, to each cation solution in the first row, until the first sign of a precipitate appears.
6. Record the number of drops of OH⁻ solution used in a copy of Results Table 4.4.
7. Repeat steps 5 and 6 with the remaining anions and cations.
8. If a precipitate appears suddenly, during the addition of a drop, then you should classify the precipitate as slight (s) or heavy (h).
9. If no precipitate appears after 40 drops, then write '40+' and regard the salt as soluble.

Results Table 4.4

Cation solution	Number of drops of anion solution added to give a precipitate			
	OH⁻	SO_4^{2-}	SO_3^{2-}	CO_3^{2-}
Mg^{2+}				
Ca^{2+}				
Sr^{2+}				
Ba^{2+}				

Question   For Group II, what are the trends in solubility of the salts listed below?
a hydroxides,
b sulphates,
c sulphites,
d carbonates.

EXPERIMENT 4.4   The solubility of the halogens in organic solvents

Aim   The purpose of this experiment is to discover whether each of the halogens chlorine, bromine and iodine is:
a soluble in organic solvents,
b more soluble in organic solvents than in water,
c the same colour in organic solvents as it is in water.

Introduction   After mixing aqueous solutions of the halogens separately with Volasil 244,* ethoxyethane, $CH_3CH_2OCH_2CH_3$, and cyclohexane, $(CH_2)_6$, you decide whether each halogen moves out of the aqueous solution into the solvent. If it does, you can compare its colour in the aqueous layer with that in the organic layer – these colours are useful in identifying the halogens.

Requirements
■ safety spectacles
■ 3 test-tubes, each fitted with a bung
■ test-tube rack
■ 6 dropping pipettes approximately graduated for 1 cm³
■ Volasil 244 (octamethylcyclotetrasiloxane)$((CH_3)_2 SiO)_4$
■ ethoxyethane (diethyl ether), $CH_3CH_2OCH_2CH_3$
■ cyclohexane, $(CH_2)_6$
■ chlorine water, $Cl_2(aq)$

*Volasil 244 is a cyclic organosilicone, octamethylcyclotetrasiloxane. Its molecule has alternating silicon and oxygen atoms in a ring structure with methyl groups attached to the silicon atoms. You will **not** be expected to remember its full name or structure! Indeed, the phrase 'inert solvent' is adequate in most contexts. We have included it here, and subsequently, because it is more environmentally friendly than most organic solvents and is safer to use, although it is flammable.

■ bromine water, $Br_2(aq)$
■ iodine solution, 0.01 M I_2 (in KI(aq))
■ 3 labelled bottles for organic residues

HAZARD WARNING

■ This experiment should be performed in a **fume cupboard** since all the halogen vapours are **toxic** and the organic vapours are dangerous to inhale. If a fume cupboard is not available then **the laboratory must be well ventilated**.
■ Check that no flames are close to where you are working because ethoxyethane and cyclohexane are extremely flammable. Volasil 244 is also flammable.

Procedure
1. In a copy of Results Table 4.5 note the colour of each aqueous halogen solution provided.
2. Into each of three test-tubes in turn put about 1 cm³ of a different aqueous halogen solution.
3. To each tube add about 1 cm³ of Volasil 244 and note whether the organic liquid becomes the upper or lower layer. How can you tell?
4. Cork and shake each tube, allow the layers to separate, and note the colour of each layer.
5. Repeat steps 2, 3 and 4 with the other two solvents.
6. Pour residues into the labelled bottles provided, **not** down the sink.

Results Table 4.5

	Nature of each layer	**Chlorine water**	**Bromine water**	**Iodine solution**
Colour of aqueous solution				
Colour of each layer after shaking with Volasil 244	Upper layer *organic/aqueous			
	Lower layer *organic/aqueous			
Colour of each layer after shaking with ethoxyethane	Upper layer *organic/aqueous			
	Lower layer *organic/aqueous			
Colour of each layer after shaking with cyclohexane	Upper layer *organic/aqueous			
	Lower layer *organic/aqueous			

*Delete organic or aqueous as appropriate.

Questions
1. Do you think the halogens are more soluble in the organic solvents than in water? Explain your answer.
2. Which of the three halogens has a significantly different colour in the organic layer from its colour in the aqueous layer? (Specify the organic solvents in your answer.)
3. How would you distinguish, other than by smell, between a dilute aqueous iodine solution and a fairly concentrated solution of bromine water?

EXPERIMENT 4.5 The action of dilute alkali on the halogens

Aim
The purpose of this experiment is to show that observable reactions occur between dilute sodium hydroxide and aqueous solutions of bromine and iodine and, furthermore, that these reactions are reversible.

Introduction
You add dilute sodium hydroxide dropwise to bromine water and iodine solution in turn. A significant change in colour in either halogen solution indicates that a reaction has occurred. If you suspect that the change in colour is only due to a dilution effect, you should set up a control experiment, where you add the same number of drops of distilled water to the halogen solution.
  To determine whether the reaction is reversible, you acidify the alkaline halogen solution and see if the original halogen colour reappears.

Requirements
- safety spectacles
- 5 test-tubes
- 1 test-tube rack
- 4 teat pipettes
- bromine water, Br_2(aq)
- iodine solution, 0.01 M I_2 (in KI(aq))
- sulphuric acid, 1 M H_2SO_4
- sodium hydroxide solution, 2 M NaOH
- distilled water

HAZARD WARNING

Bromine water is **toxic** and corrosive. The vapour is extremely irritant to the eyes, lungs and skin. Sodium hydroxide solution is corrosive. Therefore you **must**:
- **avoid contact with skin;**
- **avoid inhaling bromine vapour.**

Procedure
1. Place about 2 cm³ of bromine water in a test-tube and note the colour of the solution.
2. Add dilute sodium hydroxide, drop-by-drop, and note any change of colour in the bromine solution.
3. Now add dilute sulphuric acid to the solution from step 2, and note if the colour returns when the acid is in excess.
4. Repeat the procedure using iodine solution instead of bromine water.
5. Record your results in a copy of Results Table 4.6.

Results Table 4.6

Aqueous halogen	Original colour	Colour after adding NaOH(aq)	Colour after adding H_2SO_4(aq)
Bromine water			
Iodine solution			

Questions
1. Write equations for the reactions of bromine and iodine with dilute sodium hydroxide at room temperature. Use your textbook(s) as necessary.
2. Which of the above reactions would you class as disproportionation reactions?
3. Are these reactions reversible? Explain your answer.
4. How does chlorine differ from bromine and iodine in its reaction with cold dilute sodium hydroxide? Suggest a reason.

EXPERIMENT 4.6 Halogen–halide reactions in aqueous solution

Aim

The purpose of this experiment is to investigate the order of oxidising ability of the halogens Cl_2, Br_2 and I_2 in aqueous solution.

Introduction

You mix each of the aqueous solutions with halide ion solutions, $Cl^-(aq)$, $Br^-(aq)$, and $I^-(aq)$ in turn, and see whether a reaction takes place. The addition of Volasil 244 to the halogen–halide mixture enables you to recognise the halogen molecules present. The halogen which oxidises most of the other halide ions will clearly be the strongest oxidising agent.

Requirements

- safety spectacles
- 6 test-tubes fitted with corks
- test-tube rack
- 7 dropping pipettes
- bromine water, $Br_2(aq)$
- chlorine water, $Cl_2(aq)$
- iodine solution, I_2 (in $KI(aq)$)
- potassium bromide solution, KBr
- potassium chloride solution, KCl
- potassium iodide solution, KI
- Volasil 244
- bottle for residues

HAZARD WARNING

Halogen vapours must not be inhaled. If a fume cupboard is not available then:
- **the laboratory must be well ventilated and reagent bottles and test-tubes stoppered as much as possible;**
- **keep Volasil 244 away from flames.**

Results Table 4.7

		Chlorine water	Bromine water	Iodine solution
1.	Initial colour			
2.	Colour after shaking with KI solution			
Colour of each layer after shaking with Volasil 244	Upper			
	Lower			
Conclusion				
3.	Colour after shaking with KBr solution			
Colour of each layer after shaking with Volasil 244	Upper			
	Lower			
Conclusion				
4.	Colour after shaking with KCl solution			
Colour of each layer after shaking with Volasil 244	Upper			
	Lower			
Conclusion				

Procedure

1. **Reaction (if any) of iodide with chlorine and bromine.**
   a To each of two test-tubes add about 1 cm^3 of potassium iodide solution.
   b To one of these tubes, add about the same volume of chlorine water, and to the other add the same volume of bromine water.
   c Cork and shake the tubes and note the colour change – if any.
   d To each tube add about 1 cm^3 of Volasil 244, cork and shake, allow to settle, and note the colour of each layer. The relative volumes of the two layers will tell you which is aqueous and which is organic.
   e Decide which reactions have taken place, and complete a copy of Results Table 4.7.
2. **Reaction (if any) of bromide with chlorine and iodine.**
   Repeat the above steps, 1a–e, using potassium bromide instead of potassium iodide.
3. **Reaction (if any) of chloride with bromine and iodine.**
   Repeat steps 1a–e using potassium chloride instead of potassium iodide.

Questions

1. a Does $I_2(aq)$ oxidise $Cl^-(aq)$ and $Br^-(aq)$?
   b Does $Br_2(aq)$ oxidise $Cl^-(aq)$ and $I^-(aq)$?
   c Does $Cl_2(aq)$ oxidise $Br^-(aq)$ and $I^-(aq)$?
2. Write ionic equations for the reactions taking place.

EXPERIMENT 4.7 Reactions of solid halides

Aim

The purpose of this experiment is to study the effect of an oxidising acid (concentrated sulphuric acid) and a non-oxidising acid (phosphoric(V) acid) on three solid potassium halides: potassium chloride, potassium bromide and potassium iodide.

Introduction

In this experiment, you mix separate samples of crystalline potassium chloride, potassium bromide and potassium iodide with the following reagents in turn:
a $H_2SO_4(l)$ and $MnO_2(s)$
b $H_2SO_4(l)$ alone
c $H_3PO_4(l)$.

Possible products include the halogens, the hydrogen halides, sulphur dioxide (SO_2) and hydrogen sulphide (H_2S). You already know how to recognise the halogens. Tests to recognise the other products are as follows:

Hydrogen halides Hold a moist stopper from a bottle of ammonia solution near the source of the gas. Dense white fumes indicate the presence of a hydrogen halide (or other strongly acidic gas).

Sulphur dioxide Hold a strip of filter paper soaked in acidified potassium dichromate(VI) solution near the source of the gas. A colour change from orange to green indicates the presence of sulphur dioxide (or other strongly reducing gas).

Hydrogen sulphide The 'bad egg' smell is very characteristic, but take care – the gas is very toxic. Hold a strip of filter paper soaked in lead ethanoate (acetate) solution near the source of the gas. A silver black colour indicates the presence of hydrogen sulphide.

Requirements

- safety spectacles
- access to fume cupboard
- 12 test-tubes in rack
- spatula
- potassium bromide, solid, KBr
- potassium chloride, solid, KCl
- potassium iodide, solid, KI
- manganese(IV) oxide, MnO_2
- glass stirring rod
- sulphuric acid, concentrated, H_2SO_4

- phosphoric(V) acid, 100%, H_3PO_4
- test-tube holder
- Bunsen burner and bench mat
- distilled water
- 3 dropping pipettes
- ammonia solution, 2 M NH_3
- lead(II) ethanoate solution, $(CH_3COO)_2Pb$
- potassium dichromate(VI) solution, $K_2Cr_2O_7$
- strips of filter paper
- starch solution
- Volasil 244

HAZARD WARNING

Concentrated sulphuric acid is very corrosive and reacts violently with water. Phosphoric(V) acid and potassium dichromate are also very corrosive. Lead(II) ethanoate is **toxic**. Therefore, you **must**:

- **avoid contact with skin; if contact does occur, wash immediately under a cold tap with plenty of water;**
- **dispose of cold residues containing concentrated sulphuric acid by pouring slowly into plenty of water.**

The halogens, hydrogen halides, sulphur dioxide and hydrogen sulphide are **toxic**. Therefore you **must**:

- **carry out these experiments in a fume cupboard.**

Volasil 244 is very flammable.

- **Keep Volasil 244 stoppered and away from flames.**

Procedure

1. **Reaction with H_2SO_4 and MnO_2.**
   a Into three separate test-tubes, place enough potassium chloride, potassium bromide and potassium iodide to half-fill the rounded part at the bottom.
   b To the contents of each test-tube, add a roughly equal quantity of manganese(IV) oxide, and mix the solids together with a stirring rod.

   c Hold the tube in a fume cupboard, with its mouth pointed away from you, and cautiously add ten drops of concentrated sulphuric acid, shaking the tube gently after the addition of each drop.
   d Note whether any reaction occurs, and confirm any suspected products by appropriate tests. Complete a larger copy of Results Table 4.8.
   e If no reaction seems to occur, warm the test-tube carefully.

Results Table 4.8

Test	Chloride	Bromide	Iodide
1. **Action of conc. H_2SO_4 and MnO_2** Observations Suspected product(s) Confirmatory tests			
2. **Action of conc. H_2SO_4** Observations Suspected product(s) Confirmatory tests			
3. **Action of H_3PO_4** Observations Suspected product(s) Confirmatory tests			

2. **Reaction with H$_2$SO$_4$.**
   Repeat the above procedure without using manganese(IV) oxide.
3. **Reaction with H$_3$PO$_4$.**
   Repeat the above procedure, using phosphoric(V) acid alone in place of sulphuric acid, i.e. without using manganese(IV) oxide.

Questions 1. In many of the reactions you may have detected mixtures of the halogens and the hydrogen halides. In such cases, you should assume that at least two reactions are occurring. With this in mind and with the aid of textbooks, complete and balance the following equations:
   a $KCl(s) + H_2SO_4(l) \rightarrow$
   b $KCl(s) + H_3PO_4*(l) \rightarrow$
   c $KBr(s) + H_2SO_4(l) \rightarrow$
      $HBr(g) + H_2SO_4(l) \rightarrow$
   d $KBr(s) + H_3PO_4*(l) \rightarrow$
   e $KI(s) + H_2SO_4(l) \rightarrow$
      $HI(g) + H_2SO_4(l) \rightarrow$
   f $KI(s) + H_3PO_4*(l) \rightarrow$
2. Manganese(IV) oxide is a strong oxidising agent capable of oxidising all the hydrogen halides (except HF) to the halogens. In the light of this statement, explain the reactions between potassium chloride and concentrated sulphuric acid, with and without manganese(IV) oxide.
3. Why does the addition of manganese(IV) oxide appear to have little effect on the reaction between potassium iodide and concentrated sulphuric acid?

*We have used the formula $H_3PO_4(l)$ rather than $H_3PO_4(s)$ because the solid melts before reaction occurs.

EXPERIMENT 4.8 Reaction of halides in solution

Aim The purpose of this experiment is to find out whether the ions Cl^-, Br^- and I^- react in solution with certain reagents and, where they do react, what products are formed.

Introduction In this experiment, you add various reagents to separate samples of solutions containing Cl^-, Br^- and I^- ions. In many of the reactions, precipitates are formed. Where you are asked to add another reagent to excess, you should look carefully to see if any of the precipitate dissolves.

Requirements ■ safety spectacles
   ■ 18 test-tubes, 9 with corks
   ■ 3 test-tube racks
   ■ 8 dropping pipettes
   ■ potassium bromide solution, 0.1 M KBr
   ■ potassium chloride solution, 0.1 M KCl
   ■ potassium iodide solution, 0.1 M KI
   ■ silver nitrate solution, 0.02 M AgNO$_3$
   ■ nitric acid, dilute, 2 M HNO$_3$
   ■ ammonia solution, 5 M NH$_3$
   ■ lead(II) nitrate solution, 0.1 M Pb(NO$_3$)$_2$
   ■ hydrogen peroxide solution, H$_2$O$_2$, 20 volume
   ■ starch solution
   ■ sulphuric acid, dilute, 1 M H$_2$SO$_4$
   ■ Volasil 244

HAZARD WARNING

Volasil 244 is very flammable. Therefore you **must**:
■ **keep Volasil 244 well stoppered and away from flames.**
Silver nitrate is **toxic** and corrosive. Lead nitrate is **toxic**.
Ammonia solution and hydrogen peroxide are corrosive substances. Therefore you **must**:
■ **avoid contact with the skin.**

Procedure Add the following reagents to 1 cm³ of the chloride, bromide and iodide solutions in turn, and record your observations in a copy of Results Table 4.9.
1. Add approximately 1 cm³ of silver nitrate solution and shake gently. Note what happens. Move the three tubes to a dark cupboard, leave them there until the end of the lesson and note their appearance again.
2. Add silver nitrate solution as in 1. Leave these tubes in their racks until the end of the lesson, noting their appearance every 10–15 minutes.
3. Add approximately 1 cm³ of silver nitrate solution followed by excess (e.g. 5 cm³) dilute nitric acid. Cork the test-tube and shake vigorously.
4. Add approximately 1 cm³ silver nitrate solution followed by excess (e.g. 5 cm³) ammonia solution. Cork the test-tube and shake.
5. Add approximately 1 cm³ lead(II) nitrate solution.
6. Add approximately 1 cm³ of hydrogen peroxide solution followed by approximately 1 cm³ of dilute sulphuric acid. Cork these tubes and allow them to stand. Add any further reagent(s) which you think will help you to decide what has happened.

Results Table 4.9

Test	Chloride	Bromide	Iodide
Action of $AgNO_3$(aq)			
Effect of standing in **a** dark **b** light			
Action of $AgNO_3$(aq) followed by dilute HNO_3(aq)			
Action of $AgNO_3$(aq) followed by NH_3(aq)			
Action of $Pb(NO_3)_2$(aq)			
Action of H_2O_2(aq) and dilute H_2SO_4(aq)			

Questions 1. Write ionic equations for the reactions between each of the three halide solutions and
   a silver nitrate solution,
   b lead(II) nitrate solution.
2. What chemical tests would you perform in order to distinguish between
   a Cl^-(aq) and Br^-(aq),
   b Br^-(aq) and I^-(aq)?

3. **a** Write an ionic equation for the reaction between an aqueous iodide and acidified hydrogen peroxide.

   b Why do you think no reaction occurs between acidified hydrogen peroxide and the other halide ions?

4. Suggest a reason for the darkening effect of light on the silver chloride and silver bromide precipitates.

EXPERIMENT 4.9   Balancing a redox reaction

Aim   The purpose of this experiment is to calculate the amount of iodide ions which react with each mole of iodate(V) ions in aqueous solution.

Requirements
- safety spectacles
- 2 measuring cylinders, 10 cm^3
- potassium iodide solution, ~ 1 M KI
- 2 conical flasks, 250 cm^3
- hydrochloric acid, ~ 2 M HCl
- 2 burettes, stands and filter funnels
- 1 white tile
- potassium iodate solution, 0.10 M KIO_3
- sodium thiosulphate solution, 0.10 M $Na_2S_2O_3$
- starch solution, 0.2%
- wash-bottle of distilled water

Procedure
1. Use a measuring cylinder to pour about 10 cm^3 of potassium iodide solution into a 250 cm^3 conical flask.
2. To the solution in the conical flask add about 10 cm^3 of dilute hydrochloric acid.
3. From a burette, add precisely 5.0 cm^3 of 0.10 M potassium iodate solution to the acidified iodide solution.
4. Titrate the iodine formed against 0.10 M sodium thiosulphate solution. When the colour of the iodine has nearly gone, add 1–2 cm^3 of starch solution and continue the addition of thiosulphate solution drop-by-drop until the blue colour disappears.
5. Record your burette readings in a copy of Results Table 4.10.
6. Repeat steps 1 to 5 as a check on your accuracy.

Results Table 4.10

Solution in flask				mol dm^{-3}	cm^3
Solution in burette				mol dm^{-3}	
Indicator					
		Trial	1	2	3	4
Burette readings	Final					
	Initial					
Volume used/cm^3						
Mean titre/cm^3						

Calculations
1. Calculate the amount of sodium thiosulphate present in the volume of solution run out from the burette.
2. Calculate the amount of iodine **atoms** which must have reacted with the amount of $S_2O_3^{2-}$(aq) calculated in step 1. Use the equation:

$$2S_2O_3^{2-}(aq) + I_2(aq) \rightarrow 2I^-(aq) + S_4O_6^{2-}(aq)$$

3. Calculate the amount of iodine **atoms** present in 5.0 cm^3 of 0.10 M KIO$_3$.
4. Subtract the value obtained in step 3 from the value obtained in step 2 to obtain the amount of iodine atoms which originated from the potassium iodide.
5. State the amount of iodide ions which reacts with each mole of iodate ions.

EXPERIMENT 4.10   Observation and deduction exercise 1

Aim

The purpose of this experiment is to give you some practice in the investigation of unknown substances.

Introduction

The procedure below is taken from an A-level practical examination paper; read it carefully and report fully.

Requirements

- safety spectacles
- 5 test-tubes in rack
- test-tube holder
- alkali metal salt, F
- spatula
- Bunsen burner and bench mat
- red and blue litmus papers
- wood splints
- wash-bottle of distilled water
- silver nitrate solution, 0.02 M AgNO$_3$
- nitric acid, dilute, 2 M HNO$_3$
- chlorine water, Cl$_2$(aq)
- lead(II) ethanoate solution, 0.1 M (CH$_3$CO$_2$)$_2$Pb
- other chemicals, for testing gases, are available from your teacher

HAZARD WARNING

Silver nitrate solution and dilute nitric acid are corrosive.
Aqueous chlorine gives off a harmful vapour.
Lead ethanoate is **toxic**. Therefore you **must**:
- **wear safety spectacles and work with care, preferably at a fume cupboard.**

Procedure

You are provided with an alkali metal salt, F. Carry out the following tests and record your observations and inferences in (a larger copy of) Results Table 4.11. Then answer the question which follows.

Results Table 4.11

Test	Observations	Inferences
a Heat approximately 0.1 g of F in a Pyrex tube, at first gently and then more strongly, until the change is complete. Cool and keep the residue. Test any gases evolved		
b Make an aqueous solution of the residue from **a** and carry out the following tests on portions: i) Add aqueous silver nitrate followed by dilute nitric acid. ii) Add aqueous chlorine. iii) Add aqueous lead(II) ethanoate (lead acetate)		

Question   For a non-metal in F, give two substances or ions involved in the reactions in **a** and **b** which contain the non-metal and in which the non-metal has different oxidation numbers. Write your answer in a copy of Results Table 4.12.

Results Table 4.12

Substance provided	Name of non-metal	Name and formula of substance/ion	Oxidation number
F			

EXPERIMENT 4.11   Observation and deduction exercise 2

Aim   The purpose of this experiment is to give you some practice in the investigation of unknown substances.

Introduction   The procedure below is taken from an A-level practical examination paper; read it carefully and report fully.

Requirements
- safety spectacles
- 5 test-tubes in rack
- test-tube holder
- potassium salts, D and E
- spatula
- Bunsen burner and bench mat
- red and blue litmus papers
- wood splints
- sulphuric acid, concentrated, H_2SO_4
- potassium manganate(VII) (permanganate) solution, 0.01 M KMnO$_4$
- sulphuric acid, dilute, 1 M H_2SO_4
- wash-bottle of distilled water
- other chemicals, for testing gases, are available from your teacher

HAZARD WARNING

Concentrated sulphuric acid is very corrosive and reacts violently with water. Therefore, you **must**:
- **avoid contact with skin**; if contact does occur, wash immediately under a cold tap with **plenty** of water;
- dispose of **cold** residues by pouring **slowly** into plenty of water.

Procedure   You are provided with potassium salts, D and E. Test each salt in turn, as follows:
  a Heat a portion until any reaction ceases. Test any gases evolved.
  b Allow the residue from **a** to cool; then cautiously add a few drops of concentrated sulphuric acid.
  c Add a fresh portion of each salt to a few drops of aqueous potassium manganate(VII) previously acidified with twice its volume of dilute sulphuric acid, and warm.
  d Now make aqueous solutions of D and E and mix the two solutions.
  e Acidify the mixture from **d** with dilute sulphuric acid.
Carefully observe what happens and report fully.
     What tentative inferences do you draw from these experiments?
     Carry out and report on **two** further experiments which test your inferences. These experiments can be on D, E or on the products of the above reactions.

Full credit will not be given unless your answer discloses the method (including the scale of your experiments), careful observations, and some comment on the types of chemical reactions involved.

The record of your work must be made in the form of three tables (such as Results Tables 4.13, 4.14 and 4.15).

Results Table 4.13
Tests with unknown substance D

Test		Method	Observations	Inferences
a	Heat			
b	Concentrated sulphuric acid on cold residue from **a**			
c	Acidified potassium manganate(VII) (permanganate) and warm			

Results Table 4.14
Tests with unknown substance E

Test		Method	Observations	Inferences
a	Heat			
b	Concentrated sulphuric acid on cold residue from **a**			
c	Acidified potassium manganate(VII) (permanganate) and warm			
d	Mix aqueous solutions of D and E			
e	Dilute sulphuric acid with mixture from **d**			

Results Table 4.15
Experiments to test inferences

Inference tested	Test and observations	Conclusion

EXPERIMENT 4.12 Investigating the properties of Period 3 chlorides

Aim

The purpose of this experiment is to study the chlorides of Period 3 elements and classify them according to structural type and bonding.

Introduction

You first examine the appearance of each compound and then you find out whether it dissolves in water and/or cyclohexane. If it does dissolve you may detect a temperature change. In general, a small temperature change indicates a physical process and a large one a chemical process. This will help you to distinguish between the physical process of dissolving and the chemical one of hydrolysis when you add these substances to water.

You also determine any pH changes that take place when you mix the chlorides with water. A decrease in pH indicates that hydrolysis has taken place.

Finally, you consider physical data for each compound and reach a conclusion about its bonding and structure.

Requirements
- safety spectacles
- protective gloves
- access to fume cupboard
- 14 test-tubes (6 must be dry)
- test-tube rack
- 2 measuring cylinders, 10 cm^3 (1 must be dry)
- distilled water
- thermometer, 0–100 °C
- spatula
- universal indicator solution and colour chart
- pH paper to cover the range 1–7
- ammonia solution, 2 M NH$_3$
- sodium chloride, NaCl
- magnesium chloride, MgCl$_2$
- aluminium chloride, AlCl$_3$ (anhydrous if possible)
- 4 teat pipettes
- silicon tetrachloride, SiCl$_4$
- phosphorus trichloride, PCl$_3$
- disulphur dichloride, S$_2$Cl$_2$
- cyclohexane, C$_6$H$_{12}$
- organic residues bottle

HAZARD WARNING

Many of the chlorides in this experiment react vigorously with water. SiCl$_4$, PCl$_3$ and S$_2$Cl$_2$ are corrosive and harmful. Therefore you **must:**
- **do this experiment in a fume cupboard;**
- **keep stoppers on bottles as much as possible;**
- **wear gloves and safety spectacles.**

Old stock of silicon tetrachloride often has hydrogen chloride trapped at the neck of the bottle. Ensure the bottle has been checked by your teacher before you attempt to open it.

Cyclohexane is very flammable. Therefore you **must:**
- **keep the stopper on the bottle as much as possible;**

Procedure – Part A

Appearance
1. Examine the chloride samples provided and, in a larger copy of Results Table 4.16, note for each:
   a whether it is solid, liquid or gaseous,
   b its colour (if any).

Procedure – Part B

On mixing with water
2. Set up seven test-tubes, side by side.
3. Into each test-tube pour about 5 cm^3 of distilled water.
4. In the first test-tube place a thermometer.
   a Note the temperature.
   b Add half a spatula-tip of sodium chloride and very carefully stir with the thermometer.
   c Note, after about one minute, i) the temperature, ii) whether the solid has dissolved and iii) anything else you see. For example, is gas evolved at any time? If so, is the gas acidic? Can you identify it using a simple test?
   d Add 2–4 drops of universal indicator solution, or use a piece of pH paper, compare the colour with the chart provided, and note the pH indicated.

5. Repeat (but with more care!) the above steps 4**a–d** using, in turn, magnesium chloride, aluminium chloride, silicon tetrachloride (2 drops), phosphorus trichloride (2 drops), and disulphur dichloride (2 drops).
6. Measure the pH of the water in the seventh test-tube by adding 2–4 drops of universal indicator solution or by using pH paper, for comparison with the above.

Procedure – Part C

On mixing with cyclohexane
7. Set up another six test-tubes, side by side. These must be dry.
8. Into each test-tube pour about 5 cm³ of cyclohexane.
9. In the first test-tube place a thermometer.
   a Note the temperature.
   b Add half a spatula-tip of sodium chloride and stir very carefully with the thermometer.
   c Note, after about one minute, i) the temperature, ii) whether the solid dissolves and iii) anything else you see.
   (Dispose of cyclohexane by pouring into the residue bottle provided.)

10. Repeat the above steps 9**a–c** using, in turn, magnesium chloride, aluminium chloride, silicon tetrachloride (2 drops), phosphorus trichloride (2 drops), and disulphur dichloride (2 drops).

Results Table 4.16

	NaCl	MgCl₂	AlCl₃	SiCl₄	PCl₃	S₂Cl₂
Appearance						
On mixing with water Initial temperature Final temperature Does it dissolve? pH of solution Other observation(s) (if any)						
On mixing with cyclohexane Initial temperature Final temperature Does it dissolve? Other observation(s) (if any)						

Questions

1. Complete a copy of Table 4.1 on the next page using your experimental results and your data book. Then decide on the structure of these chlorides and the bonding found in them and fill in the last part of your table.
2. In the experiment you discovered that some of the chlorides are hydrolysed by water. Look up the equations for these reactions in your textbook(s). In the case of S_2Cl_2 you may find that most books do not give an equation for its hydrolysis. This is because a mixture of products is obtained. We suggest the following equation:

$$2S_2Cl_2(l) + 2H_2O(l) \rightarrow SO_2(aq) + 3S(s) + 4HCl(aq)$$

Table 4.1
Properties of chlorides of
Period 3

Formula of chloride	NaCl	MgCl$_2$	AlCl$_3$	SiCl$_4$	PCl$_3$	S$_2$Cl$_2$	Cl$_2$
Melting point/°C							
Boiling point/°C							
Physical state at r.t.p.*							
ΔH_f°/kJ mol^{-1}							
ΔH_f° per mole of Cl/kJ mol^{-1}							
Conductivity of liquid							
Action of water							
pH of aqueous solution							
Solubility in cyclohexane							
Structure							
Bonding							

* r.t.p. = room temperature and pressure (i.e. 20°C and 1 atm).

EXPERIMENT 4.13   Preparing anhydrous aluminium chloride

Aim
In this experiment you gain experience in setting up an assembly of glassware in order to carry out an inorganic synthesis. You also calculate the percentage yield of your product.

Introduction
You prepare chlorine by adding concentrated hydrochloric acid to potassium manganate(VII), dry it using anhydrous calcium chloride and then pass it over heated aluminium foil in a combustion tube. When the reaction is complete you weigh your collected product and calculate the percentage yield.

Requirements
- safety spectacles
- access to fume cupboard
- forceps
- glass rod
- calcium chloride, anhydrous, CaCl$_2$
- long spatula
- combustion tube
- ceramic wool
- bung fitted with a short piece of glass tubing
- access to a balance capable of weighing to within 0.01 g
- aluminium foil, Al
- absorption tube
- soda lime
- receiver bottle with two holed bung (connected to absorption and combustion tubes)
- ruler
- rubber tubing for connections
- 3 clamps, bosses and stands
- potassium manganate(VII), KMnO$_4$

- pear-shaped flask with ground-glass joint, 50 cm^3
- ground-glass adapter with T-connection
- cylindrical funnel with ground-glass joint
- hydrochloric acid, concentrated, HCl
- Bunsen burner
- specimen tube with lid
- labels
- access to a desiccator

HAZARD WARNING

Chlorine is a **toxic** gas. Therefore you **must**:
- **do the experiment at the fume cupboard.**
Concentrated hydrochloric acid is a corrosive liquid, and its vapour is harmful to eyes, lungs and skin. Therefore you **must**:

- **wear gloves;**
- **wear safety spectacles;**
- **keep the hydrochloric acid in a fume cupboard;**
- **keep the stopper on the bottle as much as possible.**

Procedure There are several steps in assembling the apparatus for this experiment. The diagram below (Fig. 4.2) gives you an idea of what you are aiming for. Details of the separate stages are given at appropriate points in the procedure.

Figure 4.2
Preparation of aluminium
chloride.

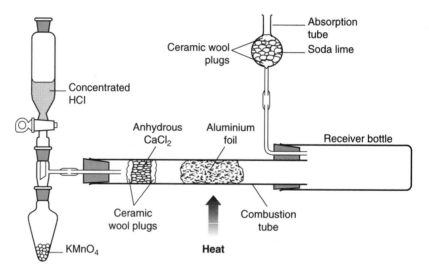

1. Using forceps and a glass rod, put some granular anhydrous calcium chloride between two loose plugs of ceramic wool near the entrance of the combustion tube. (Make sure that the calcium chloride fills the cross-section of the tube without preventing the free flow of chlorine.) Attach the bung fitted with glass tubing at the entrance of the combustion tube.
2. Weigh about 0.25 g of aluminium foil, crumple it loosely, and put it in the combustion tube as shown in Fig. 4.3.

Figure 4.3

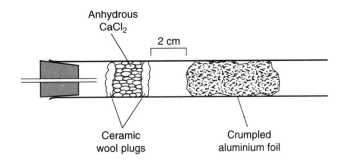

3. Loosely pack the absorption tube as follows:
   a Using forceps, push in a plug of ceramic wool.
   b Fill with soda lime.
   c Using forceps again, close with a second plug of ceramic wool. Both plugs must be loose to avoid blockage.
4. Fit the combustion tube and absorption tube to the receiver bottle as shown in Fig. 4.2. Clamp the apparatus so that the combustion tube is about 15 cm above the base of the fume cupboard.

5. Weigh about 5 g of potassium manganate(VII) and place it in the pear-shaped flask.
6. Fit the pear-shaped flask with the adapter and dropping funnel. Then clamp the flask and connect it to the combustion tube, as shown in Fig. 4.2.

You are now ready to start the preparation.

7. Get your teacher to check the apparatus.
8. Make sure that the tap of the dropping funnel is closed.

9. Pour 10 cm^3 of concentrated hydrochloric acid into the dropping funnel.
10. Allow a few drops of acid to trickle onto the potassium manganate(VII) and allow chlorine to displace air from the apparatus. Then let the acid continue dropping slowly into the flask.
11. Heat the aluminium gently near the calcium chloride until a bright glow shows that the chloride is reacting exothermically with the aluminium. If the glow is very bright, remove the heat until it subsides.
12. Continue heating, all around the tube, moving the flame slowly towards the receiver bottle, until reaction is complete.
13. When reaction is complete, stop the trickle of acid and let the combustion tube cool (about 10 minutes). Meanwhile weigh the empty specimen tube and top.
14. Remove the receiver bottle and, using your spatula, quickly scrape the product into the specimen tube. Place the top on the specimen tube and weigh it.
15. Record your results in a copy of Results Table 4.17.
16. Label the specimen tube with your name and the name of the product and store it in a desiccator.

Results Table 4.17

Mass of aluminium	g
Mass of empty specimen tube, m_1	g
Mass of specimen tube and product, m_2	g
Mass of product, $m = (m_2 - m_1)$	g
% yield	

Questions
1. Why is it important to use dry chlorine in this experiment?
2. What impurity would be present in the product if damp chlorine were used? Write an equation for the reaction giving this impurity.

3. Calculate and comment on the percentage yield of your product, using the expression

$$\% \text{ yield} = \frac{\text{actual mass of product}}{\text{maximum mass of product}} \times 100$$

4. Why is your product stored in a desiccator?

EXPERIMENT 4.14 Investigating the properties of Period 3 oxides

Aim

The purpose of this experiment is to examine the oxides of Period 3 elements and describe their bonding and structure.

Introduction

You carry out an investigation along similar lines to the work you did on the chlorides of the elements in Period 3 (Experiment 4.12). However, you will not be asked to test the oxides with cyclohexane because unlike the covalent chlorides, most of the oxides are not composed of discrete molecules. Therefore they are unlikely to dissolve in cyclohexane and simple experiments cannot distinguish between insolubility and slight solubility.

Requirements

- safety spectacles
- access to a fume cupboard
- 6 test-tubes
- test-tube rack
- 1 measuring cylinder, 10 cm^3
- 1 measuring cylinder, 100 cm^3
- distilled water
- thermometer, 0–100 °C
- 1 spatula
- universal indicator solution and colour chart
- teat pipette
- pH paper
- splints
- sodium peroxide, Na_2O_2
- magnesium oxide, MgO
- aluminium oxide, Al_2O_3
- phosphorus(V) oxide, P_4O_{10}
- silicon(IV) oxide, SiO_2
- access to sulphur dioxide cylinder or generator, SO_2
- Drechsel bottle
- glass tubing with right-angled bend
- rubber tubing for connections

HAZARD WARNING

Phosphorus(V) oxide is corrosive and irritates eyes, skin and lungs. Sodium peroxide is also corrosive and a powerful oxidant. Sulphur dioxide is a **toxic** gas with a choking smell. Therefore you **must**:
- **do the experiment at the fume cupboard;**
- **wear safety spectacles;**
- **avoid contact with skin.**

Procedure – Part A

Appearance

1. Examine your oxide samples, and in a larger copy of Results Table 4.18 note for each:
   a whether it is solid, liquid or gaseous,
   b its colour (if any).

Procedure
– Part B

On mixing with water

2. Set up six test-tubes, side by side.
3. Into each tube pour about 5 cm³ of distilled water.
4. In the first test-tube place a thermometer.
    a Note the temperature.
    b Add half a spatula-tip of sodium peroxide and stir carefully with the thermometer.
    c Note, after about one minute, i) the temperature, ii) whether the solid has dissolved and iii) anything else you see. For example, is gas evolved at any time? If so, is the gas acidic? Can you identify it using a simple test?
    d Add 2–4 drops of universal indicator solution, compare the colour with the chart provided, and note the pH indicated, or use a piece of pH paper.

5. Repeat the above steps **4a–d** using, in turn, magnesium oxide, aluminium oxide, silicon(IV) oxide and phosphorus(V) oxide.
6. Measure the pH of the water in the sixth test-tube by adding 2–4 drops of universal indicator solution for comparison with the above.
7. Bubble sulphur dioxide slowly through the water in the sixth test-tube until there is no further change in the colour of the indicator. Note the final pH of the solution. (You will probably be given sulphur dioxide in liquid form in a cylinder. To obtain the gas you carefully open the valve and the sudden decrease in pressure inside the cylinder causes the surface liquid to vaporise. Make sure there is a Drechsel bottle between the cylinder and the water in case of suck-back. Alternatively, your teacher may suggest other ways of generating the gas.)
8. To test the solubility of sulphur dioxide lower the delivery tube from your generator to the bottom of the 100 cm³ measuring cylinder filled with water. Pass a slow steady stream of gas through the water and when the air has been expelled from your apparatus look for a change in the size of the sulphur dioxide gas bubbles as they rise up through the water.

Results Table 4.18

	Na_2O_2	MgO	Al_2O_3	SiO_2	P_4O_{10}	SO_2
Appearance						
On mixing with water						
Initial temperature						
Final temperature						
Does it dissolve?						
pH of solution						
Other observation(s) (if any)						

Questions

1. Use your experimental results, your data book and your textbook(s) if necessary to complete a larger copy of Table 4.2 on the next page.

Table 4.2

Formula of oxide	Na$_2$O$_2$*	MgO	Al$_2$O$_3$	SiO$_2$	P$_4$O$_{10}$*	SO$_2$*	Cl$_2$O*
Melting point/°C							
Boiling point/°C							
State at s.t.p.							
Action of water							
pH of aq. solution							
Acid–base nature							
Conductivity of liquid							
Solubility in cyclohexane							
Structure							
Bonding							

*These substances represent the most familiar or readily available oxides of that element. In general the other oxides of that element have similar properties.

2. Write equations for any reactions which took place when you added the oxides to water.
3. Comment on the change in structure and bonding in the oxides between sodium and chlorine.
4. How does the acid–base nature of the oxides of the elements in Period 3 change with increasing atomic number?
5. Can you relate this change to the change in structure and bonding that takes place along the period?

ILPAC

5

INTRODUCTION TO
ORGANIC CHEMISTRY

EXPERIMENT 5.1 Chemical properties of alkanes

Aims

The purpose of this experiment is to test the reactivity of the alkanes using cyclohexane as an example.

Introduction

We have chosen cyclohexane as an example of an alkane because it is a liquid, which makes it easy to handle, and because it is cheap. It has virtually the same reactions as hexane and is very similar to other alkanes. It is also less hazardous to use than hexane. You use cyclohexane in five simple test-tube reactions.

Requirements

- safety spectacles
- protective gloves
- cyclohexane (with teat pipette)
- hard glass watch glass
- Bunsen burner and bench protection mat
- wood splints
- beaker, 250 cm^3
- 1 dry test-tube covered in aluminium foil
- 5 dry test-tubes with corks to fit
- test-tube rack
- bromine dissolved in an inert solvent
- lamp with 100 watt bulb
- ammonia solution, 5 M NH$_3$
- dilute sulphuric acid, 1 M H$_2$SO$_4$
- potassium manganate(VII) solution, 0.01 M KMnO$_4$
- concentrated sulphuric acid, H$_2$SO$_4$

HAZARD WARNING

Bromine is dangerously **toxic** and corrosive, especially in its liquid state. Solutions, such as those used in this experiment, must also be treated with care. Therefore you **must**:
- **do the experiment in a fume cupboard;**
- **keep the top on the bottle as much as possible;**
- **wear gloves and safety spectacles.**

Cyclohexane is very flammable. Therefore you **must**:
- **keep the top on the bottle as much as possible;**
- **keep the bottle away from flames;**
- **wear safety spectacles.**

Ammonia solution (5 M) is an irritant. Take great care when opening bottles on a hot day. You **must**:
- **wear safety spectacles.**

Concentrated sulphuric acid is very corrosive and reacts violently with water. Therefore you **must**:
- **wear gloves and safety spectacles;**
- **dispose of unwanted acid by cooling and pouring slowly into an excess of water.**

Procedure – Part A

Combustion

1. Place your watch glass on a bench protection sheet in the fume cupboard. Put on safety spectacles and make sure the extractor in the fume cupboard is switched on.
2. Using a teat pipette, place 3–4 drops of cyclohexane on the watch glass.
3. Stopper and remove the bottle of cyclohexane to a safe place away from the watch glass and any Bunsen flames.

4. Pull down the front of the fume cupboard leaving a 30 cm opening.
5. Light a long splint and use this to light the cyclohexane. Lower the front of the fume cupboard to a 10 cm opening.
6. Write down, in a larger copy of Results Table 5.1:
   a the colour of the flame,
   b whether you can see any soot produced.

Procedure – Part B

Reaction of bromine (dissolved in inert solvent)
Put on safety spectacles and make sure the extractor in the fume cupboard is switched on.
7. Place the test-tube covered with aluminium foil in a rack in the fume cupboard. Put an uncovered tube alongside. Put on safety spectacles and gloves.
8. Using a teat pipette, place approximately 2 cm^3 of cyclohexane in each test-tube.
9. Stopper the cyclohexane and remove it to a safe place away from flames.
10. Pull down the front of the fume cupboard leaving a 30 cm opening.
11. Using a teat pipette, place in each tube five drops of a solution of bromine in inert solvent.
12. Stopper the bromine bottle.
13. Shine the lamp on both test-tubes for about 3 minutes.
14. A gas is given off during this experiment. Think what gas could be given off and work out a test for the gas. Note the test and its result in your Results Table.
15. Note the appearance of the contents of the clear test-tube.
16. Pour the contents of the test-tube covered with aluminium foil into a clean test-tube. Note its appearance.

Procedure – Part C

Reaction of acidified potassium manganate(VII)
17. Place a test-tube in a rack in the fume cupboard.
18. Using a teat pipette, place 3–4 drops of cyclohexane in the test-tube.
19. Stopper and remove the bottle of cyclohexane to a safe place, away from flames.
20. Pour into the test-tube approximately 1 cm^3 of dilute sulphuric acid and gently agitate the mixture.
21. Pour into the test-tube 5–6 drops of potassium manganate(VII) solution and shake the mixture.
22. Note the appearance of the reaction mixture.

Procedure – Part D

Reaction of concentrated sulphuric acid
23. Place a test-tube in a rack in the fume cupboard.
24. Pour into the test-tube approximately 1 cm^3 of concentrated sulphuric acid.
25. Pour into the test-tube approximately 1 cm^3 of cyclohexane.
26. Stopper and remove the bottle of cyclohexane to a safe place, away from flames.
27. Note whether the substances mix or form two separate layers.
28. Dispose of this solution by adding it to a beaker of water.

Results Table 5.1
Reactions of alkanes

Reaction	Observations
A **Combustion**	
Appearance of flame	
Sootiness	
B **Action of bromine** (in inert solvent)	
1. In dark	
2. In light	
Identification of gas	
C **Action of acidified potassium manganate(VII)**	
D **Action of concentrated sulphuric acid**	

Questions

1. **a** Look up the C—C and C—H bond energies in your data book. Are these values higher or lower than most of the other single bonds listed?
   b What does your answer to part **a** suggest about the reactivity of alkanes?
   c Do the results of this experiment support your answer to part **b**?

2. **a** What are the products of complete combustion of the alkanes?
   b Use your data book to write full thermochemical equations for the combustion of methane, ethane and propane.
   c How do your answers to part **b** relate to the uses of the alkanes?

3. **a** What is meant by the term 'substitution reaction'? Refer to your organic textbook(s).
   b Complete the following equation for the substitution reaction between equal amounts of cyclohexane and bromine.

$$+ Br_2 \longrightarrow$$

   c What conditions favour the reaction shown in **b** above?
   d In the presence of excess bromine, it is possible to substitute more than one hydrogen atom per molecule of alkane. Write four equations showing all the possible substitution products of reaction between bromine and methane, CH_4, in sunlight. Name the products.

EXPERIMENT 5.2 Chemical properties of alkenes

Aim

The purpose of this experiment is to test the reactivity of the alkenes by carrying out some test-tube reactions on cyclohexene.

Introduction

You will be using cyclohexene (which is a cycloalkene) because it is one of the cheapest liquid alkenes. It has virtually the same reactions as hexene and is similar to other alkenes. You will repeat the same reactions on cyclohexene that you performed on cyclohexane. This will enable you to compare the reactivities of the two types of hydrocarbon.

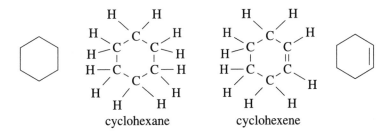

cyclohexane   cyclohexene

Requirements and Procedure

Work through the details of Experiment 5.1 again except that you substitute cyclohexene for cyclohexane. Record your results in another copy of Results Table 5.1, this time labelling it Results Table 5.2.

HAZARD WARNING

Cyclohexene is an irritant. **The vapour must not be inhaled.** In the reaction between cyclohexene and concentrated sulphuric acid **the amounts suggested must be strictly adhered to.** Use **eye protection** as usual and make sure the front of the fume cupboard is down as far as possible. All other precautions taken for Experiment 5.1 must also be adhered to here.

Questions

1. **a** Calculate the C—C bond dissociation energy in ethane, C_2H_6, given the following information:

$$2C(g) + 6H(g) \rightarrow C_2H_6(g); \quad \Delta H^\circ = -2820 \text{ kJ mol}^{-1}$$

$$\bar{E}(C—H) = 412 \text{ kJ mol}^{-1}$$

   b Calculate the C=C bond dissociation energy in ethene, C_2H_4, given the following information:

$$2C(g) + 4H(g) \rightarrow C_2H_4(g); \quad \Delta H^\circ = -2260 \text{ kJ mol}^{-1}$$

   c Assuming that the σ-bonds in ethane and ethene are identical (they are certainly very similar), calculate the approximate bond dissociation energy for the π-bond in ethene.
   d Would you expect ethene to be more or less reactive than ethane?
   e Was the answer you gave in part **d** verified by experiment?
2. Why do you think alkenes produce a sootier flame than alkanes?
3. Which test(s) could be used to distinguish between alkanes and alkenes?

EXPERIMENT 5.3 Hydrolysis of organic halogen compounds

Aim The purpose of this experiment is to find out how the rate of hydrolysis of an organic halogen compound depends on:
a the identity of the halogen atom,
b the nature of the carbon–hydrogen 'skeleton'.

Introduction In this experiment, you compare the rates of hydrolysis of 1-chlorobutane, 1-bromobutane, 1-iodobutane and chlorobenzene. A general equation for the hydrolysis is:

$$R—X + H_2O \rightarrow R—OH + H^+ + X^-$$

(where R = alkyl or aryl group; X = halogen atom).

You can follow the rate of the reaction by carrying it out in the presence of silver ions, so that any halide ions produced form a silver halide precipitate.

$$Ag^+(aq) + X^-(aq) \rightarrow AgX(s)$$

Since halogenoalkanes and halogenoarenes are insoluble in water, ethanol is added to act as a common solvent for the halogeno-compounds and silver ions.

Requirements
- safety spectacles
- Bunsen burner, tripod, gauze and bench protection sheet (or a theromostatically controlled water-bath, set at 60 °C)
- beaker, 250 cm³
- thermometer, 0–100 °C
- 5 test-tubes fitted with corks
- test-tube rack
- waterproof marker or chinagraph pencil
- protective plastic gloves
- measuring cylinder, 10 cm³
- ethanol, C_2H_5OH
- 1-chlorobutane, C_4H_9Cl
- 1-bromobutane, C_4H_9Br
- 1-iodobutane, C_4H_9I
- chlorobenzene, C_6H_5Cl
- silver nitrate solution, 0.05 M $AgNO_3$
- stopclock (or clock with seconds hand)

HAZARD WARNING

All organic halogen compounds have harmful vapours and can be **toxic** by absorption through the skin. Some are flammable. Therefore you **must**:
- **keep the stoppers on the bottles as much as possible;**
- **keep the bottles away from flames;**
- **wear safety spectacles and gloves.**

Procedure 1. Set up the apparatus shown in Fig. 5.1 (or switch on your electric water-bath). Make sure none of the test-tubes contains any tap-water; this would give an immediate precipitate with silver nitrate and spoil your results.

Figure 5.1

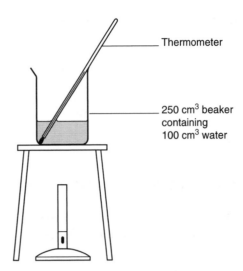

2. Pour 2 cm^3 of ethanol into each of four test-tubes and mark them with the letters A to D.
3. Add 3–4 drops of 1-chlorobutane to A, 3–4 drops of 1-bromobutane to B, 3–4 drops of 1-iodobutane to C and 3–4 drops of chlorobenzene to D.
4. Pour about 5 cm^3 of silver nitrate solution into the fifth test-tube.
5. Stand all the test-tubes in the beaker (or water-bath) and heat to 60 °C. Remove the Bunsen burner.
6. Quickly add 1 cm^3 of aqueous silver nitrate to each of the tubes A to D and start the stopclock. Shake each tube once to mix the contents, and leave in the water with the cork resting **loosely** on the tube to reduce evaporation.
7. Watch the tubes continuously for about ten minutes and note, in a copy of Results Table 5.3, the time when a precipitate first appears in each tube as a definite cloudiness. If necessary, heat the water to 60 °C again at intervals.
8. Continue observation at intervals for about 30 minutes more, noting any further changes in the appearance of the precipitates.

Results Table 5.3

Reaction	Time for precipitate to appear	Observations
A 1-Chlorobutane		
B 1-Bromobutane		
C 1-Iodobutane		
D Chlorobenzene		

Table 5.1

Bond		Bond energy /kJ mol^{-1}
C—Cl	in halogenoalkanes	338
C—Br		276
C—I		238
C—Cl	in ⬡—Cl	365

Questions
1. Use the data listed in Table 5.1 on page 75 to predict the likely order of reactivity of the following compounds:
   1-chlorobutane, 1-bromobutane, 1-iodobutane, chlorobenzene.
2. From your experimental results, list the compounds in order of speed of hydrolysis, fastest first.
3. Was the prediction you made in question 1 verified by experiment?
4. Write equations for the hydrolysis reactions which take place in this experiment.

EXPERIMENT 5.4 Preparation of a halogenoalkane

Aim
The purpose of this experiment is to prepare 2-chloro-2-methylpropane and to illustrate several practical techniques employed in organic chemistry.

Introduction
In this experiment you prepare 2-chloro-2-methylpropane from 2-methylpropan-2-ol and hydrochloric acid. The reaction takes place at room temperature because tertiary alcohols undergo substitution very readily.

$$
\begin{array}{ccccc}
& CH_3 & & & CH_3 \\
& | & & & | \\
CH_3 - & C - CH_3 & + \ HCl & \longrightarrow & CH_3 - C - CH_3 & + \ H_2O \\
& | & & & | \\
& OH & & & Cl
\end{array}
$$

  2-methylpropan-2-ol   2-chloro-2-methylpropane

In this preparation you will meet the techniques of simple distillation and use of a separating funnel, which are commonly used in the purification of an organic liquid to give the best possible yield.

Requirements
- safety spectacles and gloves
- measuring cylinder, 25 cm^3
- 2-methylpropan-2-ol, $(CH_3)_3COH$
- access to balance, sensitivity ± 0.1 g or better
- separating funnel, 50 cm^3, with stopper
- 3 retort stands, bosses and clamps
- hydrochloric acid, concentrated, HCl
- ground-glass-joint apparatus shown in Fig. 5.2 (with rubber tubing)
- Bunsen burner, tripod and gauze
- thermometer, 0–100 °C
- conical flask, 100 cm^3, with bung
- sodium hydrogencarbonate solution, saturated, $NaHCO_3$
- sodium sulphate, anhydrous, Na_2SO_4
- spatula
- anti-bumping chips

HAZARD WARNING

2-Chloro-2-methylpropane and 2-methylpropan-2-ol are flammable. Concentrated hydrochloric acid is corrosive and gives off a harmful vapour. Therefore you **must**:
- **keep stoppers on bottles as much as possible;**
- **keep flammable liquids away from flames;**
- **wear gloves and safety spectacles.**

Procedure

1. Pour about 9 cm³ of 2-methylpropan-2-ol into a measuring cylinder, weigh it, and note its mass in a copy of Results Table 5.4.
2. Pour the 2-methylpropan-2-ol into a 50 cm³ separating funnel and again weigh and record the mass of the measuring cylinder. Then add 20 cm³ of concentrated hydrochloric acid about 3 cm³ at a time. After each addition hold the stopper and tap securely in place and invert the funnel a few times; then, with the funnel in the upright position, loosen the stopper briefly to release any pressure.
3. Leave the separating funnel plus contents in the fume cupboard for about twenty minutes and shake it gently at intervals.
4. Meanwhile, set up, in a fume cupboard, a clean distillation apparatus, as shown in Fig. 5.2. Remember that the apparatus is a rigid assembly; you must be very careful when you clamp it at more than one point, to avoid strain and possible breakage.

Figure 5.2
Distillation.

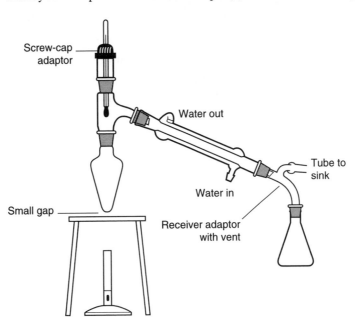

5. Weigh the small flask used as a receiver for the distillate.
6. Allow the layers in the separating funnel to separate; run off and discard the lower aqueous layer.
7. Add sodium hydrogencarbonate solution 2 cm³ at a time in order to neutralise any excess hydrochloric acid. Shake the funnel carefully after each addition and release the pressure of carbon dioxide frequently by loosening the stopper. Continue until no more carbon dioxide is produced.
8. Allow the layers to separate; run off and discard the lower aqueous layer.
9. Run the organic layer into a small, dry conical flask and add about three spatula-measures of anhydrous sodium sulphate to dry the organic liquid. Cork and swirl the flask occasionally for about five minutes.
10. Carefully decant (pour off) the dried organic liquid from the solid sodium sulphate into the pear-shaped flask set up for distillation, as in Fig. 5.2. If you decant slowly, you should be able to separate the solid and liquid completely – no solid must enter the distilling flask.
11. Add a few anti-bumping granules to the pear-shaped flask and distil the 2-chloro-2-methylpropane, collecting the fraction in the range 47–53 °C into the pre-weighed conical flask. Heat gently at first and then more strongly but only just strongly enough to keep the product distilling at about 1–2 drops per second.
12. Determine the mass of 2-chloro-2-methylpropane collected.

Results Table 5.4

Mass of measuring cylinder + 2-methylpropan-2-ol	g
Mass of measuring cylinder after emptying	g
Mass of 2-methylpropan-2-ol	g
Mass of collecting flask	g
Mass of collecting flask + 2-chloro-2-methylpropane	g
Mass of 2-chloro-2-methylpropane	g

Questions

1. From the chemical equation, calculate the maximum mass of 2-chloro-2-methylpropane that could be formed from the mass of 2-methylpropan-2-ol you used.

2. Calculate the percentage yield of 2-chloro-2-methylpropane using the expression

$$\% \text{ yield} = \frac{\text{actual mass of product}}{\text{maximum mass of product}} \times 100$$

3. Why is sodium hydrogencarbonate used to remove acid impurities, rather than a stronger alkali such as sodium hydroxide?

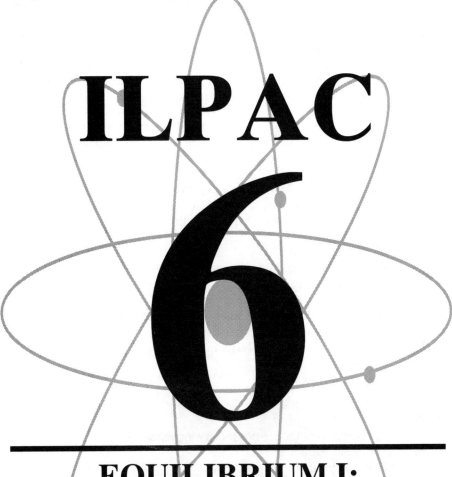

ILPAC

6

EQUILIBRIUM I:
PRINCIPLES

EXPERIMENT 6.1 The effect of concentration changes on equilibria

Aim The purpose of this experiment is to find out how a system in equilibrium responds to a change in concentration of components in the mixture.

Introduction Iron(III) ions and thiocyanate ions react in solution to produce thiocyanatoiron(III), a complex ion, according to the equation:

$$Fe^{3+}(aq) + SCN^-(aq) \rightleftharpoons Fe(SCN)^{2+}(aq)$$

pale   colourless   blood-red
yellow

The colour produced by the complex ion can indicate the position of equilibrium. (The colour of the Fe^{3+}(aq) ion is in fact a very pale violet, but solutions of iron(III) salts are usually yellow, due to the formation of other complexes.)

Requirements
- safety spectacles
- 4 test-tubes and test-tube rack
- 2 teat pipettes
- distilled water
- potassium thiocyanate solution, 0.5 M KSCN
- iron(III) chloride solution, 0.5 M $FeCl_3$

- ammonium chloride, NH_4Cl
- spatula
- glass stirring rod

HAZARD WARNING

Ammonium chloride is harmful by ingestion.
Therefore you **must**:
- **wash your hands after use.**

Procedure
1. Mix together one drop of 0.5 M iron(III) chloride solution and one drop of 0.5 M potassium thiocyanate solution in a test-tube and add about 5 cm³ of distilled water to form a pale orange–brown solution.
2. Divide this solution into four equal parts in four test-tubes.
3. Add one drop of 0.5 M iron(III) chloride to one test-tube. Add one drop of 0.5 M potassium thiocyanate to a second.
4. Compare the colours of these solutions with the untouched samples. Enter your observations in a copy of Results Table 6.1.
5. Add a spatula-measure of solid ammonium chloride to a third test-tube and stir well. Compare the colour of this solution with the remaining tube and note your observation.

     Ammonium chloride removes iron(III) ions from the equilibrium by forming complex ions such as $FeCl_4^-$. A possible reaction is:

$$Fe^{3+}(aq) + 4Cl^-(aq) \rightleftharpoons FeCl_4^-(aq)$$

The effect is to reduce the concentration of iron(III) ions.

Interpretation of results Having made three observations, suggest a **cause** for each colour change (in terms of the concentrations of the coloured species) and then suggest what can be **inferred** about a shift in the position of equilibrium.

     If a pattern has emerged, then you can make a prediction based on the results of the experiment.

Results Table 6.1

Change	Observation	Cause	Inference
$[Fe^{3+}]$ increased			
$[SCN^-]$ increased			
$[Fe^{3+}]$ decreased			

Questions
1. How would the position of equilibrium be affected by increasing the concentration of $FeSCN^{2+}$?
2. For each imposed change show how the shift in equilibrium position conforms to Le Chatelier's principle.

EXPERIMENT 6.2   Determining an equilibrium constant

Aim   The purpose of this experiment is to calculate the equilibrium constant for the reaction:

$$CH_3CO_2C_2H_5(l) + H_2O(l) \rightleftharpoons C_2H_5OH(l) + CH_3CO_2H(l)$$

ethyl ethanoate   water   ethanol   ethanoic acid

Introduction   The reaction between ethyl ethanoate and water is very slow. However, by using a catalyst, dilute hydrochloric acid, equilibrium can be attained in about 48 hours.

In part A of the experiment you prepare, in sealed containers, mixtures containing different proportions of the two reactants. To each mixture you add a fixed amount of dilute hydrochloric acid as a catalyst.

In part B, after the mixtures have reached equilibrium at room temperature, you analyse each one by titration with sodium hydroxide. Part of the added sodium hydroxide reacts with the catalyst; the rest indicates the amount of ethanoic acid in the equilibrium mixture.

Finally, from the starting amounts and the amount of ethanoic acid produced, you calculate the equilibrium amounts of all four components and use them to determine the equilibrium constant.

Requirements – Part A
- safety spectacles
- 5 specimen tubes with well-fitting caps
- labels for tubes and stoppers
- access to a balance (sensitivity ± 0.01 g or better)
- pipette, 5 cm^3, and safety filler
- dilute hydrochloric acid, 2 M HCl
- 2 measuring cylinders, 10 cm^3 (one must be dry)
- ethyl ethanoate, $CH_3CO_2C_2H_5$
- distilled water

Procedure – Part A
1. Label five specimen tubes with your name and the date. Number them 1a, 1b, 2, 3 and 4. Number the stoppers too, so that they do not get misplaced.
2. Weigh each tube, with its stopper, and record the masses in a copy of Results Table 6.2.
3. Using a pipette and safety filler, carefully add 5.0 cm^3 of 2 M hydrochloric acid to each tube, replacing the stoppers as you go. The volume of acid must be precisely the same in each tube; measure it as carefully as you can. If you think you have made a mistake, wash out the tube, dry it and start again.
4. Weigh each stoppered tube in turn and record the masses.
5. Select a **dry** measuring cylinder, and use it to add to tubes 2, 3 and 4 the volumes (approximate) of ethyl ethanoate shown in Results Table 6.2, again replacing the stoppers as you go.

6. Weigh the stoppered tubes 2, 3 and 4. Record the masses.
7. From a second measuring cylinder, add to tubes 3 and 4 the volumes (approximate) of distilled water shown in Results Table 6.2, again replacing the stoppers as you go.
8. Weigh the stoppered tubes 3 and 4. Record the masses.
9. Gently shake the tubes and set them aside for at least 48 hours. During this time, arrange to shake the tubes occasionally.

HAZARD WARNING

Ethyl ethanoate is flammable. Therefore you **must**:
■ **keep the stopper on the bottle as much as possible;**
■ **keep the liquid away from a naked flame.**
Hydrochloric acid is an irritant.

Sodium hydroxide solution is very corrosive. Even when dilute it can damage your eyes.
Therefore you **must**:
■ **wear safety spectacles throughout the experiment.**

Results Table 6.2

Tube number	1a	1b	2	3	4
Mass of empty tube/g					
Volume of HCl(aq) added/cm^3	5.0	5.0	5.0	5.0	5.0
Mass of tube after addition/g					
Volume of ethyl ethanoate added/cm^3	–	–	5.0	4.0	2.0
Mass of tube after addition/g					
Volume of water added/cm^3	–	–	–	1.0	3.0
Mass of tube after addition/g					
Mass of ethyl ethanoate added/g					
Mass of HCl(aq) added/g					
Mass of water added/g					

In addition to the two tubes containing only hydrochloric acid, you now have three tubes containing different amounts of ethyl ethanoate and water (tube 2 has water from the acid). When these mixtures have reached equilibrium, you can analyse them in part B of the experiment.

Before you begin part B, revise the technique of titration.

**Requirements
– Part B**

■ safety spectacles
■ 5 conical flasks, 250 cm^3
■ wash-bottle of distilled water
■ phenolphthalein indicator
■ burette, stand and white tile
■ small funnel
■ sodium hydroxide solution, 1 M NaOH (standardised)

**Procedure
– Part B**

1. Rinse and fill a burette with standardised sodium hydroxide solution.
2. Carefully pour the contents of tube 1a into a conical flask. Rinse the tube into the flask three times with distilled water.
3. Add two to three drops of phenolphthalein indicator solution and titrate the acid against sodium hydroxide solution. Record your burette readings in a copy of Results Table 6.3.

4. Repeat steps 2 and 3 for each of the other tubes in turn. Remember that tube 1b should require the same volume of alkali as tube 1a, but the others should require a little more. Complete Results Table 6.3.

Results Table 6.3

Solution in flask	Equilibrium mixture				
Solution in burette	Sodium hydroxide			mol dm^{-3}	
Indicator	Phenolphthalein				
Tube number	1a	1b	2	3	4
Final burette reading					
Initial burette reading					
Titre/cm^3					

Calculations

The calculations seem complex, but consist of several very simple steps. The flow scheme below summarises the procedure; refer to it as you work through so that you can see the purpose of each step.

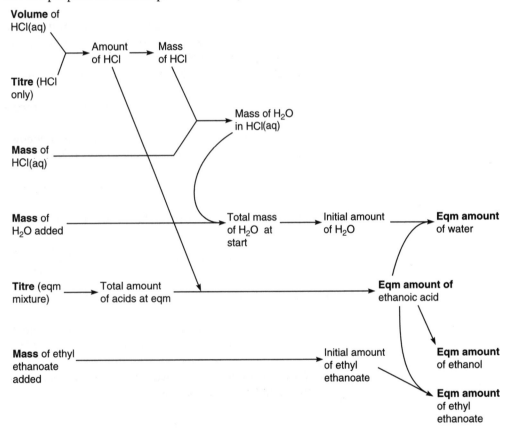

1. From the average titre for tubes 1a and 1b (or the better titre if you think one was inaccurate), calculate the amount of hydrochloric acid catalyst you added to each of the five tubes. Remember that hydrochloric acid and sodium hydroxide react in equimolar amounts and that

$$amount = concentration \times volume.$$

Record this amount in each column of a copy of Results Table 6.4.

2. From the titres for tubes 2, 3 and 4 in turn, calculate and record the total amount of acid (hydrochloric and ethanoic) in each mixture.

3. Calculate, by subtraction, the amount of ethanoic acid in each equilibrium mixture. This is the first of the four quantities you need to substitute in the equilibrium law expression. Complete the third row of Results Table 6.4.
4. The equation for the equilibrium system shows that the amount of ethanol produced is equal to the amount of ethanoic acid produced. You now have the second of the four quantities you need. Complete the fourth row of your table.
5. From the data in Results Table 6.2, calculate the amount of ethyl ethanoate added to each tube

$$\text{amount of ethyl ethanoate} = \frac{\text{mass after addition} - \text{mass before addition}}{\text{molar mass}}$$

Complete the fifth row of your table.
6. Calculate and record the equilibrium amount of ethyl ethanoate in each tube, using the relationship:

$$\begin{array}{c}\text{eqm amount of} \\ CH_3CO_2C_2H_5\end{array} = \begin{array}{c}\text{initial amount of} \\ CH_3CO_2C_2H_5\end{array} - \begin{array}{c}\text{eqm amount of} \\ CH_3CO_2H\end{array}$$

You can see from the chemical equation that the amount of ethyl ethanoate which reacts is equal to the amount of ethanoic acid produced. You now have the third of the four quantities you need.
7. Calculate and record the mass of **pure** HCl in each mixture

$$\text{mass} = \text{amount} \times \text{molar mass}$$

8. Calculate and record the mass of water in the **aqueous** HCl added to each tube. (You need to refer back to Results Table 6.2.)

$$\text{mass of water} = \text{mass of HCl(aq)} - \text{mass of HCl}$$

9. Calculate and record the total amount of water initially in each mixture

$$\text{initial amount of } H_2O = \frac{\text{mass in HCl(aq)} + \text{mass added}}{\text{molar mass}}$$

10. Calculate and record the equilibrium amount of water in each mixture

$$\begin{array}{c}\text{eqm amount} \\ \text{of } H_2O\end{array} = \begin{array}{c}\text{initial amount} \\ \text{of } H_2O\end{array} - \begin{array}{c}\text{eqm amount} \\ \text{of } CH_3CO_2H\end{array}$$

11. Write an equilibrium law expression for the reaction and calculate three values of the equilibrium constant, K_c.

Results Table 6.4

Tube number		**2**	**3**	**4**
1.	Amount of HCl/mol			
2.	Total amount of acid at eqm/mol			
3.	Eqm amount of ethanoic acid/mol			
4.	Eqm amount of ethanol/mol			
5.	Initial amount of ethyl ethanoate/mol			
6.	Eqm amount of ethyl ethanoate/mol			
7.	Mass of pure HCl/g			
8.	Mass of water in HCl(aq)/g			
9.	Initial amount of water/mol			
10.	Eqm amount of water/mol			
11.	Eqm constant, K_c			

Questions

1. In step 2 of part B some more water (one of the reactants) is added to the mixture. Furthermore, titration of the equilibrium mixture with sodium hydroxide neutralises both the catalyst acid and the ethanoic acid. In other words, one of the products is removed.

   Use Le Chatelier's principle to predict what effect these procedures should have on the equilibrium position.

2. It seems that analysis of the equilibrium mixture by this titration does not in fact disturb the equilibrium to any noticeable extent. Can you explain this?

EXPERIMENT 6.3 Determining a solubility product

Aim

The purpose of this experiment is to determine the solubility and solubility product of calcium hydroxide.

Introduction

The equilibrium between solid calcium hydroxide and its ions in an aqueous solution is

$$Ca(OH)_2(s) \rightleftharpoons Ca^{2+}(aq) + 2OH^-(aq)$$

The concentration of hydroxide ions can be determined by titration with hydrochloric acid; the concentration of calcium ions can be calculated from the titration result.

Requirements

- safety spectacles
- 4 stoppered bottles, 250 cm^3
- labels for bottles
- spatula
- calcium hydroxide, solid, Ca(OH)$_2$
- measuring cylinder, 100 cm^3
- distilled water
- 4 filter funnels, **dry,** with filter papers
- 4 conical flasks, 250 cm^3
- thermometer 0–100 °C (±1°C)
- pipette, 25 cm^3, and safety filler
- burette and stand, white tile
- small funnel
- hydrochloric acid solution, 0.1 M – standardised
- phenolphthalein indicator solution

Procedure
1. Into each of four bottles put about 2 g of powdered calcium hydroxide and about 100 cm³ of distilled water. Stopper securely.
2. Shake well for about a minute. Label each bottle with your name, experiment and date, and set aside for a day or more.
3. Rinse and fill the burette with standardised hydrochloric acid.
4. Filter the contents of one bottle, allowing the first 5 cm³ to run to waste and collecting the rest in a dry conical flask. (The first few cm³ are rejected because they are less concentrated in solute than the rest. The filter paper adsorbs solute until it attains equilibrium with the solution. Yet another equilibrium!)

To minimise absorption of carbon dioxide, steps 5 and 6 should be done quickly (with due care!) and with only the minimum shaking that will ensure mixing.

5. Rinse the pipette with the calcium hydroxide solution and transfer 25.0 cm³ to a conical flask (this need not be dry).
6. Add two drops of phenolphthalein to the flask and titrate the solution until the pink colour just disappears. Record your burette readings in a copy of Results Table 6.5.
7. Repeat steps 4, 5 and 6 for the other three solutions.
8. Record the temperature.

Results Table 6.5

Solution in flask			mol dm^{-3}	cm³
Solution in burette			mol dm^{-3}	
Indicator				

		Trial	1	2	3	4
Burette readings	Final					
	Initial					
Volume used/cm³						
Mean titre/cm³						

Calculation
1. Calculate the concentration of hydroxide ions in a saturated solution of calcium hydroxide.
2. From the equilibrium concentration of hydroxide ions calculate the equilibrium concentration of calcium ions.
3. Calculate the solubility of calcium hydroxide at the temperature of your experiment. Compare your result with the value listed in your data book.
4. Calculate the solubility product from:
   a your result,
   b the solubility of calcium hydroxide given in your data book.

EXPERIMENT 6.4 Illustrating the common ion effect

Aim
The purpose of this experiment is to demonstrate an example of the application of Le Chatelier's principle.

Introduction
Although sodium chloride is quite soluble, we can use it to demonstrate the common ion effect.

Requirements
■ safety spectacles
■ 2 test-tubes with corks, in a rack
■ sodium chloride solution, saturated, NaCl
■ hydrochloric acid, concentrated, HCl

- teat pipette
- sodium hydroxide, pellets, NaOH
- spatula or forceps

HAZARD WARNING

Concentrated hydrochloric acid is a corrosive liquid, and its vapour is harmful to eyes, lungs and skin.
Sodium hydroxide is corrosive. Therefore you **must**:
- **wear safety spectacles;**
- **keep the stoppers on the bottles as much as possible.**

Procedure

1. Carefully pour about 10 cm^3 of saturated sodium chloride solution into each of two test-tubes. Do not transfer any solid.
2. To the first test-tube carefully add four to five drops of concentrated hydrochloric acid. Cork the tube, shake gently and set aside.
3. To the second test-tube add one pellet of sodium hydroxide. **Use forceps or spatula to handle the sodium hydroxide.** Cork the tube, shake gently and set aside.
4. Note any observations.

Questions
1. What did you see happen in each test-tube?
2. Interpret your observations in terms of Le Chatelier's principle.
3. In the saturated solution of sodium chloride, what is the concentration of each ion? (Use your data book.)
4. The concentration of concentrated hydrochloric acid is approximately 12 mol dm^{-3}. Explain what happened to the sodium ions in solution when the hydrochloric acid was added.
5. Explain what happened to the chloride ions in solution when the sodium hydroxide pellet was added.
6. Why is no solubility product value given for sodium chloride in any data book?

EXPERIMENT 6.5   Distribution equilibrium

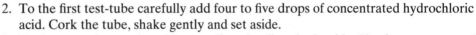

Aim
The purpose of this experiment is to determine the value of the distribution coefficient for the equilibrium that exists when ammonia is distributed between water and an organic solvent, Volasil 244.

Introduction
In this experiment you shake some ammonia solution with Volasil 244 to establish equilibrium, and then determine the concentration of ammonia in each solvent by titration. This enables you to calculate the distribution coefficient, K_D.

$$NH_3(Vol) \rightleftharpoons NH_3(aq) \quad (Vol = Volasil\ 244)$$

$$K_D = \frac{[NH_3(aq)]}{[NH_3(Vol)]}$$

Requirements

- safety spectacles
- measuring cylinder, 50 cm^3
- ammonia solution, 1.0 M NH$_3$
- Volasil 244
- separating funnel, 150 cm^3
- 2 beakers, 100 cm^3
- pipette, 10 cm^3, and safety filler
- 2 conical flasks, 150 cm^3
- wash-bottle of distilled water

■ methyl orange indicator solution
■ white tile
■ burette, 50 cm^3, and stand
■ hydrochloric acid, 0.010 M HCl (standardised)
■ hydrochloric acid, 0.50 M HCl (standardised)

HAZARD WARNING

Volasil 244 is flammable. Therefore you **must**:
■ **keep the stopper on the bottle as much as possible;**
■ **keep the liquid away from naked flames.**

Procedure
1. Pour about 50 cm^3 of ammonia solution into a separating funnel.
2. Pour about 50 cm^3 of Volasil 244 into the same separating funnel.
3. Holding the tap firmly in position with one hand and the stopper with the other, shake the separating funnel vigorously for about 10 seconds. Release the pressure inside by loosening the stopper for a moment.
4. Continue shaking for about half a minute, releasing the pressure every 10 seconds. Set aside until two layers separate.
5. Transfer the lower aqueous layer to a beaker. Rinse the pipette thoroughly, transfer 10.0 cm^3 to a flask, add about 20 cm^3 of water and a few drops of indicator solution, and titrate to the end-point with 0.50 M HCl.
6. Titrate two more 10 cm^3 samples and complete a copy of Results Table 6.6.
7. Transfer the organic layer to a beaker. Using a **dry** pipette, transfer 10.0 cm^3 to a conical flask. Add about 20 cm^3 of distilled water, a few drops of indicator and titrate the mixture with 0.010 M HCl until the yellow solution just changes to red and remains red after shaking. (It may take a few moments for all the ammonia to transfer from the organic layer and react with the acid.)
8. Titrate two more 10 cm^3 samples and complete another copy of Results Table 6.6, this time labelling it Results Table 6.7.

Results Table 6.6

Solution in flask			mol dm^{-3}			cm^3
Solution in burette			mol dm^{-3}			
Indicator						
		Trial	1	2	3	4
Burette readings	Final					
	Initial					
Volume used/cm^3						
Mean titre/cm^3						

Calculation
1. Calculate the average concentration of ammonia in the aqueous layer from your Results Table 6.6.
2. Calculate the average concentration of ammonia in the organic layer from your Results Table 6.7.
3. Calculate the distribution coefficient.

$$K_D = \frac{[NH_3(aq)]}{[NH_3(Vol)]}$$

4. Compare your results with others in the class.

ILPAC

7

EQUILIBRIUM II: ACIDS AND BASES

EQUILIBRIUM III: REDOX REACTIONS

EXPERIMENT 7.1 **The pH of a weak acid at various concentrations**

Aim The purpose of this experiment is to examine the effect of dilution on the pH of ethanoic acid, a weak acid.

Introduction Ethanoic acid dissociates according to the following equation:

$$CH_3CO_2H(aq) \rightleftharpoons CH_3CO_2^-(aq) + H^+(aq)$$

The extent of dissociation depends on the initial concentration of acid. By measuring the pH at different concentrations, you can see the effect of dilution. These results can be generalised for any weak acid.

Requirements ■ pH meter with glass electrode
■ wash-bottle of distilled water
■ buffer solution (to calibrate the pH meter)
■ 50 cm^3 beaker
■ 0.10 M, 0.010 M, 0.0010 M and 0.00010 M ethanoic acid solutions

Procedure 1. Calibrate the pH meter by dipping the glass electrode into a solution of known pH (a buffer solution) and turning the adjusting knob so that the scale shows the correct pH value. (If you are in doubt about this, ask your teacher.)
2. Rinse the glass electrode with distilled water and dip it into a beaker containing 0.00010 M ethanoic acid. Record the pH value in a copy of Results Table 7.1. Return the electrode to water; it must never be dry.
3. Rinse the beaker with the next solution, and repeat step 2, working from the most dilute solution to the most concentrated.
4. Enter calculated pH values for hydrochloric acid in the second column of Results Table 7.1.

Results Table 7.1

Concentration of acid/mol dm^{-3}	Observed pH of solutions of ethanoic acid	Calculated pH of solutions of hydrochloric acid
0.000 10		
0.0010		
0.010		
0.10		

Questions 1. Compare the pH of ethanoic acid with hydrochloric acid at each concentration.
   a In which of the two acids is the concentration of hydrogen ions greater?
   b What does this tell you about the extent of dissociation of ethanoic acid compared to hydrochloric acid?
2. **a** What happens to the **difference** between the pH of the two acids as concentration decreases? What does this tell you about the effect of dilution on dissociation?
   b Use Le Chatelier's principle to explain the effect of dilution on the extent of dissociation of ethanoic acid.

EXPERIMENT 7.2 The pH of different acids at the same concentration

Aim The purpose of this experiment is to compare the strengths of acids by measuring pH at the same concentration.

Introduction You measure the pH of 0.010 M solutions of benzoic acid, $C_6H_5CO_2H$, dihydrogenphosphate(V) ion, $H_2PO_4^-$, boric acid, H_3BO_3, and ethanoic acid, CH_3CO_2H. From these measurements you can rank the acids in order of strength.

Requirements
- pH meter with glass electrode
- wash-bottle of distilled water
- buffer solution (to calibrate the pH meter)
- beaker, 50 cm^3
- ethanoic acid solution, 0.010 M CH_3CO_2H
- benzoic acid solution, 0.010 M $C_6H_5CO_2H$
- boric acid solution, 0.010 M H_3BO_3
- dihydrogenphosphate(V) ion solution, 0.010 M $H_2PO_4^-$

Procedure Measure the pH of each solution, rinsing the electrode first each time, and record the values in a copy of Results Table 7.2.

Results Table 7.2

Acid	Concentration /mol dm^{-3}	pH
Boric acid	0.010	
Benzoic acid	0.010	
Ethanoic acid	0.010	
Dihydrogenphosphate(V) ion	0.010	

Question List these acids in order of **decreasing** acid strength.

EXPERIMENT 7.3 The action of a buffer solution

Aim The purpose of the experiment is to compare the effects of adding small amounts of acid and alkali to buffered and unbuffered solutions of the same pH.

Introduction You are provided with a buffer solution designed to maintain a pH of 7.0 at 25 °C and some pure water which, if it is pure enough, should also have a pH of 7.0 at 25 °C.

To samples of these two liquids, you add small measured amounts of 0.1 M NaOH and 0.1 M HCl, measuring the pH at each addition.

By comparing the pH changes in the two solutions you can demonstrate the action of a buffer solution.

Requirements
- safety spectacles
- 2 burettes, 50 cm^3, and stands
- 2 funnels, small
- 2 beakers, 100 cm^3
- hydrochloric acid, 0.1 M HCl
- sodium hydroxide solution, 0.1 M NaOH
- measuring cylinder, 25 cm^3
- beaker, 50 cm^3
- wash-bottle of distilled water
- buffer solution, pH 7.0

■ pH meter (If no pH meter is available use: full range pH paper, 1–14; narrow range pH paper; thin glass stirring rod)
■ pure water – fresh de-ionised water or freshly boiled distilled water

HAZARD WARNING

Sodium hydroxide solution is very corrosive. Even when dilute it can damage your eyes. Therefore you **must**:
■ **wear safety spectacles throughout the experiment.**

Procedure

1. Fill a burette with 0.1 M HCl and another with 0.1 M NaOH.
2. Using a measuring cylinder, put 25 cm³ of the buffer solution in a 50 cm³ beaker.
3. Rinse the pH meter electrode with distilled water from a wash-bottle, and put it into the beaker, making sure that the glass bulb is completely immersed. Set the meter to read 7.0.
4. Place the beaker under the burette containing NaOH and, making sure the alkali does not fall directly on to the electrode, add 1 drop of 0.1 M NaOH. Stir gently to ensure thorough mixing and record the pH in a copy of Results Table 7.3.
   If you cannot use a pH meter, measure the pH by transferring 1 drop of the mixed solution on a glass rod to a piece of pH paper. Use full range paper first, and then narrow range paper to obtain a more accurate value.
5. Add more NaOH to make the total volume added 1.0 cm³; measure and record the pH as before.
6. Add more NaOH to make the total volume added 5.0 cm³; measure and record the pH. Rinse the electrode in distilled water and stand it in a flask of distilled water.
7. Take another 25 cm³ portion of the buffer, and measure the pH on the addition of 1 drop, 1.0 cm³, and 5.0 cm³ of 0.1 M HCl in the same way as you did for NaOH. Again, rinse the electrode carefully and stand it in distilled water.
8. Put 25 cm³ of pure water in the beaker and, keeping its exposure time to the air as short as possible, measure its pH. If it is absolutely pure, its pH will be 7.0, but it is very difficult to achieve this. If the pH is less than 6.0, wash the beaker and electrode more carefully and try again.
9. When you have a pH between 6.0 and 7.0 for the 'pure' water, measure and record the pH changes on addition of 0.1 M NaOH and 0.1 M HCl just as you did for the buffer solution. Take special care to wash the electrode when you change from using alkali to acid. Record your results in Results Table 7.3.
10. Take another 25 cm³ of pure water, measure the pH and then leave it to stand open to the air for 10 minutes. Measure the pH again and record the results.

Results Table 7.3

Volume added	pH on addition of 0.1 M NaOH to		pH on addition of 0.1 M HCl to	
	Buffer	Pure water	Buffer	Pure water
0 1 drop 1.0 cm³ 5.0 cm³				
pH of pure water with minimum air exposure				
pH of pure water after 10 minutes air exposure				

Questions
1. By how much (to the nearest unit) does the pH of 25 cm^3 of pure water change for the addition of 1.0 cm^3 of 0.1 M HCl?
2. Calculate the ratio:
$$\frac{[H^+(aq)] \text{ after addition of 1.0 cm}^3 \text{ of HCl to pure water}}{[H^+(aq)] \text{ in pure water}}$$
3. By contrast, the addition of 1.0 cm^3 of 0.1 M HCl to 25 cm^3 of the buffer solution should decrease the pH by about 0.1, and this corresponds to increasing [H$^+$(aq)] by a factor of only about 1.25. However, the same number of hydrogen ions were added to both solutions. What must have happened to most of the hydrogen ions added to the buffer?
4. Why does the pH of pure water decrease when exposed to the air?

EXPERIMENT 7.4   Determining the pH range of some acid–base indicators

Aim
The purpose of this experiment is to show that different acid–base indicators change colour over different ranges of pH.

Introduction
To determine the pH range, you add an alkali, 1.0 cm^3 at a time, to a solution containing an indicator and a buffer, and measure the pH at each addition. The pH values at which a colour change begins and ends defines the pH range.

It is best to measure the pH with a pH meter. However, if one is not available, you can calculate the pH from an equation we give at the end of the experiment.

Requirements
- ■ safety spectacles
- ■ 3 burettes, 50 cm^3, and stands ⎫
- ■ 4 beakers, 250 cm^3 ⎬ 2 of these may be shared
- ■ 3 funnels, small, for burettes ⎭
- ■ distilled water
- ■ hydrochloric acid, 0.1 M HCl
- ■ sodium hydroxide solution, 0.1 M NaOH
- ■ pipette, 25 cm^3, and safety filler
- ■ buffer solution, B
- ■ 3 beakers, 100 cm^3
- ■ indicator solutions, in dropping bottles, as follows:
  - – litmus
  - – methyl orange
  - – phenolphthalein
  - – bromophenol blue
  - – methyl red
- ■ pH meter (if available)

HAZARD WARNING

Sodium hydroxide solution is very corrosive. Even when dilute it can damage your eyes. Therefore you **must**:
- ■ **wear safety spectacles throughout the experiment.**

Procedure
1. Fill three burettes with distilled water, 0.1 M NaOH, and 0.1 M HCl respectively.
2. From burettes, run 25.0 cm^3 of 0.1 M HCl and 10.0 cm^3 of water into a small beaker. Similarly, run 25.0 cm^3 of 0.1 M NaOH and 10.0 cm^3 of water into a second small beaker.
3. Pipette 25.0 cm^3 of solution B into a third beaker, add two drops of any one of the indicators provided, and mix. If the colour is very pale, add a few more drops of indicator, but always add the minimum amount which gives a distinct colour.

4. Add the same number of drops of indicator to the first two beakers as you did to the third. Put these two beakers aside to use for comparison purposes.
5. Add 0.1 M NaOH, 1.0 cm³ at a time, to the third beaker (containing B) and mix the contents thoroughly after each addition. At the **first sign** of a colour change, measure the pH of the mixture with a meter or, if a meter is not available, record the volume of alkali added. You will be able to detect a change in colour by comparing with the beaker containing 0.1 M HCl. Record the pH, or volume of alkali added, in a copy of Results Table 7.4.

   To match colours precisely, you may find it helpful to dilute the 0.1 M HCl with water so that it has the same volume as the mixture of buffer solution and NaOH.
6. Continue adding 0.1 M NaOH, 1.0 cm³ at a time as before, until the colour change appears to be complete. Compare the solution with the beaker containing 0.1 M NaOH to help you to judge the end. Record the pH or the volume of added alkali at this point in Results Table 7.4.

   To match colours precisely, you may find it helpful to dilute the 0.1 M NaOH with water so that it has the same volume as the mixture of buffer and added NaOH.
7. Repeat steps 1 to 6 for as many other indicators as time permits. If you have not measured the pH values, calculate them using the equation under Results Table 7.4.

Results Table 7.4

Indicator used	Initial colour	Colour change starts		Colour change ends		Final colour
		Volume*	pH	Volume*	pH	

* These columns need only be filled in if the pH has not been measured. The pH can then be calculated from the volume, V cm³, of alkali added by using the equation: pH = 3.0 + 0.23 V (max. V = 35).

8. Complete a copy of Figure 7.1, using your experimental results and/or your data book. Choose suitable indicators so that their pH ranges, as shown by boxes similar to the two examples given, form a straight diagonal line from bottom left to top right.

Figure 7.1

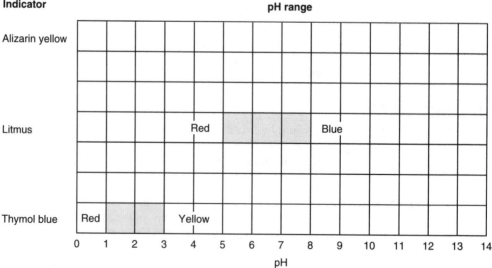

Question   Why was the indicator range measured in a buffer solution as opposed to a water solution?

EXPERIMENT 7.5 Determining the ionisation constant for an indicator

Aim The purpose of this experiment is to determine the ionisation constant, K_{In}, for bromophenol blue.

Introduction You make use of the equation:

$$\text{pH} = \text{p}K_{In} - \log \frac{[\text{HIn(aq)}]}{[\text{In}^-(\text{aq})]}$$

You prepare two solutions: one with a high hydrogen ion concentration in which the indicator exists almost entirely as HIn, and the other with a high hydroxide ion concentration in which the indicator exists almost entirely as In^-.

These solutions are used to show the colour of the indicator at different values of the ratio: $[\text{HIn(aq)}]/[\text{In}^-(\text{aq})]$. From this measurement, you can determine the value of K_{In}.

You prepare two sets of test-tubes in which the concentrations of the two coloured forms of the indicator vary regularly as shown in Fig. 7.2. You can observe colours corresponding to different values of $[\text{HIn(aq)}]/[\text{In}^-(\text{aq})]$ by looking through two tubes at once.

Figure 7.2

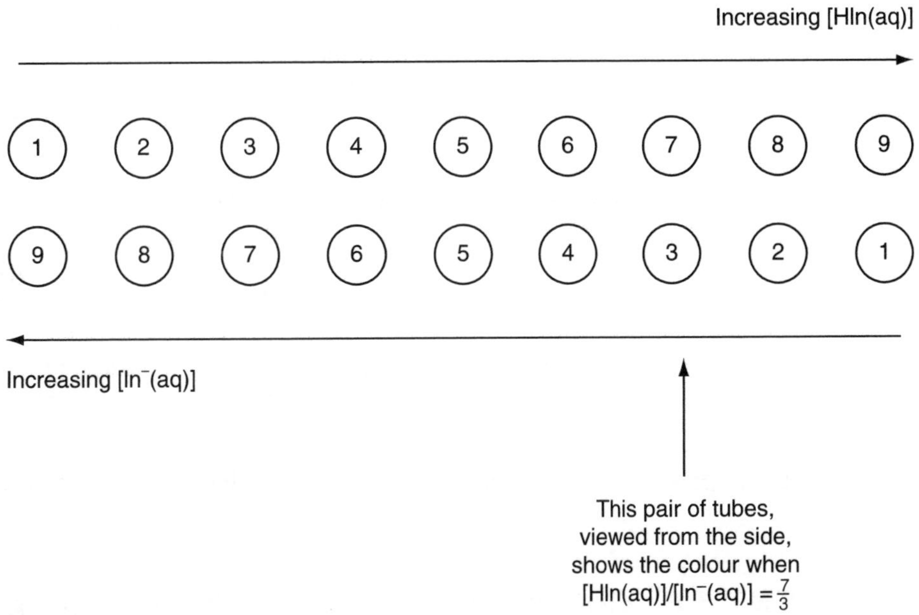

Increasing [HIn(aq)]

Increasing [In$^-$(aq)]

This pair of tubes, viewed from the side, shows the colour when $[\text{HIn(aq)}]/[\text{In}^-(\text{aq})] = \frac{7}{3}$

Requirements
- safety spectacles
- measuring cylinder, 10 cm^3
- 20 test-tubes
- rack or racks to hold 2 rows of 9 tubes each
- bromophenol blue solution
- 2 teat pipettes
- hydrochloric acid, concentrated, HCl
- stirring rod
- sodium hydroxide solution, 4 M NaOH
- distilled water
- buffer solution, pH 3.7

HAZARD WARNING

Concentrated hydrochloric acid is a corrosive liquid, and its vapour is harmful to eyes, lungs and skin.

Sodium hydroxide solution is also corrosive. Therefore you **must**:
■ **wear safety spectacles.**

Procedure

1. Pour about 5 cm^3 of bromophenol blue solution into a test-tube and add 1 drop of concentrated hydrochloric acid. In this solution, almost all of the indicator is in the form HIn. Call this solution 'X'.
2. Pour about 5 cm^3 of bromophenol blue solution into a test-tube and add 1 drop of 4 M sodium hydroxide solution. In this solution, almost all of the indicator is in the form In$^-$. Call this solution 'Y'.
3. Arrange 18 test-tubes in a rack (or racks) as shown in Fig. 7.2 and carefully add drops of solutions X and Y corresponding to the numbers in Fig. 7.2.
4. Add 10 cm^3 of distilled water to each tube and stir if necessary so that the colour is even from top to bottom.
5. Pour 10 cm^3 of the buffer solution (pH = 3.7) into a test-tube and add 10 drops of bromophenol blue solution. Shake the tube to mix the contents.
6. By holding the buffer tube alongside the pairs of tubes in the rack, find the pair which is nearest to the same colour.
   You will find it helpful to view the tubes against a brightly lit white background.
7. Record the value of [HIn(aq)]/[In$^-$(aq)] in the pair of tubes which best matches the buffer solution.

Calculation

Substitute your measured value of [HIn(aq)]/[In$^-$(aq)] and the given pH of the buffer in the equation:

$$pH = pK_{In} - \log \frac{[HIn(aq)]}{[In^-(aq)]}$$

and obtain a value for pK_{In}. Obtain K_{In} from pK_{In} in the same way as you calculated hydrogen ion concentration from pH. Compare your result with the value given in your data book.

Questions

1. Why was as much as 10 drops of indicator solution added to the buffer solution?
2. Could a buffer of pH 8 have been used in this experiment?

EXPERIMENT 7.6 Obtaining the pH curve for an acid–alkali titration

Aim

The purpose of this experiment is to obtain a curve which shows how pH changes during the titration of a weak acid with a strong base. This curve can be used to determine the equivalence point of the titration, the suitability of an indicator and the value of K_a for the weak acid.

Introduction

You add the alkali from a burette, in small steps, into 25 cm^3 of the acid and measure the pH at each addition. You then plot the pH against volume of alkali added. It is best to measure pH with a pH meter but it is possible to get adequate results using narrow range pH paper if a meter is not available. Using a magnetic stirrer speeds up the experiment but it is not essential.

Requirements

■ safety spectacles
■ pH meter **or** narrow range pH papers to cover pH 3–11
■ pipette, 25 cm^3, and safety filler

- beaker (preferably tall form), 100 or 150 cm^3
- conical flask, 250 cm^3
- thin glass rod
- magnetic stirrer (if available)
- burette, 50 cm^3, and stand
- funnel, small, for filling burette
- 2 beakers, 100 or 250 cm^3
- distilled water
- ethanoic acid solution, approx. 0.1 M CH$_3$CO$_2$H
- sodium hydroxide solution, approx. 0.1 M NaOH
- phenolphthalein indicator
- indicator 'A'
- standard buffer solution, pH 4.0

HAZARD WARNING

Sodium hydroxide solution is very corrosive. Even when dilute it can damage your eyes. Therefore you **must**:
- **wear safety spectacles throughout the experiment.**

Procedure

1. Pipette 25 cm^3 of the ethanoic acid solution into a 250 cm^3 conical flask, add 2–3 drops of phenolphthalein indicator and titrate with the sodium hydroxide solution to a permanent faint pink end-point. Record the volume (V cm^3). This value will be useful to you in judging the size of volume additions in the rest of the experiment.
2. Set up the pH meter (if available) and fit the combined electrode unit. Standardise the pH meter with the buffer provided.
3. Pipette 25 cm^3 of the ethanoic acid solution into the tall form beaker, add about 3 drops of the indicator 'A' and set the beaker on the magnetic stirrer. If a magnetic stirrer is not available you will have to swirl the beaker by hand.
4. Carefully clamp the electrode so that the bulb is completely immersed in the acid and is clear of the stirrer follower. Add distilled water to cover the electrode if necessary.
5. Record the pH (to 0.1 unit), burette reading (to 0.05 cm^3) and colour of the solution in a copy of Results Table 7.5. If a pH meter is not used, measure the pH by removing **one small drop** of the solution on a glass rod and testing with narrow range indicator paper. If you are not sure which range to use, test first with full range universal indicator paper. It is important not to remove more than the minimum acid from the flask.
6. Add sodium hydroxide solution from the burette in varying portions. After each addition record the burette reading, pH and colour of the solution. Add 5 cm^3 portions until about $(V - 5)$ cm^3, then 1 cm^3 and finally 0.1 cm^3 portions in the region of the equivalence point. (V is the volume determined in step 1.)
7. Continue adding sodium hydroxide solution in suitable volumes until about 5 cm^3 beyond the equivalence point, again recording pH, burette volume and solution colour.
8. As soon as you have finished, remove the combined electrode and rinse it with distilled water. Do not leave it in a solution of high pH.
9. Plot a graph of pH (y-axis) against volume of sodium hydroxide solution (x-axis). Indicate clearly on the graph where the colour change of the indicator occurred, showing the pH range. Also indicate clearly on the graph the equivalence point.

Questions and calculations

1. What is the colour change and the pH range of the indicator 'A'?
2. Would indicator 'A' have been a suitable end-point detector for this titration in the absence of a pH meter? Comment.

3. What was the volume of the sodium hydroxide solution as shown by your graph at the equivalence point?
4. Calculate the molarity of the ethanoic acid solution, assuming that the sodium hydroxide solution was exactly 0.100 M NaOH.
5. From your graph find the pH of the solution at exactly half-way to the equivalence point, i.e. at volume $V/2$ cm^3. What special property does this solution have?

Results Table 7.5

Burette reading/cm³	pH	Colour of solution
0.00		
5.00		
10.00		
etc.		

Note: It is not necessary to add the exact volumes as suggested above. It is sufficient to add approximately 5 cm^3 portions at first, so long as the burette readings are recorded accurately.

EXPERIMENT 7.7 Preparation of buffers

Aim The purpose of this experiment is threefold:

1. To prepare two buffer solutions of pH values of 5.2 and 8.8.
2. To check the pH and buffering capacity of the prepared buffers.
3. To examine the effect of dilution of the prepared buffers on their pH and buffering capacity.

Introduction This experiment lends itself to a planning exercise where you have to work out for yourself the detailed procedure on the basis of the hints given below. When you have worked out the details, check with your teacher that your proposals are sensible and that apparatus will be available at a suitable time. Try not to waste laboratory time on planning.

Hints 1. The following solutions will be available:
■ ammonia solution, 1.0 M NH$_3$
■ ethanoic acid, 1.0 M CH$_3$CO$_2$H
■ ammonium chloride solution, 1.0 M NH$_4$Cl
■ sodium ethanoate solution, 1.0 M CH$_3$CO$_2$Na

HAZARD WARNING

Ammonia solution is harmful and the vapour is irritating to the eyes and lungs. Therefore you **must**:
■ **wear safety spectacles;**
■ **prepare the alkaline buffer at the fume cupboard.**

2. Use the following equation to calculate how much of the above solutions you need to make 100 cm^3 of each buffer.

$$pH = pK_a - \log \frac{[HA(aq)]}{[A^-(aq)]}$$

3. Your experience of Experiment 7.3 will be very useful.
4. For the dilution effect, try diluting your buffer to 1/10 and 1/100 of its initial concentration.
5. Prepare a suitable table to record your results. This should be handed to your teacher with your answers to the questions below.

Questions

1. What did you use to make 100 cm^3 of a buffer of pH 5.2?
2. What did you use to make 100 cm^3 of a buffer of pH 8.8?
3. How close to the required values were the measured pH values of your prepared buffers?
4. Describe the effect of dilution on the pH of your prepared buffers. Was this effect expected?
5. Describe the effect of dilution on the buffering capacity of your prepared buffers.
6. Suggest a reason for the pH 8.8 buffer being less stable over a period of time than many other buffers.

EXPERIMENT 7.8 Determining the dissociation constant of a weak acid

Aim

The purpose of the experiment is to prepare a buffer solution from benzoic acid and sodium benzoate, and then to determine its pH by a visual method as used in Experiment 7.5. pK_a for the acid can then be calculated from the pH by the usual buffer formula.

Introduction

First you prepare a buffer solution from benzoic acid and sodium benzoate. Then you measure its pH using the same procedure as in Experiment 7.5. Having determined the pH, you calculate K_a for benzoic acid using the equation:

$$pH = pK_a - \log \frac{[C_6H_5CO_2H(aq)]}{[C_6H_5CO_2^-(aq)]}$$

You should read the introduction to Experiment 7.5.

Requirements

- safety spectacles
- benzoic acid solution, 0.020 M $C_6H_5CO_2H$
- sodium benzoate solution, 0.020 M $C_6H_5CO_2Na$
- measuring cylinder, 10 cm^3
- 20 test-tubes
- rack or racks to hold 2 rows of 9 tubes each
- bromophenol blue solution
- 2 teat pipettes
- hydrochloric acid, concentrated, HCl
- stirring rod
- sodium hydroxide solution, 4 M NaOH
- distilled water

HAZARD WARNING

Concentrated hydrochloric acid is a corrosive liquid, and its vapour is harmful to eyes, lungs and skin.

Sodium hydroxide solution is also corrosive. Therefore you **must**:
- **wear safety spectacles.**

Procedure
1. Prepare a buffer solution by mixing 5.0 cm³ of 0.020 M benzoic acid and 5.0 cm³ of 0.020 M sodium benzoate in a test-tube.
2. Follow the procedure for Experiment 7.5. In step 5, use the buffer you have just prepared.

Calculation
1. Obtain the pH of the buffer solution by substituting in the equation:

$$pH = pK_{In} - \log \frac{[HIn(aq)]}{[In^-(aq)]}$$

2. Obtain pK_a, and hence K_a, by substituting in the equation:

$$pH = pK_a - \log \frac{[C_6H_5CO_2H(aq)]}{[C_6H_5CO_2^-(aq)]}$$

EXPERIMENT 7.9 Some simple redox reactions

Aim
The purpose of this experiment is to illustrate some redox reactions by means of some simple test-tube reactions between metals and salt solutions.

Introduction
You place zinc, copper and silver into salt solutions containing the ions Zn^{2+}, Cu^{2+} and Ag^+. The observations you record will provide a starting point for your study of redox reactions.

Requirements
■ safety spectacles
■ 6 test-tubes in a rack
■ 2 strips of copper foil
■ 2 strips of zinc foil
■ 2 pieces of silver wire
■ emery paper
■ copper sulphate solution, 0.5 M $CuSO_4$
■ zinc sulphate solution, 0.5 M $ZnSO_4$
■ silver nitrate solution, 0.1 M $AgNO_3$
■ silver residues bottle

HAZARD WARNING

Copper sulphate is harmful.
Silver nitrate is corrosive and **toxic**. Therefore you **must**:
■ **wear safety spectacles**.

Procedure
1. If necessary, clean the strips of metal with emery paper. Avoid cross-contamination by using three different pieces of emery paper, one for each metal.
2. Dip a piece of each metal into solutions of salts of each of the other two metals. Leave for about two minutes.
3. Examine each test-tube and record your observations in a copy of Results Table 7.6.

Results Table 7.6

Solution	Observations		
	Zn	Cu	Ag
$Zn^{2+}(aq)$			
$Cu^{2+}(aq)$			
$Ag^{+}(aq)$			

Questions
1. Write ionic equations for the reactions you have observed.
2. In each case, state which of the reactants has been oxidised and which has been reduced. Show any changes in oxidation number.
3. Which of the metals has acted as both reducing agent and oxidising agent?

EXPERIMENT 7.10   Measuring the potential difference generated by electrochemical cells

Aim   The purpose of this experiment is to construct three electrochemical cells, and to measure the potential difference between the electrodes, noting the polarity.

Introduction   You combine the following half-cells and measure the potential difference between the metal electrodes using a high resistance voltmeter.

Table 7.1

Cell	Half-cells	
1	$Zn^{2+}(aq) + 2e^- \rightleftharpoons Zn(s)$	$Cu^{2+}(aq) + 2e^- \rightleftharpoons Cu(s)$
2	$Ag^{+}(aq) + e^- \rightleftharpoons Ag(s)$	$Cu^{2+}(aq) + 2e^- \rightleftharpoons Cu(s)$
3	$Ag^{+}(aq) + e^- \rightleftharpoons Ag(s)$	$Zn^{2+}(aq) + 2e^- \rightleftharpoons Zn(s)$

When you measure the potential difference between the electrodes of each cell, the polarity of each electrode is indicated by the positive sign and negative sign on the voltmeter (or red and black terminals respectively). Thus, you can determine at which electrode electrons are needed and at which electrode electrons are produced. From this, you can work out the direction in which the overall reaction proceeds.

Requirements
■ safety spectacles
■ strip of copper foil
■ strip of zinc foil
■ silver wire
■ emery paper, 3 small pieces

- 4 beakers, 50 cm^3
- 3 connecting leads with crocodile clips attached
- copper sulphate solution, 1.0 M CuSO$_4$
- zinc sulphate solution, 1.0 M ZnSO$_4$
- silver nitrate solution, 0.10 M AgNO$_3$
- filter paper strips
- potassium nitrate solution, saturated, 3 M KNO$_3$
- voltmeter, high resistance

HAZARD WARNING

Copper sulphate is harmful.
Silver nitrate is corrosive and **toxic**. Therefore you **must**:
- **wear safety spectacles**.

Procedure

1. If necessary, clean each metal strip (or wire) with a separate piece of emery paper. Again, as in Experiment 7.9, avoid cross-contamination of the metal strips.
2. Place each metal strip in a separate beaker. Hold each strip vertically against the inside of the beaker so that about 2 cm projects above the rim. Fold the projection down over the rim of the beaker and clamp it in position with a crocodile clip attached to a lead.
3. Pour about 20 cm^3 of the appropriate salt solution into each beaker so that each metal strip dips into a solution of its own ions. Make sure the crocodile clips keep dry.
4. Prepare a salt bridge by soaking a strip of filter paper in saturated potassium nitrate solution. Let the surplus solution drain off by hanging the strip over the fourth beaker.
5. Connect the zinc and copper electrodes to a high resistance voltmeter, as shown in Fig. 7.3, and complete the circuit with the salt bridge.

Figure 7.3

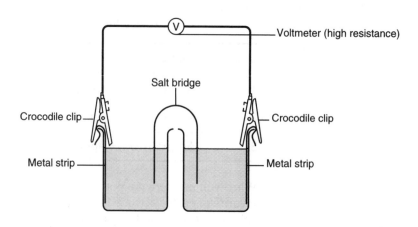

6. If the reading on the voltmeter is negative, reverse the connections to obtain a positive reading. Record the potential difference in a copy of Results Table 7.7, noting which electrode is positive (connected to the red terminal of the voltmeter) and which is negative.
7. Remove the salt bridge as soon as possible and throw it away. Disconnect the voltmeter.
8. Repeat steps 4 to 7 for the other two cells.

Results Table 7.7

Cell	Positive electrode	Negative electrode	Potential difference/V
1			
2			
3			

Questions

1. Consider cell 1:
   a What reaction is taking place at the zinc electrode to make it negative?
   b What reaction is taking place at the copper electrode to make it positive?
2. Similarly for the other cells, write the half-reactions which make the negative electrode negative and the positive electrode positive.
3. Add each pair of half-reactions together to give the **overall cell reaction** for each cell.
4. Compare these cell reactions to the test-tube reactions you performed in Experiment 7.9.
5. What is the function of the salt bridge in the cells?

EXPERIMENT 7.11   Testing predictions about redox reactions

Aim

The purpose of this experiment is to test whether predictions you will make for some redox reactions are borne out in practice.

Introduction

A. $\underline{Br_2(aq) + 2I^-(aq)} \rightarrow 2Br^-(aq) + I_2(aq)$

B. $\underline{Br_2(aq) + 2Cl^-(aq)} \rightarrow 2Br^-(aq) + Cl_2(aq)$

C. $\underline{Zn(s) + 2Fe^{3+}(aq)} \rightarrow Zn^{2+}(aq) + 2Fe^{2+}(aq)$

D. $\underline{2MnO_4^-(aq) + 16H^+(aq) + 10Br^-(aq)} \rightarrow 8H_2O(l) + 2Mn^{2+}(aq) + 5Br_2(aq)$

E. $\underline{2MnO_4^-(aq) + 16H^+(aq) + 5Cu(s)} \rightarrow 8H_2O(l) + 2Mn^{2+}(aq) + 5Cu^{2+}(aq)$

F. $\underline{3S_2O_8^{2-}(aq) + 2Cr^{3+}(aq) + 7H_2O(l)} \rightarrow 6SO_4^{2-}(aq) + Cr_2O_7^{2-}(aq) + 14H^+(aq)$

First you use standard electrode potential values to predict whether reactions A to F above are spontaneous under standard conditions. Then you mix the reactants underlined in equations A to F above and by simple observation or simple tests decide whether a reaction has taken place.

Requirements

■ safety spectacles
■ 10 test-tubes with corks or bungs to fit
■ test-tube rack
■ potassium iodide solution, 0.1 M KI
■ bromine water, $Br_2(aq)$
■ Volasil 244
■ potassium chloride solution, 0.1 M KCl
■ iron(III) chloride solution, 0.1 M $FeCl_3$
■ spatula
■ zinc powder, Zn
■ potassium hexacyanoferrate(III) (ferricyanide) solution, 0.1 M $K_3Fe(CN)_6$
■ potassium manganate(VII) (permanganate) solution, 0.02 M $KMnO_4$
■ sulphuric acid, dilute, 1 M H_2SO_4

- potassium bromide solution, 0.1 M KBr
- copper powder, Cu
- potassium peroxodisulphate (persulphate) solution, 0.1 M $K_2S_2O_8$
- chromium(III) chloride solution, 0.1 M $CrCl_3$

HAZARD WARNING

  Bromine vapour must not be inhaled. If a fume cupboard is not available then:
- **the laboratory must be well ventilated and reagent bottles and test-tubes stoppered as much as possible.**

 - **Keep Volasil 244 away from flames.**

 Potassium hexacyanoferrate(III) is toxic.

 Bromine vapour and all the chemical solutions used in this experiment are irritants. Therefore you **must**:
- **wear safety spectacles.**

Procedure – Part A

Reaction between $Br_2(aq)$ and $I^-(aq)$

1. Place about 3 cm³ of potassium iodide solution in a test-tube and add, dropwise, about the same volume of bromine water.
2. Cork and shake the tube and note any colour change.
3. Add a little Volasil 244, shake and observe the colour of the upper layer. Record your observations and deductions in a copy of Results Table 7.8.

Results Table 7.8

Reaction	Additional test	Observations	Deductions
A			
B			
C			
D			
E			
F			

Procedure – Part B

Reaction between $Br_2(aq)$ and $Cl^-(aq)$

4. Place about 3 cm³ of potassium chloride solution in a test-tube and add about the same volume of bromine water.
5. Cork and shake the tube. Record your observations and deductions.

Procedure – Part C

Reaction between $Fe^{3+}(aq)$ and $Zn(s)$

6. Place about 3 cm³ of iron(III) chloride solution in a test-tube and add a **very** small amount of zinc powder (a mere pinch).
7. Cork and shake the tube and allow any solid to settle.
8. Test for the presence of $Fe^{2+}(aq)$ by adding a few drops of potassium hexacyanoferrate(III) solution ($Fe^{2+}(aq)$ will give a dark blue precipitate if present). Record your observations and deductions.

Procedure – Part D

Reaction between $MnO_4^-(aq)$, $H^+(aq)$ and $Br^-(aq)$

9. Place about 3 cm³ of potassium manganate(VII) solution in a test-tube and add about 1 cm³ of dilute sulphuric acid. Mix the solutions.
10. Place about 3 cm³ of potassium bromide solution in another test-tube and add, dropwise, the mixture from step 9.
11. Cork and shake the tube and note any colour change.
12. Add a little Volasil 244, shake and observe the colour of the upper layer.

Procedure – Part E

Reaction between $MnO_4^-(aq)$, $H^+(aq)$ and $Cu(s)$

13. Place about 3 cm³ of potassium manganate(VII) solution in a test-tube and add about 1 cm³ of dilute sulphuric acid.
14. Mix the contents and add a **very** small amount of copper powder (the smallest amount on the tip of a spatula).
15. Cork and shake the tube well and note any change.

Procedure – Part F

Reaction between $S_2O_8^{2-}(aq)$ and $Cr^{3+}(aq)$

16. Place about 3 cm³ of potassium peroxodisulphate(VI) solution in a test-tube and add about 3 cm³ of chromium(III) chloride solution.
17. Cork and shake the tube and note any change. Complete Results Table 7.8.

Question

Were your predictions made from standard electrode potential values confirmed by experiment?

EXPERIMENT 7.12 Variation of cell e.m.f. with concentration

Aim

The purpose of this experiment is to investigate the effect of changes in ionic concentration on the e.m.f. of a cell and to check whether the results are in accordance with Le Chatelier's principle.

Introduction

The cell you study in this experiment is represented as follows:

$$Zn(s) \mid Zn^{2+}(aq) \mid\mid Cu^{2+}(aq) \mid Cu(s)$$

This was one of the cells involved in Experiment 7.10.

You vary the concentration of the copper ions, keeping the zinc ion concentration constant, and measure the cell e.m.f. for each concentration of copper ions. You then repeat this procedure, keeping the copper ion concentration constant and varying the zinc ion concentration.

Requirements
- safety spectacles
- copper foil
- zinc foil
- emery paper, 2 small pieces
- 5 beakers, 50 cm^3
- 4 strips of filter paper
- saturated potassium nitrate solution, 3 M KNO$_3$
- voltmeter (high resistance)
- 2 connecting leads, with crocodile clips attached
- copper sulphate solutions, 1.0 M, and 0.10 M CuSO$_4$
- zinc sulphate solutions, 1.0 M, and 0.10 M ZnSO$_4$

HAZARD WARNING

Copper sulphate is harmful.
Therefore you **must**:
- **wear safety spectacles**.

Procedure   Using 1.0 M ZnSO$_4$ solution in the zinc half-cell, carry out the same procedure as you did in Experiment 7.10, using each of the copper sulphate solutions in turn.

Again repeat the above procedure, using 1.0 M CuSO$_4$ in the copper half-cell and using 0.10 M ZnSO$_4$ in the zinc half-cell.

Record your results in a copy of Results Table 7.9.

Results Table 7.9

[Zn^{2+}(aq)]/mol dm^{-3}	[Cu^{2+}(aq)]/mol dm^{-3}	ΔE/V
1.0	1.0	
1.0	0.10	
0.10	1.0	

Questions
1. How does the e.m.f. of the cell change as the copper ion solution becomes more dilute?
2. How does the e.m.f. of the cell change as the zinc ion solution becomes more dilute?
3. Use Le Chatelier's principle to explain your answers to questions 1 and 2 above.

EXPERIMENT 7.13 Rusting of iron and steel

Aims   The purpose of this experiment is to identify the anodic and cathodic sites in the corrosion of iron and to investigate some methods of rust prevention.

Introduction   The reagent used in this investigation is known as 'Ferroxyl' indicator. It is a solution containing potassium hexacyanoferrate(III), K$_3$Fe(CN)$_6$, phenolphthalein and sodium chloride. The hexacyanoferrate(III) ion can be used to detect iron(II), zinc(II) and copper(II) ions. With iron(II) ions it forms a dark blue precipitate (Prussian Blue), with zinc ions it forms a white precipitate and with copper(II) ions it forms a chocolate brown precipitate. The phenolphthalein detects hydroxide ions, of course, forming a red solution. The sodium chloride is included to speed up the corrosion process.

Requirements
- safety spectacles
- Petri or crystallising dish
- beaker, 250 cm^3

- dropping pipette
- emery paper
- piece of steel sheet
- 5 iron nails
- strip of zinc foil
- strip of copper foil
- grease
- cotton wool or cloth
- methanol
- Ferroxyl indicator
- phosphoric acid, 1 M H_3PO_4

HAZARD WARNING

Ferroxyl indicator contains potassium hexacyanoferrate(III) which is poisonous. Boiling dilute phosphoric acid solution is hazardous. Therefore you **must**:
- **wear safety spectacles.**

Procedure
1. Clean a piece of steel sheet with emery paper and then, using a dropping pipette, carefully add a fairly large drop of Ferroxyl indicator. Observe what happens in the first minute, then inspect it again after about ten minutes.
   Record your observations in a copy of Results Table 7.10.
2. Clean five iron nails by wiping them carefully with cotton wool or a cloth moistened with methanol. Treat the nails as follows:
   Nail A   No further treatment.
   Nail B   Fold a narrow strip of copper foil in half, then push a nail between the two halves, slide the copper strip until it is halfway up the nail, then crimp it tightly to make a good electrical contact, as in Fig. 7.4.

Figure 7.4

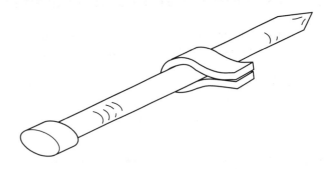

   Nail C   Proceed as for nail B, but using zinc foil instead of copper.
   Nail D   Put the nail in a beaker, cover with phosphoric acid solution and heat just to boiling for a few minutes. Discard the phosphoric acid and rinse the nail with water.
   Nail E   Cover the nail completely with grease.
   Pour some Ferroxyl indicator into a Petri dish to a depth of about 5 mm and place the dish over a sheet of white paper marked with the letters A, B, C, D and E in the positions where you expect to place the nails. Carefully place each nail in the Ferroxyl indicator solution above its appropriate letter and observe what happens over a period of about ten minutes.
   Record your observations in a copy of Results Table 7.10.

Results Table 7.10

Experiment	Observations
Steel sheet	
Nail A	
Nail B (+Cu)	
Nail C (+Zn)	
Nail D (H_3PO_4)	
Nail E (grease)	

Questions

1. In the experiment on the steel sheet you may have observed colours appearing at different sites. Can you explain what has happened at each site? Write ion-electron half-equations.
2. For nail A, where did corrosion occur most rapidly?
3. How did the rate of corrosion of nail B compare with that of nail A? Explain what happened at the surfaces of the nail and the copper foil. Write ion-electron half-equations.
4. How did the rate of corrosion of nail C compare with that of nail A? Explain what happened at the surfaces of the nail and the zinc foil. Write ion-electron half-equations.
5. How did the rates of corrosion of nails D and E compare with that of nail A? Can you explain any differences in rate?

EXPERIMENT 7.14 Determination of the Faraday constant

Aim

The purpose of this experiment is to determine the value of the Faraday constant from measurements made during electrolysis of aqueous copper(II) sulphate.

Introduction

You electrolyse some copper(II) sulphate solution using copper electrodes, measuring the current, the time and the increase in mass of the cathode. From the results you can evaluate the Faraday constant.

Figure 7.5

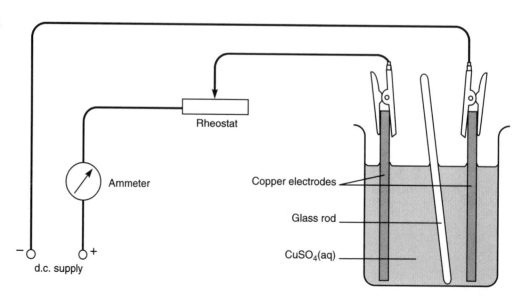

Rheostat

Ammeter

Copper electrodes

Glass rod

$CuSO_4$(aq)

− +

d.c. supply

Requirements
- d.c. power source (a few volts)
- ammeter ⎫ the power source may contain these
- rheostat ⎭
- connecting wire
- 2 leads with crocodile clips
- 2 pieces of copper foil or plate, approximately 6 cm × 3 cm
- emery paper
- beaker, 150 or 250 cm³
- glass rod
- stopclock
- balance weighing to ±0.01 g or ±0.001 g
- copper(II) sulphate solution, 0.5 M CuSO₄
- propanone (acetone)
- wash-bottle of distilled water

HAZARD WARNING

Copper sulphate is harmful. Propanone is flammable. Therefore you **must**:
- **wear safety spectacles;**
- **keep propanone away from flames.**

Procedure
1. Clean one of the pieces of copper with the emery paper, then stand both pieces of copper in the beaker with the glass rod between them so that they cannot make electrical contact.
2. Pour copper(II) sulphate solution into the beaker until the liquid level is no higher than about 1.5 cm from the top edge of the copper.
3. Connect the power source to the ammeter, rheostat and electrolysis cell as shown in Fig. 7.5. Use crocodile clips to connect to the copper electrodes, with the cleaned electrode connected to the negative supply. Do not let the crocodile clips touch the solution.
4. With the rheostat set to maximum resistance, switch on the d.c. supply and slowly adjust the rheostat until the current is 0.20 A. After a minute or two, switch off the d.c. supply and remove the negative electrode (cathode).
5. Holding the electrode by the top part (which has not been wetted by the copper sulphate solution), rinse the electrode with distilled water, then with propanone and allow to dry. Do not touch the freshly plated surface.
6. Weigh the electrode and record the mass.
7. Replace the electrode in the cell and connect up the circuit.
8. Switch on the d.c. supply and note the time or start a stopclock. Maintain a current of 0.20 A for 45 minutes, then switch off.
9. Repeat steps 5 and 6 above.

Calculations
1. From your weighings find the mass of the copper deposited.
2. Calculate the amount of copper deposited (Cu = 63.5) and hence the amount of electrons transferred:

$$Cu^{2+}(aq) + 2e^- \rightarrow Cu(s)$$

3. From time and current readings calculate the quantity of electricity passed.
4. From the results of 2 and 3 above calculate the value of the Faraday constant.

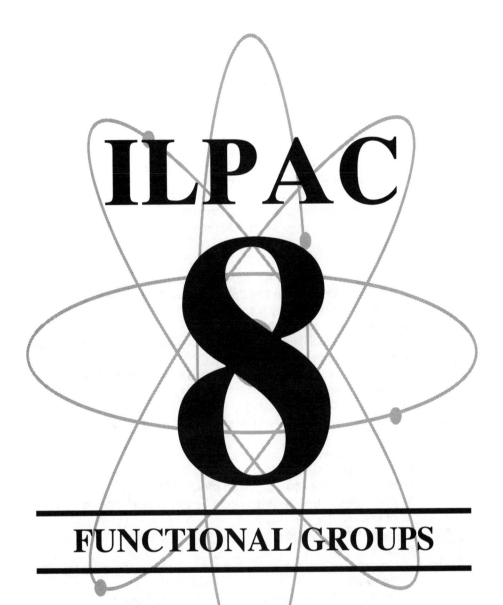

ILPAC

8

FUNCTIONAL GROUPS

EXPERIMENT 8.1 Chemical properties of ethanol

Aim The purpose of this experiment is to study some of the reactions of ethanol, a typical primary alcohol.

Introduction The reactions to be investigated, with approximate times required, are:

A. Solubility in water – 5 minutes
B. Mild oxidation – 30 minutes
C. Further oxidation – 40 minutes
D. Reaction with sodium – 5 minutes
E. Esterification – 5 minutes
F. Dehydration – 30 minutes

HAZARD WARNING

Ethanol is very flammable. Therefore you **must**:
■ **keep the stopper on the bottle as much as possible;**
■ **keep the bottle away from flames;**
■ **wear safety spectacles.**

Bromine and glacial ethanoic acid (acetic acid) have dangerous fumes and burn the skin. Therefore you **must**:
■ **keep the stoppers on the bottles as much as possible;**
■ **wear gloves;**
■ **wear safety spectacles.**

Concentrated sulphuric acid is very corrosive and reacts violently with water. Therefore you **must**:
■ **wear gloves;**
■ **wear safety spectacles;**
■ **mop up minor spillages with plenty of water;**
■ **dispose of unwanted residues by cooling and pouring slowly into an excess of water.**

Tollens reagent for the silver mirror test becomes explosive if dry. Therefore you **must**:
■ **wash away the solutions from experiments A and B immediately you have finished.**

Sodium is extremely dangerous. Therefore you **must**:
■ **use as little as possible (1 mm cube);**
■ **use forceps to handle it;**
■ **keep it under oil;**
■ **wear safety spectacles.**

Sodium dichromate(VI) is a powerful oxidant and can damage the skin. Therefore you **must**:
■ **wear safety spectacles and gloves.**

Sodium hydroxide solution is very corrosive. Even when dilute it can damage your eyes. Therefore you **must**:
■ **wear safety spectacles.**

Fehling's solution 2 is corrosive because it contains sodium hydroxide. It is likely to spurt out of a clean test-tube during heating. Therefore you **must**:
■ **wear safety spectacles.**

Your teacher may want you to divide up the experiment among a group, with each member reporting back on two parts.

You will use Fehling's solution in some of your tests. This solution contains a blue copper(II) compound which, in the presence of a reducing agent, changes to a red copper(I) compound.

$$Cu^{2+} + e^- \rightarrow Cu^+ \rightarrow Cu_2O$$

blue   red

You will also use an ammoniacal solution of silver oxide (Tollens reagent) which, in the presence of a reducing agent, produces a 'silver mirror' (and/or a grey precipitate):

$$Ag^+ + e^- \rightarrow Ag(s)$$

Each of these tests confirms the presence of a reducing agent.

**Requirements
– Part A**

■ safety spectacles
■ test-tube
■ distilled water
■ universal indicator
■ ethanol, C_2H_5OH

**Procedure
– Part A**

Solubility in water
1. Pour about 1 cm^3 of distilled water into a test-tube, add a few drops of universal indicator and shake gently.
2. Add about 1 cm^3 of ethanol and shake the mixture. Note, in a copy of Results Table 8.1, whether the addition of ethanol has any effect on the colour of universal indicator. (Your distilled water may be weakly acidic due to the absorption of atmospheric carbon dioxide.)

**Requirements
– Part B**

■ safety spectacles
■ protective gloves
■ ground-glass-joint apparatus in Fig. 8.1
■ measuring cylinder, 10 cm^3
■ sulphuric acid, dilute, 1 M H_2SO_4
■ spatula and 3 teat pipettes
■ small funnel, wide stem
■ sodium dichromate(VI), solid, $Na_2Cr_2O_7$
■ balance, ±0.1 g
■ anti-bumping granules
■ ethanol, C_2H_5OH
■ 2 retort stands, bosses and clamps
■ Bunsen burner, tripod, gauze, bench mat
■ test-tube and holder
■ boiling-tube
■ Fehling's solution 1
■ Fehling's solution 2
■ sodium hydroxide solution, 2 M NaOH
■ silver nitrate solution, 0.05 M $AgNO_3$
■ ammonia solution, 2 M NH_3
■ beaker, 250 cm^3

Procedure – Part B

Mild oxidation

1. Into a pear-shaped flask, pour 10 cm^3 of 1 M sulphuric acid. Using a small wide-stemmed funnel, add 3.0 g of sodium dichromate(VI) and 2–3 anti-bumping granules.
2. Swirl the flask gently until all the sodium dichromate(VI) has dissolved.
3. Slowly add 5 cm^3 of ethanol and swirl to mix.
4. Set up the apparatus shown in Fig. 8.1.* Ensure that water enters the condenser from the bottom and leaves at the top.

Figure 8.1
Distillation.

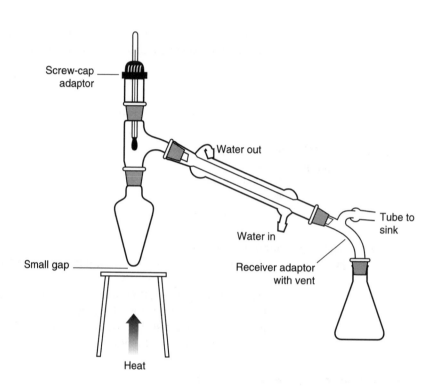

*If you are using a receiver adaptor without a vent, you should perform the experiment at a fume cupboard or in a well-ventilated room.

5. Heat very gently until 2–3 cm^3 of liquid has distilled over.
6. Keep the distillate and test it in the following ways:
    a Smell cautiously (compare with ethanol).
    b Transfer about 1 cm^3 of the distillate to a test-tube. Add about 1 cm^3 of Fehling's solution 1 followed by 1 cm^3 of Fehling's solution 2. Fehling's solution 2 is corrosive, so wear safety spectacles. Boil this mixture very gently. Note your observations in a copy of Results Table 8.1.
    c Pour about 5 cm^3 of silver nitrate solution into a boiling-tube. Add one drop of sodium hydroxide solution. Drop by drop, add aqueous ammonia until the precipitate disappears. Add 2–3 drops of the distillate and warm the tube in a beaker containing hot water. Note your observations. (This is called the 'silver mirror test' or the 'Tollens test'.)
    (Do not keep this solution – it becomes explosive on evaporation.)

Requirements – Part C

- safety spectacles
- protective gloves
- ground-glass-joint apparatus in Fig. 8.1
- measuring cylinder, 10 cm^3
- sulphuric acid, dilute, 1 M H$_2$SO$_4$
- spatula and teat pipette

■ small funnel, wide stem
■ sodium dichromate(VI), solid, $Na_2Cr_2O_7$
■ balance, ± 0.1 g
■ sulphuric acid, concentrated, H_2SO_4
■ anti-bumping granules
■ ethanol, C_2H_5OH
■ 2 retort stands, bosses and clamps
■ Bunsen burner, tripod, gauze, bench mat
■ universal indicator papers
■ test-tube
■ sodium carbonate, anhydrous, Na_2CO_3

Procedure – Part C

Further oxidation

1. Into a pear-shaped flask, pour 10 cm^3 of 1 M sulphuric acid. Through a wide-stemmed funnel add 5 g of sodium dichromate(VI) and 2 or 3 anti-bumping granules.
2. Swirl the flask gently until all the sodium dichromate(VI) has dissolved.
3. **With care**, add 2 cm^3 concentrated sulphuric acid.
4. Cool the flask under a running tap.
5. Set up the apparatus shown in Fig. 8.2, preferably in a fume cupboard.
6. Drop-by-drop, add 1 cm^3 of ethanol down the condenser.
7. Boil gently under reflux for 20 minutes. (While you are waiting you could do reactions D and E.)
8. Rearrange your equipment so it is set up as in Fig. 8.1 above.
9. Distil 2–3 cm^3 of liquid.
10. Test the distillate as follows, and note your observations.
    a Smell cautiously (compare with ethanol).
    b Add a drop to moistened universal indicator paper.
    c Add a few drops to about 1 g of solid sodium carbonate.

Figure 8.2
Heating under reflux.

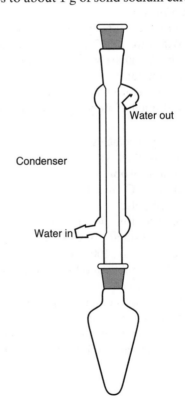

Water out

Condenser

Water in

**Requirements
– Part D**
■ safety spectacles
■ test-tube, in rack
■ ethanol, C_2H_5OH
■ sodium, Na, small pieces under oil
■ forceps
■ filter paper
■ splint
■ watch glass

**Procedure
– Part D**

Reaction with sodium
(Work at a fume cupboard, with your teacher present.)
1. Pour about 1 cm^3 of ethanol into a test-tube.
2. Using forceps, pick up a 1 mm cube of sodium and remove the oil from its surface on filter paper. Drop the sodium into the ethanol.
3. With the front of the fume cupboard pulled down as far as is practically possible, test the gas with a lighted splint.
4. Pour a little of the product from step 2 onto a watch glass, leave in the fume cupboard and allow to evaporate. Describe what remains.

**Requirements
– Part E**
■ safety spectacles
■ test-tube and holder
■ ethanol, C_2H_5OH
■ ethanoic acid, glacial, CH_3CO_2H
■ sulphuric acid, concentrated, H_2SO_4
■ Bunsen burner, and bench mat
■ beaker, 100 cm^3
■ sodium carbonate solution, 1 M Na_2CO_3
■ teat pipette

**Procedure
– Part E**

Esterification
1. Into a test-tube, pour 2 cm^3 of ethanol and 1 cm^3 of glacial ethanoic acid.
2. **With care**, add 2–3 drops of concentrated sulphuric acid.
3. Check you are wearing your safety spectacles and warm gently for a few minutes but do not boil.
4. Pour the product carefully into a beaker containing sodium carbonate solution. Stir and smell. Note your observations.

**Requirements
– Part F**
■ safety spectacles
■ 3 test-tubes, with corks
■ ceramic wool
■ ethanol, C_2H_5OH
■ teat pipette
■ pumice stone, 4–8 mesh
■ 2 retort stands, bosses and clamps
■ conical flask, 100 cm^3
■ delivery tubes and bungs as in Fig. 8.3
■ water trough
■ Bunsen burner and bench mat
■ bromine water, $Br_2(aq)$
■ potassium manganate(VII) solution, 0.01 M $KMnO_4$
■ sulphuric acid, dilute, 1 M H_2SO_4

**Procedure
– Part F**

Dehydration

1. Push enough ceramic wool down to the bottom of the test-tube to fill it to a depth of 2 cm.
2. Using a pipette, drop 2 cm^3 of ethanol onto the ceramic wool and allow to soak into the wool.
3. Fill up the rest of the test-tube with the pumice stone.
4. Set up the apparatus shown in Fig. 8.3, in the fume cupboard, making sure clamp A is at the open end of the test-tube. (The centre conical flask in Fig. 8.3 prevents any water which may be sucked back from the trough entering the heated test-tube. **Under no circumstances** attempt this experiment without it.)

Figure 8.3
Dehydration of ethanol.

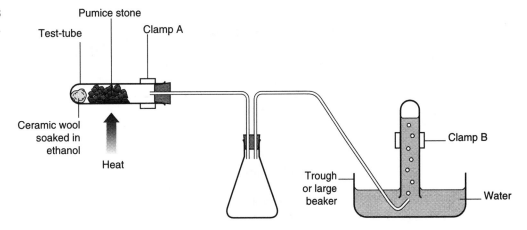

5. Holding the Bunsen burner in your hand, heat the pumice stone quite strongly (without melting the tube!) and occasionally heat the ethanol **gently** to drive the vapour over the hot pumice.
6. Allow the first bubbles to escape (this is displaced air) before collecting the gas over water.
7. Collect a tube of gas (two if possible), cork and place in a rack.
8. Test separate tubes of gas as follows and note your observations:
   a Shake with 1–2 drops of bromine water.
   b Shake with 1–2 drops of acidified potassium manganate(VII) solution.

Results Table 8.1
Reactions of ethanol

Property/Reaction	Observations
A **Solubility in water** pH of solution	

B **Mild oxidation**
   a Smell
   b Fehling's solution
 	
   c Silver mirror (Tollens) test	

C **Further oxidation**
   a Smell
   b Universal indicator paper
   c Sodium carbonate	

D **Reaction with sodium**	
E **Esterification**	

F **Dehydration**
   a Bromine water
   b Acidified potassium
      manganate(VII) solution	

Questions

1. Which of the reactions of ethanol produced a reducing agent? Use your textbook to find out its name and formula.
2. Why did the orange dichromate(VI) turn green in reactions B and C?
3. Which of the reactions of ethanol produced an acidic compound? The smell should give you a clue as to what it might be.
4. What conditions and relative proportions of reactants are used in the oxidation of ethanol to favour the production of:
   a ethanal,
   b ethanoic acid?
5. In the reaction with sodium, what type of fission has taken place in the ethanol molecule – is it C—OH or CO—H fission? Explain.
6. What functional group must be in the product of dehydration of ethanol?
7. Which of the reactions produced a pleasant, sweet-smelling compound?

EXPERIMENT 8.2 Chemical properties of phenol

Aim

The purpose of this experiment is to see the effect of the benzene ring on the behaviour of the hydroxyl group, and vice versa.

Introduction

The reactions you investigate are with the following reagents:

A. water
B. sodium hydrogencarbonate
C. sodium hydroxide
D. sodium
E. bromine water
F. neutral iron(III) chloride solution.

Requirements
- safety spectacles
- protective gloves
- 6 test-tubes, with corks
- test-tube holder and rack
- wash-bottle of distilled water
- 2 beakers, 250 cm^3
- phenol, C_6H_5OH
- spatula and wood splint
- Bunsen burner, tripod, gauze and bench mat
- universal indicator solution
- sodium hydrogencarbonate, $NaHCO_3$
- sodium hydroxide solution, 2 M NaOH
- hydrochloric acid, concentrated, HCl
- teat pipette
- thermometer, 0–100 °C
- sodium, Na (1 mm cubes)
- forceps
- filter paper
- bromine water, $Br_2(aq)$
- iron(III) chloride solution, 0.5 M $FeCl_3$
- sodium carbonate solution, 1 M Na_2CO_3

HAZARD WARNING

  Both phenol and bromine water attack the skin and give off irritating vapours. Therefore you **must**:
- **wear gloves and safety spectacles;**
- **avoid contact with skin;**
- **keep stoppers on bottles as much as possible.**

 Sodium is dangerously reactive. Therefore you **must**:
- **use as little as possible (1 mm cube);**
- **handle with forceps;**
- **keep it under oil;**
- **wear safety spectacles.**

 Sodium hydroxide solution is very corrosive. Even when dilute it can damage your eyes. Therefore you **must**:
- **wear safety spectacles.**

Procedure – Part A

Solubility in water

1. Pour about 5 cm^3 of water into a test-tube and add a heaped spatula-measure (about 1.5 g) of phenol. Cork and shake the tube. Note, in a copy of Results Table 8.2, whether phenol dissolves in water.
2. Add a further 3–4 measures of phenol, shake and note your observations.
3. Place the test-tube in a beaker of hot water for a few minutes, shake the tube and note your observations.
4. Allow the solution in the test-tube to cool and note your observations.
5. Add a few drops of universal indicator solution to the phenol–water mixture in one test-tube and distilled water in another.

Procedure – Part B

Reaction with sodium hydrogencarbonate

6. Into a test-tube pour about 1 cm^3 of water and add 2–3 small crystals of phenol. Cork and shake until the phenol has dissolved.
7. Add about 0.5 g of solid sodium hydrogencarbonate and note your observations.

Procedure – Part C

Reaction with sodium hydroxide

8. Pour about 5 cm³ of 2 M sodium hydroxide into a test-tube and add a spatula-measure of phenol. Cork and shake the test-tube.
9. Add 3 more measures of phenol, cork and shake. Compare the solubility of phenol in water from part A. Note your observations.
10. Drop-by-drop, add 2 cm³ of concentrated hydrochloric acid. Shake the test-tube and note your observations.

Procedure – Part D

Reaction with sodium
(Your teacher must supervise this experiment.)

11. In a fume cupboard, heat about 100 cm³ water in a beaker to about 60 °C.
12. Put a spatula-measure of phenol in a dry test-tube, and stand it in the hot water until the phenol melts.
13. Using forceps, pick up a 1 mm cube of sodium and remove the excess oil from its surface on a piece of filter paper.
14. Use a holder to remove the test-tube from the hot water and, with the front of the fume cupboard down as far as is practically possible, drop the dry sodium into the molten phenol.
15. Apply a lighted splint to the mouth of the test-tube.

Procedure – Part E

Reaction with bromine water

16. Into a test-tube pour about 5 cm³ of water and add a spatula-measure of phenol.
17. Cork and shake until the phenol has dissolved.
18. Pour half the solution into another test-tube for part F.
19. Add about 6 drops of bromine water to the aqueous phenol, shaking the test-tube after the addition of each drop. Note your observations.

Procedure – Part F

Reaction with neutral iron(III) chloride solution

20. Into a test-tube, pour about 1 cm³ of iron(III) chloride solution. Add sodium carbonate solution, drop-by-drop, until a **trace** of the brown precipitate **just** remains after shaking.
21. Add a few drops of this 'neutral' iron(III) chloride solution to the phenol solution prepared in part E. Note your observations.
22. Add a few drops of 'neutral' iron(III) chloride solution to about 1 cm³ of ethanol. Note the difference between ethanol and phenol in this test.

Results Table 8.2
Reactions of phenol

Test		Observations
A	**Solubility in water** **a** A little phenol **b** A lot of phenol **c** pH of solution	
B	**Reaction with sodium hydrogencarbonate**	
C	**Reaction with sodium hydroxide** Subsequent addition of hydrochloric acid	
D	**Reaction with sodium**	
E	**Reaction with bromine water**	
F	**Action of neutral iron(III) chloride solution**	

Questions   1. What does the smell of phenol remind you of?
2. How does the solubility and pH of phenol compare with ethanol? Explain the difference.
3. In the reaction with sodium, what bond has been broken, C—O or O—H? How does this compare with ethanol?
4. Which tests distinguish between ethanol and phenol?
5. Explain why phenol is more soluble in sodium hydroxide than in water.
6. Which tests indicate that phenol is a stronger acid than ethanol?
7. Which test indicates that phenol is a weaker acid than dilute mineral acids such as HCl, H_2SO_4 and HNO_3?
8. How do you account for the fact that phenol decolorises bromine water and forms a white precipitate whereas ethanol does not?

EXPERIMENT 8.3   Reactions of amines

Aim   The purpose of this experiment is to study some of the chemical properties of butylamine (an alkylamine) and phenylamine (an arylamine) and to compare them with the properties of ammonia.

This will enable you to see how the nature of the carbon–hydrogen skeleton affects the properties of the amine group and how the amine group affects the properties of the benzene ring.

Introduction   You will be carrying out some test-tube reactions on butylamine, phenylamine and aqueous ammonia.

| ammonia | butylamine | phenylamine |

We have chosen butylamine as a typical alkylamine because it is a liquid and not too volatile. We have chosen phenylamine, which is also a liquid, as a typical arylamine.

The reactions or properties to be investigated are:

A. Solubility in water
B. Reaction with hydrochloric acid
C. Reaction with copper(II) sulphate
D. Reaction with nitrous acid
E. Reaction with bromine water

Since nitrous acid, HNO_2, is unstable, it is made *in situ* for reaction D by adding sodium nitrite to dilute hydrochloric acid.

$$NaNO_2(aq) + HCl(aq) \rightarrow NaCl(aq) +\ HNO_2(aq)$$

Requirements   ■ safety spectacles
■ protective gloves
■ 6 test-tubes, with bungs or corks
■ test-tube rack
■ phenylamine, $C_6H_5NH_2$, with teat pipette
■ wash-bottle of distilled water
■ butylamine, $C_4H_9NH_2$, with teat pipette
■ ammonia solution, 2 M NH_3
■ universal indicator paper
■ glass stirring rod
■ hydrochloric acid, concentrated, HCl, with teat pipette

- 3 watch glasses
- copper(II) sulphate solution, 1 M $CuSO_4$
- 4 boiling-tubes, with bungs or corks
- labels for test-tubes and beakers
- crushed ice
- sodium chloride, $NaCl$
- 2 beakers, 600 cm^3
- spatula
- ammonium chloride, NH_4Cl
- sodium nitrite, $NaNO_2$
- measuring cylinder, 25 cm^3
- 6 beakers, 100 cm^3
- phenol, C_6H_5OH
- naphthalen-2-ol, $C_{10}H_7OH$
- sodium hydroxide solution, 2 M $NaOH$
- thermometer, 0–100 °C
- lime-water
- wood splint
- Bunsen burner, tripod, gauze and bench mat
- bromine water, $Br_2(aq)$

HAZARD WARNING

 Phenylamine is **toxic**, by ingestion and by skin absorption.

  Phenylamine and butylamine are flammable and give off harmful vapours.

  Sodium hydroxide solution is very corrosive. Even when dilute it can damage your eyes. Concentrated hydrochloric acid, phenol and bromine water are corrosive and give off harmful vapours.

Therefore you **must**:
- **wear safety spectacles and gloves;**
- **work in a fume cupboard where possible;**
- **keep bottles away from flames;**
- **keep stoppers on bottles as much as possible.**

Procedure – Part A

Solubility in water
1. Into a test-tube add 2 drops of phenylamine, 10 drops of water and shake. Note whether the amine appears to dissolve.
2. Using a clean glass rod, test one drop of the solution with universal indicator paper. Compare the pH of the solution with that of distilled water alone and that of ammonia solution. Record your observations in a copy of Results Table 8.3.
3. Repeat steps 1 and 2 using butylamine instead of phenylamine. Also test the pH of ammonia solution.

Procedure – Part B

Reaction with hydrochloric acid
1. Into a test-tube, add 5 drops of phenylamine, 5 drops of water and shake.
2. Drop-by-drop, add enough concentrated hydrochloric acid to obtain a clear solution (about 5 drops).
3. In a fume cupboard, pour the contents of the test-tube on to a watch glass and, if the product is not already solid, allow to evaporate slowly. Note your observations.
4. Repeat steps 1 to 3 using butylamine.
5. Repeat steps 2 and 3, starting with 10 drops of ammonia solution.

Procedure – Part C

Reaction with copper(II) sulphate solution
1. Into a test-tube, add about 2 cm³ of copper(II) sulphate solution.
2. Drop-by-drop add phenylamine, shaking the mixture all the time until the phenylamine is present in excess. Note your observations.
3. Repeat with butylamine and aqueous ammonia.

Procedure – Part D

Reaction with nitrous acid
You carry out the initial reaction at low temperature (<5 °C), and then do further tests on the product (if any).

1. Prepare acidic solutions of salts of ammonia, phenylamine and butylamine as follows, and label them clearly.
   a In a boiling-tube, dissolve about 5 spatula-measures (~5 g) of ammonium chloride in about 15 cm³ of distilled water.
   b Into another boiling-tube, pour about 10 cm³ of water and add about 1 cm³ of phenylamine. A little at a time, carefully add about 4 cm³ of concentrated hydrochloric acid, shaking gently to obtain a clear solution.
   c Repeat **b** above, using butylamine instead of phenylamine.
2. For purposes of comparison, prepare a fourth labelled tube containing 15 cm³ of water and 2 drops of concentrated hydrochloric acid.
3. Stand the four labelled tubes in a beaker containing a 'freezing mixture' of crushed ice and salt (sodium chloride).
4. Into a fifth tube, pour about 20 cm³ of water, add two spatula-measures (1.5 g) of sodium nitrite. Cork the tube, shake to dissolve, and stand it in the freezing mixture to cool.
5. While the tubes are cooling, label 6 small beakers P_1, P_2, P_3, N_1, N_2 and N_3. (P for phenol, N for naphthalen-2-ol.)
6. Into beaker P_1, put a spatula-measure of phenol and about 10 cm³ of sodium hydroxide solution. Stir to dissolve the solid, and add about 25 cm³ of water. Divide the solution into three portions in beakers P_1, P_2 and P_3.
7. Into beaker N_1, put a spatula-measure of naphthalen-2-ol and about 10 cm³ of sodium hydroxide solution. Stir to dissolve the solid, and add about 25 cm³ of water. Divide the solution into three portions in beakers N_1, N_2 and N_3.
8. Check that the temperature of the cooled solutions (from steps 1 to 4) is below 5 °C, then add one quarter of the sodium nitrite solution to each of the other four tubes.
9. Shake each of the four boiling-tubes and look for signs of a reaction between nitrous acid (formed from the nitrite and excess acid) and the salts of the amines or ammonia. In particular, look for any evolution of gas in excess of that produced by the decomposition of nitrous acid alone in the fourth tube.
10. If a gas is evolved, test it with lime-water and with a lighted splint.
11. Into beaker P_1, pour one third of the phenylamine/nitrous acid mixture.
    Into beaker P_2, pour one third of the butylamine/nitrous acid mixture.
    Into beaker P_3, pour one third of the ammonia/nitrous acid mixture.
    Swirl the beakers to mix, and note your observations.
12. Into beaker N_1, pour one third of the phenylamine/nitrous acid mixture.
    Into beaker N_2, pour one third of the butylamine/nitrous acid mixture.
    Into beaker N_3, pour one third of the ammonia/nitrous acid mixture.
    Swirl the beakers to mix, and note your observations.
13. Stand the four labelled boiling-tubes containing the unused nitrous acid and salt mixtures in a beaker of hot water. Look for any evolution of gas in excess of the brown fumes obtained from nitrous acid alone. Test any gas with lime-water and a lighted splint.

Procedure
– Part E

Reaction with bromine water

1. Into a test-tube, place 5 drops of phenylamine and carefully add concentrated hydrochloric acid, dropwise, to obtain a clear solution.
2. Drop-by-drop, add about 1 cm^3 of bromine water. Note your observations.
3. Repeat steps 1 and 2 using butylamine. Check that the solution is acidic; if it is not, add more acid.
4. In a test-tube, dissolve a spatula-measure of ammonium chloride in about 3 cm^3 of water. Add bromine water as before and note your observations.

Results Table 8.3

Test		Phenylamine	Butylamine	Ammonia
A	**a** Solubility in water			
	b pH of solution			
B	**a** Reaction with hydrochloric acid			
	b Evaporation of water from product			
C	Reaction with copper(II) sulphate solution			
D	**a** Reaction with cold nitrous acid below 5 °C			
	b Reaction of product from **a** with: i) phenol			
	ii) naphthalen-2-ol			
	c Effect of heat on product from **a**			
E	Reaction with bromine water			

Questions
1. Are butylamine and phenylamine stronger or weaker bases than ammonia?
2. How do you account for the different solubility of the amines in water and in dilute hydrochloric acid?
3. Which reactions might enable you to distinguish between a primary alkylamine and a primary arylamine?

EXPERIMENT 8.4   Reactions of aldehydes and ketones

Aim
The purpose of this experiment is to compare some reactions of ethanal and propanone.

Introduction
We have chosen ethanal and propanone as relatively safe examples of aldehydes and ketones to illustrate their reactions in simple test-tube experiments.

$$\begin{array}{cc} \underset{H}{\overset{CH_3}{\diagdown}}C=O & \underset{CH_3}{\overset{CH_3}{\diagdown}}C=O \\[6pt] \text{ethanal} & \text{propanone} \end{array}$$

The reactions or properties to be investigated are as follows:

A. Condensation (addition–elimination)
B. Oxidation
C. Triiodomethane (iodoform) reaction

You have already used Fehling's solution and Tollens reagent (ammoniacal silver nitrate) earlier in Experiment 8.1 to test for an aldehyde as an oxidation product of a primary alcohol. Check that you understand the reactions in these tests.

HAZARD WARNING

Ethanal and propanone are irritants to eyes, skin and lungs and are highly flammable. Therefore you **must:**
- ■ **perform the experiment at a fume cupboard;**
- ■ **keep the bottles well away from flames;**
- ■ **keep the stoppers on the bottles as much as possible;**
- ■ **wear safety spectacles and gloves.**

Tollens reagent becomes explosive on evaporation. Therefore you **must:**
- ■ **wash away residues immediately after use.**

Sodium hydroxide solution is very corrosive. Even when dilute it can damage your eyes. Therefore you **must:**
- ■ **wear safety spectacles.**

Fehling's solution 2 is corrosive because it contains sodium hydroxide. It is likely to spurt out of a clean test-tube during heating. Therefore you **must:**
- ■ **wear safety spectacles.**

2,4-dinitrophenylhydrazine is **toxic** (very poisonous). Therefore you **must:**
- ■ **wear safety spectacles and gloves.**

Requirements
- safety spectacles and gloves
- 6 test-tubes
- ethanal, CH_3CHO
- propanone, CH_3COCH_3
- 2,4-dinitrophenylhydrazine solution, $C_6H_3(NO_2)_2NHNH_2$
- sodium hydroxide solution, 2 M NaOH
- Bunsen burner, tripod, gauze and bench mat
- beaker, 250 cm^3
- potassium dichromate(VI) solution, 0.1 M $K_2Cr_2O_7$
- sulphuric acid, dilute, 1 M H_2SO_4
- Fehling's solutions 1 and 2
- silver nitrate solution, 0.05 M $AgNO_3$
- ammonia solution, 2 M NH_3
- iodine solution, 10% (in KI (aq))

Procedure – Part A

Condensation reaction with 2,4-dinitrophenylhydrazine

1. Put 1–2 drops of ethanal in a test-tube and add about 2 cm^3 of 2,4-dinitrophenylhydrazine solution. Note your observations.
2. Repeat for propanone.

Procedure – Part B

Oxidation reactions

a With acidified potassium dichromate(VI)

3. Into a test-tube, put 5 drops of ethanal, 2 drops of potassium dichromate(VI) solution and 10 drops of dilute sulphuric acid.
4. Shake the tube gently and warm in a beaker of hot water. Note your observations.
5. Repeat for propanone.

b With Fehling's solution

6. Into a test-tube, put about 1 cm^3 of Fehling's solution 1 and then add Fehling's solution 2 dropwise until the precipitate just dissolves.
7. Add about 7 drops of ethanal. Shake the tube gently and place in a beaker of boiling water for 5–10 minutes – until no further colour change occurs. Note your observations.
8. Repeat for propanone.

c With Tollens reagent

9. Put about 1 cm^3 of 0.05 M $AgNO_3$ into a **very clean** test-tube and add 3–4 drops of sodium hydroxide solution.
10. Drop-by-drop, add ammonia solution until the precipitate of silver oxide nearly dissolves (do not try to get rid of all the little black specks of silver oxide).
11. Add 1 or 2 drops of ethanal, shake the tube gently and place in a beaker of warm water. Note your observations and immediately rinse out the test-tube.
12. Repeat with propanone.

Procedure – Part C

Triiodomethane reaction

13. Into a test-tube, place 5 drops of ethanal followed by 1 cm^3 of iodine solution, cork and shake.
14. Drop-by-drop, add sodium hydroxide solution until the colour of iodine just disappears (about 2 cm^3) and a straw-coloured solution remains. Note your observations.
15. Repeat with propanone.

Results Table 8.4

Test	Observations	
	Ethanal	**Propanone**
A Condensation reaction with 2,4-dinitrophenylhydrazine		
B Oxidation reactions: **a** acidified dichromate(VI)		
b Fehling's solution		
c Tollens reagent		
C Triiodomethane reaction		

Questions
1. Which tests serve to distinguish between ethanal and propanone?
2. Which reagent could be used as a general test for a carbonyl compound?

EXPERIMENT 8.5 Identifying an unknown carbonyl compound

Aim

The purpose of this experiment is to classify a carbonyl compound by a simple test and to identify it by the preparation of a derivative.

Introduction

You are provided with a sample of compound X, which is known to be an aldehyde or a ketone from a given list. In the first part of the experiment, you identify the compound as either an aldehyde or a ketone using Tollens and Fehling's tests. In the second part, you prepare a derivative of the compound with 2,4-dinitrophenylhydrazine. Finally, you determine the melting point of the derivative in order to name the particular aldehyde or ketone.

HAZARD WARNING

Aldehydes, ketones and alcohols are flammable. Therefore you **must**:
- **keep stoppers on bottles of flammable liquids as much as possible;**
- **keep flammable liquids away from flames;**
- **wear safety spectacles.**

Tollens reagent becomes explosive on evaporation. Therefore you **must**:
- **wash away the solution immediately after use.**

Sodium hydroxide solution is very corrosive. Even when dilute it can damage your eyes. Therefore you **must**:
- **wear safety spectacles.**

Fehling's solution 2 is corrosive because it contains sodium hydroxide. It is likely to spurt out of a clean test-tube during heating. Therefore you **must**:
- **wear safety spectacles.**

2,4-dinitrophenylhydrazine is **toxic** (very poisonous). Therefore you **must**:
- **wear safety spectacles and gloves.**

**Requirements
– Part A**
- safety spectacles and protective gloves
- 2 test-tubes
- teat pipette
- silver nitrate solution, 0.05 M $AgNO_3$
- sodium hydroxide solution, 2 M NaOH
- ammonia solution, 2 M NH_3
- Fehling's solutions 1 and 2
- unknown carbonyl compound, X
- beaker, 250 cm^3
- Bunsen burner, tripod, gauze and bench mat

**Procedure
– Part A**
Identification of the carbonyl compound as an aldehyde or ketone
Carry out Tollens and Fehling's tests on samples of the unknown compound. Try to remember the procedures before checking (see Experiment 8.4). Classify the compound as an aldehyde or a ketone.

**Requirements
– Part B**
- beaker, 100 cm^3 (or boiling-tube)
- methanol, CH_3OH
- 2,4-dinitrophenylhydrazine solution
- glass stirring rod
- sulphuric acid, dilute, 1 M H_2SO_4
- retort stand, boss and clamp
- apparatus for suction filtration (see Fig. 8.4)
- spatula
- beaker, 150 cm^3
- steam bath or 250 cm^3 beaker
- ethanol
- ice
- filter paper

**Procedure
– Part B**
Preparation of a crystalline derivative
1. Into a 100 cm^3 beaker (or boiling tube) put 0.5 cm^3 (10 drops) of the unknown compound. (If the substance is solid dissolve 0.5 g in a minimum amount of methanol.) Add 5 cm^3 of the 2,4-dinitrophenylhydrazine solution and stir.
2. If precipitation does not occur, carefully add 1 cm^3 of dilute sulphuric acid.

Figure 8.4
Suction filtration.

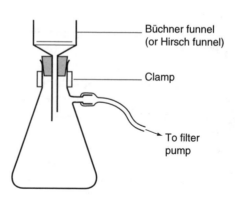

3. Using the suction filtration apparatus in Fig. 8.4, filter the precipitate.
4. Stop suction, either by lifting the funnel or by disconnecting the tubing, and soak the precipitate in about 1 cm^3 of methanol. (If you turn off the tap, you may get a 'suck-back' of water.)

5. Resume suction and dry the crystals by drawing air through them for a few minutes.
6. Recrystallise the solid using the following procedure.
   a Transfer the crystals to a 150 cm^3 beaker standing on a steam bath (or in a 250 cm^3 beaker of hot water).
   b Dissolve the crystals in the **minimum** amount of hot ethanol.
   c When the crystals have dissolved, cool the solution in an ice–water mixture until crystals reappear.
   d Filter the crystals as before. If necessary, rinse the beaker with the **filtrate** (not extra solvent) to complete the transfer. Finally, wash the crystals with a few drops of cold ethanol.
   e Press the crystals thoroughly between two wads of filter paper to remove excess solvent. Then put the crystals on another dry piece of filter paper placed alongside a Bunsen burner and gauze, turning the crystals over occasionally until they appear dry.

**Requirements
– Part C**
■ melting-point tubes (at least 2)
■ watch glass
   Either
■ rubber ring or band
■ thermometer, 0–360 °C, long stem
■ boiling-tube, fitted with cork and stirrer (see Fig. 8.5)
■ dibutyl-benzene-1,2-dicarboxylate (dibutyl phthalate)
   or
■ electrical melting point apparatus

**Procedure
– Part C**
Determination of the melting point of the derivative
1. Take a melting-point tube and push the open end through a pile of the derivative on a watch glass, until a few crystals have entered. If the crystals are large, you may need to crush or grind them first.
2. Tap the closed end of the tube vertically against a hard surface, or rub with the milled edge of a coin, to make the solid fall to the bottom.
3. Repeat the filling and tapping procedure until a total length of about 0.5 cm is compacted at the bottom of the tube. Prepare another tube in this way. If you have an electrical melting point apparatus go to step 7. If not go to step 4.
4. Attach one of the prepared melting-point tubes to the thermometer, as shown in Fig. 8.5.

Figure 8.5
Melting point determination.

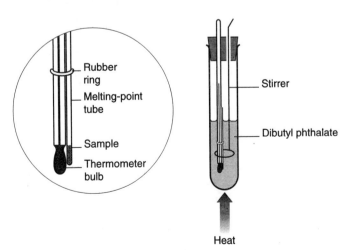

5. Half-fill the boiling-tube with dibutyl phthalate and position the thermometer with attached tube and the stirrer through the bung, as shown in Fig. 8.5.

6. Position the apparatus over a micro-burner (or low Bunsen flame) and gauze and **gently** heat the apparatus, stirring the dibutyl phthalate all the time by moving the stirrer up and down.

7. Keep an eye on the crystals and note the temperature as soon as signs of melting are seen (usually seen as a contraction of the solid followed by a damp appearance). Record the range of temperature over which your sample melts. This first reading gives only a rough melting point but is a guide for the second determination.

8. Remove the burner and the old tube containing derivative. Allow the temperature to drop about 10 °C before positioning a fresh melting-point tube containing another portion of the derivative.

9. Repeat the above procedure in order to obtain a more accurate value of the melting point. Raise the temperature very slowly (about 2 °C rise per minute) until the crystals melt (take the formation of a visible meniscus as a sign of melting).

10. Compare the melting point of your crystals with the values given in Table 8.1 and identify the unknown compound.

11. Check with your teacher or the technician whether you have identified compound X correctly.

Table 8.1
Melting points of some 2,4-dinitrophenylhydrazones

Name	Formula	Boiling point /°C	Melting point of 2,4-dinitro-phenylhydrazone/°C
Aldehydes			
Methanal	$HCHO$	−21	167
Ethanal	CH_3CHO	21	164, 146 (2 forms)
Propanal	CH_3CH_2CHO	48	156
Butanal	$CH_3CH_2CH_2CHO$	75	123
2-methylpropanal	$(CH_3)_2CHCHO$	64	187
Benzaldehyde	C_6H_5CHO	178	237
Ketones			
Propanone	CH_3COCH_3	56	128
Butanone	$CH_3CH_2COCH_3$	80	115
Pentan-2-one	$CH_3CH_2CH_2COCH_3$	102	141
Pentan-3-one	$CH_3CH_2COCH_2CH_3$	102	156
Hexan-2-one	$CH_3CH_2CH_2CH_2COCH_3$	128	107
4-methyl-pentan-2-one	$(CH_3)_2CHCH_2COCH_3$	117	95
Cyclohexanone	=O	156	162

Questions

1. What factors decide the choice of solvent in the recrystallisation procedure?
2. How were soluble impurities removed from the derivative?
3. In the recrystallisation procedure, why were the crystals dissolved in only the **minimum** amount of ethanol?
4. If your sample had contained insoluble impurities, such as pieces of filter paper, cork, etc., suggest how these might have been removed.
5. Why is it not satisfactory to identify aldehydes and ketones by measuring their boiling points?

EXPERIMENT 8.6 Reactions of carbohydrates

Aim The purpose of this experiment is to illustrate the reactions of some sugars and the polysaccharide starch.

Introduction This experiment is divided into five parts:

A. **Dehydration**. Here you examine the effect of heat and of concentrated sulphuric acid on sugars.
B. **Oxidation**. You use Fehling's and Tollens reagents to test sugars for reducing power.
C. **Carbonyl derivatives**. You make the 2,4-dinitrophenylhydrazone of a sugar.
D. **Hydrolysis**. You examine the effects of hot dilute acid and saliva on sucrose and starch.
E. **Polarimetry**. You use a polarimeter to observe the rotation of plane-polarised light by sugars and to follow the hydrolysis of sucrose.

General requirements for Parts A, B, C and D
- safety spectacles
- 6 test-tubes in a rack
- beaker, 250 cm^3 (for use as a water-bath)
- Bunsen burner, tripod, gauze and bench mat
- wash-bottle of distilled water
- spatula
- glucose, $C_6H_{12}O_6$
- fructose, $C_6H_{12}O_6$
- sucrose, $C_{12}H_{22}O_{11}$
- maltose, $C_{12}H_{22}O_{11}$
- starch, $(C_6H_{10}O_5)n$
- sulphuric acid, dilute, 1 M H_2SO_4

HAZARD WARNING

Concentrated sulphuric acid is very corrosive and reacts violently with water, especially when hot. Therefore you **must**:
- **wear safety spectacles and protective gloves;**
- **use small quantities and cool residues before disposal;**
- **pour cold residues slowly into plenty of cold water, stirring to disperse heat.**

Fehling's solution 2 is corrosive because it contains sodium hydroxide. It is likely to spurt out of a test-tube during heating. Therefore you **must**:
- **wear safety spectacles;**
- **ensure that nobody is in line with a test-tube during heating.**

Tollens reagent can become explosive if allowed to evaporate to dryness. Therefore you **must**:
- **wash away residues with plenty of water.**

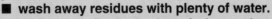
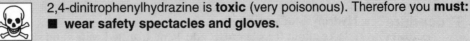

2,4-dinitrophenylhydrazine is **toxic** (very poisonous). Therefore you **must**:
- **wear safety spectacles and gloves.**

Requirements – Part A
- protective gloves
- sulphuric acid, concentrated, H_2SO_4
- wood splint
- lime-water, $Ca(OH)_2(aq)$
- potassium dichromate(VI) solution, 0.1 M $K_2Cr_2O_7$
- filter paper strips

Procedure – Part A

Dehydration

1. Warm about 0.5 g of glucose or sucrose in a dry test-tube. Use a low flame and heat the tube gently. Record your observations in a copy of Results Table 8.5, noting particularly any changes in state, colour, viscosity and smell.
2. Carefully add about 1 cm^3 of concentrated sulphuric acid to about 0.5 g of glucose or sucrose in a test-tube.
3. Warm the mixture gently and then remove the tube from the flame to observe and record the changes which occur without further heating.
4. Heat the mixture more strongly and test for carbon monoxide, carbon dioxide and sulphur dioxide.

Requirements – Part B

■ Fehling's solutions 1 and 2
■ ammonia solution, 2 M NH$_3$
■ silver nitrate solution, 0.05 M AgNO$_3$

Procedure – Part B

Oxidation

1. Dissolve about 0.1 g of glucose in 2 cm^3 distilled water in a test-tube.
2. Add 1 cm^3 each of Fehling's solutions 1 and 2. Heat the tube carefully to keep the mixture **just** boiling for about 30 seconds.
3. Note the colour of the solution and whether any precipitate is formed.
4. Repeat steps 1 to 3 using fructose, maltose and sucrose.
5. Prepare some ammoniacal silver nitrate solution (Tollens reagent) for your own use as follows. Add ammonia solution drop-by-drop to about 5 cm^3 of silver nitrate solution until the resulting buff precipitate **almost** redissolves on shaking.
6. Dissolve about 0.1 g of glucose in 2 cm^3 distilled water in a **clean** test-tube.
7. Add about 2 cm^3 of Tollens reagent and heat the tube in a beaker of boiling water. Note any colour change that takes place.
8. Repeat steps 6 and 7 with fructose, maltose and sucrose.

Requirements – Part C

■ 2,4-dinitrophenylhydrazine solution, C$_6$H$_3$(NO$_2$)$_2$NHNH$_2$
■ sulphuric acid, 1 M H$_2$SO$_4$

Procedure – Part C

Carbonyl derivatives

1. Dissolve about 0.5 g of glucose in 1 cm^3 distilled water and add 5 cm^3 of 2,4-dinitrophenylhydrazine solution.
2. If crystals do not form, add a little dilute sulphuric acid, warm the test-tube and then cool under running cold water.
3. Repeat steps 1 and 2 with fructose.

Requirements – Part D

■ boiling water-bath
■ ammonia solution, 2 M NH$_3$
■ litmus paper
■ Fehling's solution or Tollens reagent as in part B
■ iodine solution, 0.1 M I$_2$ in KI(aq)

Procedure – Part D

a Hydrolysis of sucrose

1. Take about 0.3 g sucrose, add 4 cm^3 distilled water and shake to dissolve. Add 1 cm^3 of dilute sulphuric acid.
2. Heat the tube in a boiling water-bath for 5 minutes.
3. Add enough dilute aqueous ammonia to neutralise the solution.
4. Carry out a test with either Fehling's solution or Tollens reagent to see whether you can detect any reducing sugar.

b Hydrolysis of starch

5. Place about 2 cm^3 of starch solution in each of four test-tubes labelled A, B, C and D.
6. Add a little saliva solution to each of tubes A and B.

7. Boil the contents of tube A for 2–3 minutes, then place both tubes A and B in a water-bath at 40 °C for 20 minutes.
8. Add 1 cm³ of dilute sulphuric acid to C and place it in a boiling water-bath for 15 minutes.
9. Neutralise solution C with dilute aqueous ammonia.
10. Divide the contents of each of the four tubes into two parts. Add two or three drops of iodine solution to one part and test the other with Fehling's solution or Tollens reagent as in part B of this experiment.

Results Table 8.5

Experiments	Observations				
	Glucose	Fructose	Sucrose	Maltose	Starch
A **Dehydration** **a** Action of heat **b** Sulphuric acid					
B **Oxidation** **a** Fehling's solution **b** Tollens reagent					
C **Carbonyl derivatives** 2,4-dinitro- phenylhydrazone					
D **Hydrolysis**					

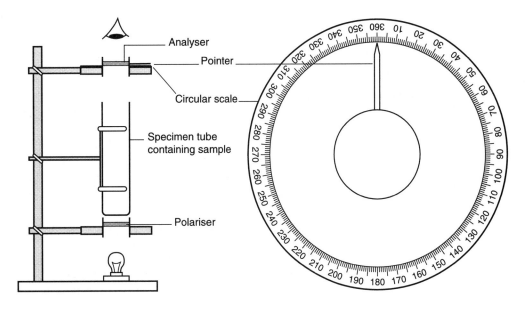

Figure 8.6
A simple polarimeter.

**Requirement
– Part E**

■ simple polarimeter

**Procedure
– Part E**

Polarimetry

We assume that you will use a polarimeter like the one shown in Fig. 8.6 (see page 133). If this is not the case, ask your teacher to modify our instructions.

1. Remove the specimen tube and look vertically down at the light source through both polaroid films. If possible, insert a filter to limit the light to a narrow band of wavelengths.
2. Rotate the analyser until you find a position which allows no light (or hardly any) to pass, and set the pointer to zero.
3. Fill the specimen tube with a fairly concentrated solution of glucose.
4. Place the specimen tube in position. Note, in a copy of Results Table 8.6, the new setting of the analyser which extinguishes the light.
5. Halve the light path in the liquid by pouring away half of the solution. Note the new setting of the analyser which extinguishes the light.
6. Refill the specimen tube by adding distilled water. Again, adjust the analyser and note the new setting.

If you have time (at least one hour), you may like to try another short experiment.

1. Dissolve 50 g of sucrose in 50 cm^3 of hot water and leave to cool.
2. Add 20 cm^3 of concentrated hydrochloric acid, mix well and pour into the polarimeter tube.
3. Take a reading, α_t, of the setting of the analyser and note the time, t. Record your results in a copy of Results Table 8.6.
4. Take further readings at intervals as shown until there is no further change. Sixty minutes should be enough for α_∞.

Results Table 8.6

	Movement of analyser from zero							
Glucose	Initial $\quad$ $\frac{1}{2}$ volume $\quad$ Diluted			+ indicates clockwise$\\$ − indicates anticlockwise				
	Time, t/min	0	3	6	10	15	20	30	∞
Sucrose	Analyser reading, α_t/°								
	$\alpha_t - \alpha_\infty$/°								

Questions

1. Why are sugars very soluble in water?
2. What are the main products when concentrated sulphuric acid reacts with glucose?
3. Why is the reaction in question 2 called dehydration?
4. What happens to the sulphuric acid during the reaction in question 2?
5. Would you have predicted positive Tollens and Fehling's tests with fructose?
6. Name the products formed when Tollens reagent and Fehling's solution react with glucose.
7. Write an equation for the reaction between glucose and 2,4-dinitrophenylhydrazine.
8. Write an equation for the hydrolysis of sucrose.
9. Why is the reaction known as inversion of sucrose?
10. Hydrolysis of sucrose in the experiment required heat. Explain why this reaction is possible in a human's digestive system at much lower temperatures.

11. Interpret the results from part **Db** of the experiment – hydrolysis of starch.
12. Why is it that sucrose and starch give a positive Fehling's test only after hydrolysis?
13. What is the importance of the hydrolysis reaction of disaccharides and starch in the human digestive system?
14. Which test is used to identify the presence of starch?
15. Calculate the concentration of the solution of glucose which you used, given the following information.
   The rotation caused by a 1 dm* column of solution at a concentration of 1 g cm^{-3}* is constant for a given substance and is known as the specific rotation, $[\alpha]$.
   $[\alpha]$ (D-glucose) = +52.5° cm^3 g^{-1} dm^{-1}*.
   Specific rotation is related to observed rotation, α, by the expression:

$$[\alpha] = \frac{\alpha}{lc}$$

   l (in dm*) is the length of the light path in the solution, c is the concentration (g cm^{-3}*)
   (Strictly speaking, the wavelength of the polarised light and the temperature should also be constant at specified values, but you may ignore these for an approximate calculation.)
16. If you did the hydrolysis of sucrose experiment with the polarimeter, plot a graph of $(\alpha_t - \alpha_\infty)$ against t. Comment on its shape.
   *Note the unusual units.

EXPERIMENT 8.7   Observation and deduction exercise 3

Aim and introduction

The experiment which follows is taken from two A-level practical examination papers. Since you should preferably work under examination conditions, all the apparatus and chemicals should be provided for you so we have not included a requirements list. However, take note of the hazard warning.

You are provided with three organic compounds, labelled C, D and E. C and D contain the elements carbon, hydrogen and oxygen only. Carry out the following experiments. Record your observations and inferences in (larger copies of) the tables provided. Comment on the types of chemical reaction occurring and, where possible, deduce the functional groups present in these compounds.

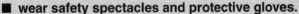

Procedure and results

Results Table 8.7

Test	Observations	Inferences
1. **a** Place 1 cm^3 of C in a test-tube and add an equal volume of water. Now add a little anhydrous sodium carbonate **b** Repeat test **1a** using D		
2. (The reactions **2a** and **2b** should be performed at a fume cupboard) **a** Place 2 or 3 cm^3 of C in a dry beaker. Add a little phosphorus pentachloride (**care**) **b** Repeat test **2a** using D (**care**)		
3. Mix, in a small beaker, about 2 cm^3 of each of C, D and concentrated sulphuric acid (**care**). Warm gently but do not boil. Pour the mixture into an excess of aqueous sodium carbonate in a large beaker. Smell the product		
4. Mix about 5 cm^3 of D with an equal volume of aqueous potassium dichromate in a test-tube. Pour the mixture into about 10 cm^3 of nearly boiling dilute sulphuric acid in a small beaker. Smell the mixture		
5. In a small beaker dissolve a few crystals of potassium iodide in about 10 cm^3 of D. Add a few drops of aqueous sodium hydroxide. Now add 2 or 3 cm^3 of aqueous sodium chlorate(I) (hypochlorite). Warm the mixture but do not boil. Cautiously smell the products		
6. Make a solution of E in distilled water and use portions for the following tests: **a** To 2–3 cm^3 of the solution add aqueous bromine **b** To 2–3 cm^3 of the solution add aqueous silver nitrate. Then add dilute nitric acid. Finally add dilute aqueous ammonia		
7. Dissolve a little E in about 1 cm^3 of concentrated hydrochloric acid and dilute to about 4 cm^3 with distilled water. Cool the tube in an ice–water mixture and add a few drops of aqueous sodium nitrite (to be prepared by dissolving sodium nitrite in distilled water). Leave the tube in the ice–water mixture. Dissolve a few crystals of phenol (**care**) in 7–8 cm^3 of aqueous sodium hydroxide, cool this solution, and then add it to the cold solution prepared as above		

1. Complete the following table as far as possible.

Results Table 8.8

	Reasoning
Functional group in C Functional group in D	

2. Give the structural features of compound E.

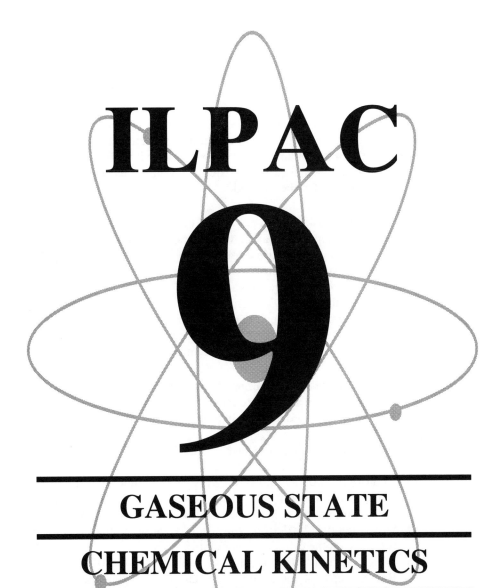

ILPAC

9

GASEOUS STATE

CHEMICAL KINETICS

EXPERIMENT 9.1 Determining the molar mass of a gas

Aim The purpose of this experiment is to measure the volume and mass of a sample of carbon dioxide, and to use these values to determine the molar mass.

Introduction You weigh a clean dry flask full of air and then full of carbon dioxide. By filling the flask with water and reweighing, you can find its volume. Knowing the density of air, you calculate the mass of air filling the flask and use it to find the mass of the empty flask, and hence the mass of carbon dioxide. You then use the ideal gas equation to determine the molar mass of carbon dioxide.

Requirements
- volumetric flask, 100 cm^3, dry, with stopper
- balance(s) capable of taking volumetric flask and of weighing:
    up to 100 g with accuracy of 0.001 g,
    up to 200 g with accuracy of 0.1 g
- carbon dioxide cylinder or generator
- delivery tube, glass, 20–30 cm long
- rubber tubing, 30–90 cm, to connect gas cylinder to delivery tube
- thermometer, 0–100 °C
- access to barometer (or telephone number of local meteorological office)

Procedure
1. Get instructions from your teacher on how to operate the gas cylinder – there will be some valves you must not touch. Alternatively, you can use a simple carbon dioxide generator, provided you purify the gas from acid spray and dry it before use. Again, ask your teacher.
2. Weigh the **dry** volumetric flask together with its stopper to the nearest 0.001 g. Enter the mass in Results Table 9.1.
3. Remove the stopper, insert the glass delivery tube from the carbon dioxide cylinder or generator so that it reaches the bottom of the flask, and open the valve so that gas passes through for at least one minute. Keep the flask upright throughout.
4. Slowly remove the delivery tube, quickly close the flask with the stopper and close the valve on the cylinder or generator.
5. Weigh the flask with stopper again to the nearest 0.001 g.
6. Repeat steps 3, 4 and 5, and check that there is no further change in mass (i.e. that the carbon dioxide has indeed displaced all the air from the flask). If this is not the case, repeat these steps again – and then yet again, if necessary, until the mass is constant.
7. Fill the flask with water and insert the stopper, so that excess water is pushed out. Dry the outside of the flask and weigh it, full of water, on a robust balance to the nearest 0.1 g.
8. Note room temperature and atmospheric pressure.
9. Complete Results Table 9.1.

Results Table 9.1

Mass of flask filled with air	g
Mass of flask filled with CO_2	g
Mass of flask filled with water	g
Room temperature	°C
Atmospheric pressure	mmHg
Density of air under conditions of experiment	g cm^{-3}

The following table gives values for the density of the air under various conditions of temperature and pressure. If your conditions do not correspond to any of those quoted, you should estimate the appropriate value.

Table 9.1
Density of air (g cm^{-3}) at different temperatures and pressures

	15 °C	17 °C	19 °C	21 °C	23 °C	25 °C
740 mmHg	0.00119	0.00119	0.00118	0.00117	0.00116	0.00115
750 mmHg	0.00121	0.00120	0.00119	0.00119	0.00118	0.00117
760 mmHg	0.00123	0.00122	0.00121	0.00120	0.00119	0.00119
770 mmHg	0.00124	0.00123	0.00123	0.00122	0.00121	0.00120
780 mmHg	0.00126	0.00125	0.00124	0.00123	0.00122	0.00122

Calculation

You need to calculate the mass of carbon dioxide from your experimental results, before using the ideal gas equation in the form $pV = mRT/M$. The steps in the calculation are as follows. Calculate:
1. The volume of the flask (from the mass and density of water).
2. The mass of air in the flask.
3. The mass of the empty stoppered flask (i.e. with no air in it).
4. The mass of carbon dioxide in the flask.
5. The molar mass of carbon dioxide.

Questions

1. What value does the experiment give for the **relative** molecular mass of CO_2?
2. Calculate the density of CO_2 at s.t.p. from your results.
3. In step 4 why were you told to remove the delivery tube slowly?
4. Why is a less accurate balance adequate for weighing the flask full of water?

EXPERIMENT 9.2   Determining the molar mass of a volatile liquid

Aim

The aim of the experiment is to determine the molar mass of ethyl ethanoate, $CH_3CO_2C_2H_5$, at the temperature of boiling water and at atmospheric pressure. The same method can be used for other liquids which boil at a temperature below 80 °C, but we have chosen this one because it is non-toxic.

Introduction

You obtain the mass of a sample of the liquid by weighing a small hypodermic syringe before and after injection into a large gas syringe. The large syringe is heated in a steam jacket (see Fig. 9.1) and you measure the volume of the vapour at the temperature of condensing steam. Finally you apply the ideal gas equation as before to calculate the molar mass.

Requirements

- safety spectacles
- 100 cm^3 gas syringe, glass
- self-sealing rubber cap for gas syringe
- steam jacket for gas syringe
- thermometer, 0 °C to 105 °C, to fit steam jacket
- Bunsen burner, tripod, gauze and bench mat
- steam generator, with safety tube
- 2 cm^3 hypodermic syringe, glass, and needle
- ethyl ethanoate, $CH_3CO_2C_2H_5$
- filter paper
- self-sealing silicone rubber to make temporary seal for needle
- balance (accuracy 0.001 g)
- access to barometer (or telephone number of local meteorological office)

Figure 9.1

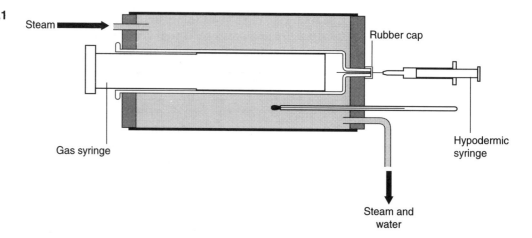

Steam

Rubber cap

Gas syringe

Hypodermic syringe

Steam and water

HAZARD WARNING

- Steam can cause serious scalding.
- Make sure your generator has a safety tube so that pressure cannot build up if the outlet tube becomes blocked. Also, make sure the steam inlet to the jacket is secure and the outlet from the jacket is directed downwards. **Wear safety spectacles.**

- Ethyl ethanoate is flammable. **Work well away from the Bunsen burner and do not leave the stopper off the bottle longer than is necessary.**

Procedure

1. Place the gas syringe into the steam jacket and draw in about 5 cm^3 of air before sealing it with the rubber cap.
2. Pass steam through the steam jacket until the temperature reading and the volume of air in the syringe reach steady values. You can begin the next step while you are waiting for this steady state to be established.
3. Draw about 1 cm^3 of ethyl ethanoate into the hypodermic syringe through the needle, rinse the syringe with the liquid and expel it into the sink. Draw in another 1 cm^3 of liquid and, holding the syringe vertically with the needle uppermost, slowly push in the piston till every bubble of air is expelled and a few drops of liquid emerge.
4. Dry the outside of the needle with filter paper and seal it with a small piece of silicone rubber.
5. Weigh the hypodermic syringe with its cap and liquid contents and record the mass in Results Table 9.2. Keep the syringe horizontal and avoid touching the piston or warming the barrel with your hand, either of which could result in loss of liquid.
6. When the temperature and volume of the air in the gas syringe are constant, record the volume of air and, with steam still passing through the jacket, push the hypodermic needle through its own seal and through the rubber seal of the gas syringe so that its tip projects well into the air space. Inject about 0.2 cm^3 of the liquid into the gas syringe. See Fig. 9.2.

Figure 9.2

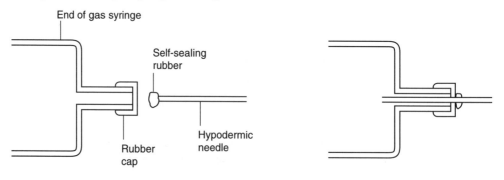

End of gas syringe

Self-sealing rubber

Rubber cap

Hypodermic needle

7. Withdraw the needle into its own self-sealing cap, and re-weigh the syringe, cap and contents immediately so that no more liquid escapes. Record the mass.
8. Make sure, by twirling it, that the piston in the gas syringe can move freely so that the pressure inside is the same as atmospheric pressure, which should also be recorded.
9. Watch the temperature, and the volume of air and vapour in the syringe, until both reach steady values. Record these steady values.
10. Remove the cap from the gas syringe and push the piston in and out several times to expel the vapour.
11. If you, or another student, wish to use the apparatus again immediately, leave the steam generator going. Otherwise turn off the Bunsen burner.

Results Table 9.2

Mass of hypodermic syringe and liquid before injection	g
Mass of hypodermic syringe and liquid after injection	g
Temperature of vapour	°C
Atmospheric pressure	mmHg
Volume of air in syringe	cm^3
Volume of air and vapour in syringe	cm^3

Calculation   From your results, calculate the molar mass of ethyl ethanoate using the ideal gas equation in the form $pV = mRT/M$.

Questions
1. What value does the experiment give for the relative molecular mass of ethyl ethanoate?
2. What might happen if the hypodermic needle were shorter than the nozzle of the gas syringe, and what effect would this have on your final results?
3. Calculate the molar mass from your experimental results in a different way, using the known value for molar volume at s.t.p.

EXPERIMENT 9.3   Determining the molar mass of a gas by effusion

Aim   The purpose of this experiment is to apply Graham's law to determine the molar mass of domestic gas.

Introduction   You fill a gas syringe with hydrogen, and allow it to escape through a small pin-hole under the weight of the piston. You measure the rate of escape and repeat the experiment using domestic gas. Assuming the molar mass of hydrogen, you use Graham's law to calculate the molar mass of domestic gas.

Requirements
■ small piece of aluminium foil
■ quick-setting glue
■ three-way tap and connector to fit syringe
■ gas syringe, 100 cm^3
■ retort stand and clamp
■ needle or pin
■ stopclock or stopwatch (preferably to 0.1 s)
■ hydrogen cylinder or generator with rubber delivery tube
■ tubing to gas tap

Figure 9.3 (left)

Figure 9.4 (right)

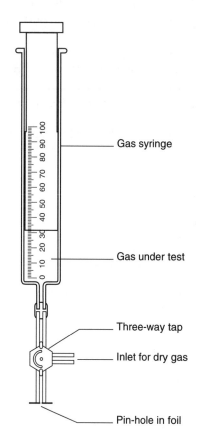

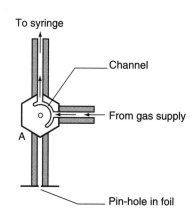

Procedure (Steps 1 to 3 may already be done for you.)
1. Cut a piece of smooth aluminium foil about 1 cm square and lay it on a flat surface, ready to be glued to the three-way tap. Do not pierce the foil yet.
2. Apply a little glue to the flat end of one of the tubes of the three-way tap. There must be enough to form a complete seal between the foil and the glass, but not so much as to close the aperture.
3. Lower the three-way tap vertically on to the foil, press gently together, and leave until the glue has dried.
4. Check that the syringe piston moves freely (it must not be greased), attach the three-way tap and clamp the syringe carefully as shown in Fig. 9.3. Turn the tap so that there is a channel between side tube and syringe (position A – Fig. 9.4) and fill the syringe with air.
5. Turn the tap so that the side tube is closed but gas can pass between syringe and foil (position B – Fig. 9.5).
6. Watch the volume reading of the syringe for half a minute – it should not change. If the volume does change, air must be escaping from the three-way tap, or from the connector, or from the joint between foil and glass. Check these in turn, re-greasing the tap if necessary, until you are satisfied that the apparatus does not leak.
   (There is always **some** leakage between the piston and the syringe, but in a good syringe this will be so slow as to be negligible over half a minute. If it is **not**

negligible, you can dispense with the three-way tap and the foil, seal the nozzle with a bung, and use the gap between piston and syringe for the effusion!)

7. With the tap still in position B, carefully pierce the foil with a needle making a **very small** hole at first. Watch the rate of fall of the piston and increase the size of the hole as necessary until the piston falls at a rate equivalent to about 1 cm³ air expelled each second. This sets the size of hole for the complete experiment – do not touch it again!

Figure 9.5

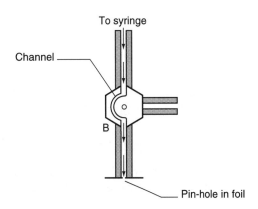

8. Turn the tap to position A and expel the air from the syringe through the side tube.
9. Check with your teacher on any instructions for using the hydrogen cylinder or generator (**no flames near!**) and obtain a slow flow of gas through the delivery tube **before** connecting it to the side tube of the three-way tap.
10. Fill the syringe to about 50 cm³, remove the delivery tube and expel the gas from the syringe to ensure that no air remains. Refill to about 75 cm³, turn off the cylinder or generator and turn the tap to position B.
11. Allow the piston to fall to the 60 cm³ mark and start the stopclock at the moment it passes the mark.
12. Stop the clock when the piston passes the 10 cm³ mark and record the time in Results Table 9.3.
13. Repeat steps 9 to 12 at least twice. The times should not vary by more than 10 per cent – if they do, check again for leaks, particularly from the tap, and for a sticking piston. Repeat if necessary to obtain reproducible results.
14. Expel the hydrogen from the syringe, obtain a slow flow of domestic gas through a rubber tube from a gas tap and fill the syringe as before, repeating steps 10 to 13 as necessary to complete Results Table 9.3.

Results Table 9.3

	1	2	3	4	Mean
Time for effusion of 50 cm³ of hydrogen /s					
Time for effusion of 50 cm³ of domestic gas /s					

Calculation Use your results to calculate the molar mass of domestic gas by using Graham's law.

Questions
1. What is the main constituent of domestic gas? Is your result for the molar mass consistent with your answer?
2. Does your result suggest that impurities in domestic gas have molar masses greater or smaller than the molar mass of the main constituent? What might these impurities be?
3. Why were you told to allow the piston to fall from the 75 cm³ mark to the 60 cm³ mark before starting the stopclock?

4. What difference would you expect if you repeated the experiment with the same apparatus and the same pin-hole at a higher temperature? Explain.
5. What difference would you expect if you repeated the experiment with the same apparatus at the same temperature but with a larger hole?

EXPERIMENT 9.4 Investigating the hydrolysis of benzenediazonium chloride

Aim The purpose of this experiment is to determine the rate equation for the reaction in which benzenediazonium chloride is hydrolysed and hence find the order of reaction with respect to benzenediazonium chloride.

Introduction Benzenediazonium chloride is an unstable substance, which decomposes when heated above 5 °C to give phenol, nitrogen and hydrochloric acid:

$$C_6H_5N_2{}^+Cl^-(aq) + H_2O(l) \rightarrow C_6H_5OH(aq) + N_2(g) + HCl(aq)$$

There are several stages in the preparation of the reaction mixture, so you do this at a temperature low enough for the rate of reaction to be negligible. When you are ready, you warm the mixture quickly to a fixed temperature and measure the volume (V_t) of gas produced at one-minute intervals for about 25 minutes. You then leave the mixture until no further reaction appears to be occurring, and measure the total volume (V_∞) of gas produced since the stopclock was started.

Because the volume of gas produced in time t is proportional to the amount of benzenediazonium chloride used up, it follows that:

$$V_\infty \propto [C_6H_5N_2{}^+Cl^-(aq)] \text{ at the start}$$

$$(V_\infty - V_t) \propto [C_6H_5N_2{}^+Cl^-(aq)] \text{ at time } t$$

A plot of $(V_\infty - V_t)$ against time will therefore have the same form as the concentration/time graph and can be used to obtain information about the rate of reaction.

Note that, in this experiment, you need not attempt to judge the time when the reaction begins. The stopclock can be started at any time after the mixture has reached a steady temperature. Even if some benzenediazonium chloride has reacted by then, the amount remaining can be taken as giving the 'initial' concentration, and this can be calculated, if necessary, from V_∞.

Requirements
■ safety spectacles and protective gloves
■ water-bath, thermostatically controlled, set between 40 and 50 °C
■ thermometer, 0–100 °C
■ side-arm test-tube with bung
■ three-way tap
■ glass syringe, 100 cm^3
■ rubber tubing (2 short lengths)
■ 2 retort stands, bosses and clamps
■ wash-bottle of distilled water
■ measuring cylinder, 10 cm^3
■ test-tube
■ sodium nitrite, NaNO$_2$
■ spatula
■ beaker, 250 cm^3
■ crushed ice
■ hydrochloric acid, concentrated, HCl

- pumice or anti-bumping granules
- graduated pipette, 5 cm^3 or 10 cm^3
- pipette filler
- phenylamine, $C_6H_5NH_2$
- teat pipette
- stopclock or stopwatch

HAZARD WARNING

  Phenylamine is **toxic**, by ingestion and by skin absorption. It is also flammable and gives off a harmful vapour.

  Concentrated hydrochloric acid is corrosive and gives off a harmful vapour.

  Sodium nitrite is an oxidising agent and is **toxic**.

Therefore you **must**:
- **wear safety spectacles and gloves;**
- **work at a fume cupboard where possible;**
- **keep bottles away from flames;**
- **keep stoppers on bottles as much as possible.**

Procedure

1. Set the control on the water-bath to a temperature between 40 and 50 °C and hang a thermometer in it. If possible this should be done before the lesson so that it has time to reach a steady temperature.
2. Set up the apparatus, without the chemicals, as shown in Fig. 9.6.

Figure 9.6

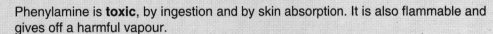
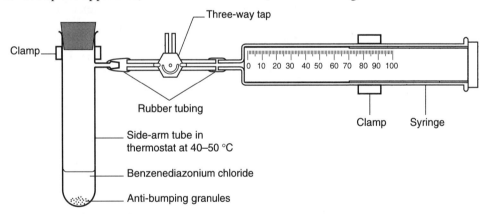

3. When you have connected the three-way tap between the side-arm tube and the syringe, turn the tap so that it connects the syringe with the open air as in Fig. 9.7, A. Press the plunger in, so that the syringe is empty, and then turn the tap so that it connects the side-arm tube with the air as in Fig. 9.7, B.

Figure 9.7

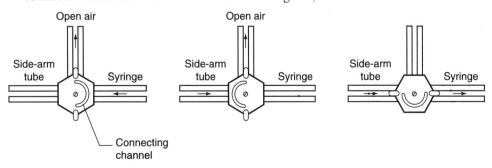

A Emptying syringe   B Allowing gas to escape   C Collecting gas

4. Using a 10 cm^3 measuring cylinder, add 2.0 cm^3 of distilled water into a test-tube. Weigh 0.80 g of sodium nitrite and dissolve it in the water. Cool this solution in a beaker of crushed ice and keep it handy.

5. Remove the side-arm tube and, using a measuring cylinder, measure into it 5.0 cm^3 of distilled water and 2.5 cm^3 of concentrated hydrochloric acid.

6. Add a few anti-bumping or pumice granules to the side-arm tube and seal its mouth with a rubber bung.

7. Place the side-arm tube in a beaker of crushed ice and, using a pipette and filler, add 1.0 cm^3 of phenylamine. Mix the contents of the tube thoroughly and allow them to cool.

8. Using a teat pipette, add the sodium nitrite solution a few drops at a time to the phenylamine solution in the side-arm tube. Shake the tube gently to swirl its contents as you do so.

9. Check that the thermostat temperature has become constant (at about 45 °C), then clamp the side-arm tube in position in the thermostat (see Fig. 9.6) so that the solution is completely immersed in water.

10. Wait four minutes with the tap open to the air, so that the solution warms to the temperature of the water-bath. Record the temperature.

11. After four minutes, turn the tap so that it connects the side-arm tube with the syringe (Fig. 9.7, C), reset the stopclock and take a reading. Regard this as time zero. Don't shake the tube now or hereafter.

12. Continue taking readings each minute for about 25 minutes. Enter your results in a larger copy of Results Table 9.4. The total volume of gas produced is over 100 cm^3, so as you see the volume approaching the 100 cm^3 mark, get ready to turn the tap to the position shown in Fig. 9.7, A (emptying the syringe into the air). Just as it reaches 100 cm^3, turn the tap, expel the collected nitrogen, then turn the tap back to the position shown in Fig. 9.7, C (connecting the side-arm tube with the syringe). Depending on how you make up your mixture, you may have to do this twice during the experiment.

13. After 25 minutes, leave the apparatus for at least another half hour for the reaction to finish completely. This gives you the total volume of nitrogen produced in the reaction, V_∞ (i.e., the volume produced at infinite time). If you want to speed things up, immerse the side-arm tube into a beaker of hot water at about 60 °C. If the syringe is nearly full, empty it first, noting the volume of nitrogen expelled. The volume of nitrogen should reach its maximum in a few minutes. Remember to allow the syringe to cool back down to the temperature of the water-bath before taking your final reading (V_∞).

Results Table 9.4

Time, t/min							
Volume of N_2, V_t/cm^3							
$(V_\infty - V_t)$/cm^3							
Time, t/min							
Volume of N_2, V_t/cm^3							
$(V_\infty - V_t)$/cm^3							
Time, t/min							
Volume of N_2, V_t/cm^3							
$(V_\infty - V_t)$/cm^3							
Time, t/min							
Volume of N_2, V_t/cm^3							
$(V_\infty - V_t)$/cm^3							

Calculations

1. Work out the values of $(V_\infty - V_t)$ and enter them into your copy of Results Table 9.4.
2. Plot $(V_\infty - V_t)$ (vertical axis) against time (horizontal axis). Draw a smooth curve through the points.
3. Construct tangents to your curve and measure the slope at each point. Draw one at time 0 and at least four others evenly spaced.
4. Use your graph to complete a copy of Results Table 9.5.

Results Table 9.5

Time /min	Slope /cm^3 min^{-1}	Rate /cm^3 min^{-1}	$(V_\infty - V_t)$ /cm^3

5. Plot another graph of rate of reaction against $(V_\infty - V_t)$, which is proportional to the concentration of benzenediazonium chloride.

Questions
1. Use the information from your second graph to write a rate equation for the reaction.
2. Use your second graph to work out a value for the rate constant, k, for the reaction, including its units.
3. Explain why the escape of gas during the first four minutes, before recording the first volume reading, can be neglected.

EXPERIMENT 9.5 The kinetics of the reaction between iodine and propanone in aqueous solution

Aim
The purpose of this experiment is to obtain the rate equation for the reaction between iodine and propanone by determining the order of reaction with respect to each reactant and to the catalyst (hydrogen ions). The equation is:

$$I_2(aq) + CH_3COCH_3(aq) \rightarrow CH_3COCH_2I(aq) + H^+(aq) + I^-(aq)$$

Introduction
A catalyst does not necessarily appear in the stoichiometric equation (here it appears as a product) but it can appear in the rate equation. The other species which are likely to appear are the reactants and so you may assume that the rate equation is:

$$\text{rate} = k[CH_3COCH_3]^p[I_2]^q[H^+]^r$$

You will be determining the order of reaction with respect to each reactant by varying the concentration of each species in turn, keeping the others constant and following the reaction colorimetrically. As the intensity of the iodine colour decreases more light is transmitted through the solution (i.e. the absorbance decreases).

There are three parts to the experiment:
1. choosing the right filter for the colorimeter;
2. calibrating the colorimeter so that meter readings can be converted to concentrations of iodine;
3. obtaining values for the concentration of iodine at intervals of time for a series of experiments with the following sets of conditions:
   a initial $[CH_3COCH_3]$ varying; $[I_2]$, $[H^+]$ constant,
   b initial $[I_2]$ varying; $[CH_3COCH_3]$, $[H^+]$ constant,
   c initial $[H^+]$ varying; $[CH_3COCH_3]$, $[I_2]$ constant.

Each set of experiments gives you the order of reaction with respect to one component. If there are three groups of students in your class working on this experiment, then we suggest that each group assumes responsibility for one set of conditions. Sharing your results will speed up matters considerably.

Requirements
■ safety spectacles
■ colorimeter with a set of filters
■ set of optically matched test-tubes to fit colorimeter (with stoppers)
■ wash-bottle of distilled water
■ 4 burettes with stands, filling funnels and beakers
■ iodine solution, 0.020 M I_2 (in KI(aq))
■ propanone solution, 2.0 M CH_3COCH_3
■ hydrochloric acid, 2.0 M HCl
■ stopclock or stopwatch
■ thermometer, 0–100 °C

Procedure
Figure 9.8
Colour wheel of complementary colours.

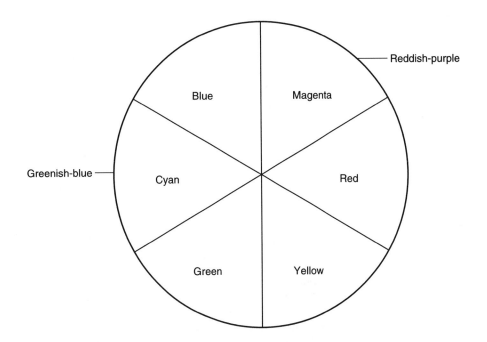

1. **Choose a filter**. First, switch on the colorimeter to allow it to warm up. (Leave it switched on until you have finished, unless your teacher advises otherwise.) Ideally, the filter should let through **only** light of the particular wavelength absorbed by the coloured solution. So, for a red solution which absorbs cyan light, you would use a cyan filter – cyan is the complementary colour to red (see Fig. 9.8). Since iodine solution is reddish, use a filter in the blue–green range. To select the best, proceed as follows.

   a Put any one of the likely filters into the slot in the colorimeter and insert a tube of distilled water, covering it to exclude stray light. Turn the adjusting knob so that the meter shows zero absorbance (or, on some colorimeters, 100% transmission). Mark the rim of the tube so that you can replace it without rotation.

   b Replace the tube with a tube containing the most concentrated iodine solution you will use (see Results Table 9.6 below) and take a reading of absorbance (or % transmission). Mark this tube too so that you can replace it in the same position (i.e. without rotation).

Results Table 9.6

Volume of 0.020 M I$_2$ solution/cm^3	Volume of distilled water/cm^3	[I$_2$(aq)] /10^{-3} mol dm^{-3}	Meter reading (% absorbance or transmission)
0.0	10.0	0.0	
1.0	9.0	2.0	
2.0	8.0	4.0	
3.0	7.0	6.0	
4.0	6.0	8.0	
5.0	5.0	10.0	

   c Repeat steps **a** and **b** above for other possible filters in turn.
   d Choose the filter which gives the greatest absorbance (or least transmission).

2. **Prepare a calibration curve**, so that you can convert your meter readings taken during the experiment to concentration of iodine.

   a To do this, prepare a series of iodine solutions as suggested in Results Table 9.6. Measure and record the absorbance of each one. Most colorimeters are liable to 'drift', so you should zero the machine before each reading, by inserting the distilled water 'blank' and resetting the needle to 100% transmission.

   b Plot a graph of meter reading against concentration of iodine and keep this to use in analysing your results.

3. Decide which series of experiments you will do from Table 9.2 below and note their letters. The figures in **bold** will help you choose. If no other students are working on this investigation then you will need to do all the experiments.

Table 9.2

	Experiment						
	a	b	c	d	e	f	g
Volume of 2 M propanone/cm^3	2	4	6	2	2	2	2
Volume of 0.02 M iodine/cm^3	2	2	2	4	1	2	2
Volume of 2 M HCl /cm^3	2	2	2	2	2	4	6
Volume of water /cm^3	4	2	0	2	5	2	0
[Propanone] /mol dm^{-3}	**0.4**	**0.8**	**1.2**	0.4	0.4	0.4	0.4
[I$_2$]/mol dm^{-3}	**0.004**	0.004	0.004	**0.008**	**0.002**	0.004	0.004
[H$^+$]/mol dm^{-3}	**0.4**	0.4	0.4	0.4	0.4	**0.8**	**1.2**

4. For your first mixture, measure out iodine solution, acid and water from burettes into a test-tube. Wipe the tube clean and handle only at the top.

5. Measure the propanone solution into another test-tube, again using a burette. Keep the outside of all tubes clean and dry.

6. Adjust the colorimeter to zero using the tube of distilled water.

7. Add the propanone solution to the first mixture and start the clock. Quickly stopper the test-tube and invert it six or seven times to mix the contents thoroughly.

8. Put the tube in the colorimeter in time to take a reading at 30 seconds after the clock was started.

9. Take further readings at 30-second intervals for six minutes, or until the colour disappears, if this occurs sooner. Record your results in a copy of Results Table 9.7.

10. Record the temperature of the room and the temperature of the mixture after the final reading. If they differ by more than 2 or 3 °C you may be advised to repeat the experiment, modifying the procedure as in step 12.

11. Repeat steps 4 to 10 for the other two mixtures in your set of experiments.

12. If time permits, repeat your measurements. Some colorimeters may give better results if you remove the tube after each reading, and reset the meter to zero just before re-inserting the reaction tube in time for the next reading.

Results Table 9.7

t = time/min		% = meter reading		$I = [I_2(aq)]/10^{-3}$ mol dm^{-3}											
	t	0	$\frac{1}{2}$	1	$1\frac{1}{2}$	2	$2\frac{1}{2}$	3	$3\frac{1}{2}$	4	$4\frac{1}{2}$	5	$5\frac{1}{2}$	6	
a	%														
	I														
b	%														
	I														
c	%														
	I														
d	%														
	I														
e	%														
	I														
f	%														
	I														
g	%														
	I														

Analysis of results

1. Use your calibration curve to convert the meter readings to iodine concentrations and enter these values in Results Table 9.7. Calculate a value of initial concentration from the data in Table 9.2.
2. Plot graphs of concentration of iodine (y-axis) against time (x-axis) for each mixture in the set of experiments you have done. Plot all three on the same sheet of graph paper.
3. From these graphs obtain values for the initial rate of reaction. Note that, under the conditions used in this experiment, the graphs will probably be straight lines. In this case the initial rate is simply the slope of the line. If the graphs are curves, simply draw a tangent to the curve at time zero and measure its slope.
4. Determine the order of reaction with respect to the component you have been varying, by comparing the initial rates at different concentrations.

Questions

1. Study the graphs plotted by other groups of students for varying the concentrations of the other two components. Work out the order of reaction with respect to each of these components by comparing the initial rates at different concentrations. Use all the information you have collected to write the rate equation for the reaction.
2. What is the overall order of the reaction?
3. Compare the rate equation with the stoichiometric equation for the reaction. What is the main difference between the two? How do you explain this difference?
4. Calculate the rate constant for the overall reaction using each of the three initial rates from your set of experiments and average the results. Compare this with values obtained from the other sets of experiments.
5. What are the main sources of error in this experiment?

EXPERIMENT 9.6 Determining the activation energy of a reaction

Aim The purpose of this experiment is to determine the activation energy, E_a, for the reduction of peroxodisulphate(VI) ions, $S_2O_8^{2-}$(aq), by iodide ions, I^-(aq), using a 'clock' reaction.

Introduction The equation for the reduction of peroxodisulphate(VI) ions by iodide ions is:

$$S_2O_8^{2-}(aq) + 2I^-(aq) \rightarrow 2SO_4^{2-}(aq) + I_2(aq)$$

A small, known amount of thiosulphate ions is added to the reaction mixture, which also contains some starch indicator. The thiosulphate reacts with the iodine formed in the above reaction as in the following equation:

$$2S_2O_3^{2-}(aq) + I_2(aq) \rightarrow S_4O_6^{2-}(aq) + 2I^-(aq)$$

At the instant that all the thiosulphate has reacted, free iodine is produced in the solution and its presence is shown by the appearance of the blue–black colour of the iodine–starch complex, i.e. the thiosulphate ions act as a 'monitor' indicating the point at which a certain amount of iodine has been formed. For this reason the reaction is often referred to as an iodine 'clock' reaction. In general, for a 'clock' reaction:

$$\text{rate of reaction} \propto \frac{1}{t}$$

where t is the time taken to reach a specified stage.

You carry out the experiment at five different temperatures between about 20 °C and 50 °C. You then find the activation energy for the reaction by plotting a graph of $\ln(1/t)$ against $1/T$. (T is the absolute temperature.)

Requirements
■ safety spectacles
■ beaker, 400 cm^3
■ 2 thermometers, 0–100 °C
■ Bunsen burner, tripod, gauze and mat
■ 4 burettes and stands, with beakers and funnels for filling
■ 2 boiling-tubes
■ clamp and stand
■ potassium peroxodisulphate(VI) solution, 0.020 M K$_2$S$_2$O$_8$
■ potassium iodide solution, 0.50 M KI
■ sodium thiosulphate solution, 0.010 M Na$_2$S$_2$O$_3$
■ starch solution, 0.2%
■ stopclock or stopwatch

Procedure
1. Half-fill the beaker with water and heat it to between 49 °C and 51 °C. This will be used as a water-bath.
2. Using a burette, measure out 10 cm^3 of potassium peroxodisulphate(VI) solution into the first boiling-tube. Clamp this in the water-bath and place a thermometer in the solution in the boiling-tube.
3. Using burettes, measure out 5 cm^3 each of the potassium iodide and sodium thiosulphate solutions and 2.5 cm^3 of starch solution into the second boiling-tube. Place another thermometer in this solution and stand it in the water-bath.
4. When the temperatures of the two solutions are equal and constant (to within ±1 °C), pour the contents of the second boiling-tube into the first, shake to mix, and start the clock.

5. When the blue colour of the starch–iodine complex appears, stop the clock and write down the time in a copy of Results Table 9.8.

6. Repeat the experiment at temperatures close to 45 °C, 40 °C, 35 °C, 30 °C. (The temperatures you use may differ from those by a few degrees but must, of course, be recorded carefully.)

Results Table 9.8

Temperature /°C					
Temperature, *T*/K					
Time *t*/s					
$\ln\dfrac{1}{t}$					
$\dfrac{1}{T}$/K^{-1} (or K/*T*)					

Calculations

1. Plot a graph of $\ln(1/t)$ (*y*-axis) against $1/T$ (*x*-axis).
2. Use your graph to calculate a value for the activation energy.

EXPERIMENT 9.7 Determining the activation energy of a catalysed reaction

Aim   The purpose of this experiment is to determine the activation energy for the oxidation of iodide ions by peroxodisulphate(VI) ions in the presence of iron(III) ions. You then compare the value obtained with that for the uncatalysed reaction, determined in Experiment 9.6.

Introduction   Because this is a planning experiment, we give fewer details and instructions than you have been used to. It is, of course, very similar to Experiment 9.6 but you should consider carefully which concentrations of solutions to use since the reaction is catalysed. You should also consider the effect of temperature on reaction rate.

Requirements   Make a list of requirements including the masses and amounts needed: discuss the list with your teacher or technician at least a day before you want to do the experiment.

Procedure   Work out the procedure for yourself and keep an accurate record.

Results
1. Tabulate your results in an appropriate form.
2. Calculate a value for the activation energy of this reaction.

Question   Compare your result with the activation energy you calculated in Experiment 9.6. Comment on the two values, and discuss them with your teacher.

EXPERIMENT 9.8   A bromine 'clock' reaction

Aim   The purpose of this experiment is to determine the rate equation for the reaction between bromide and bromate(V) ions in aqueous solution.

Introduction   Bromide and bromate(V) ions in acid solution react according to the equation:

$$5Br^-(aq) + BrO_3^-(aq) + 6H^+(aq) \rightarrow 3Br_2(aq) + 3H_2O(l) \qquad (1)$$

In order to follow the reaction, two other substances are added to the reaction mixture.
  a A precisely known, small amount of phenol. This reacts immediately with the bromine produced, removing it from solution:

$$3Br_2(aq) + C_6H_5OH(aq) \rightarrow C_6H_2Br_3OH(aq) + 3H^+(aq) + 3Br^-(aq) \qquad (2)$$

  b Methyl orange solution, which is bleached colourless by free bromine:

$$Br_2(aq) + \text{methyl orange} \rightarrow \text{bleached methyl orange} \qquad (3)$$
$$\text{(acid form: pink)} \qquad \text{(colourless)}$$

As soon as all the phenol has reacted with bromine produced in reaction *(1)*, free bromine will appear in solution and bleach the methyl orange. If the time taken for the methyl orange solution to be bleached is *t*, then the rate of reaction *(1)* is proportional to $1/t$.

In the experiment you study the effect on the rate of reaction *(1)* of varying the concentration of bromide ions, bromate(V) ions, and hydrogen ions in turn, with the concentrations of the others held constant. To save time, you could cooperate with other students and pool your results.

Requirements   ■ safety spectacles
■ phenol solution, 0.0001 M C$_6$H$_5$OH
■ wash-bottle of distilled water
■ 3 burettes and stands
■ measuring cylinder, 25 cm^3
■ potassium bromide solution, 0.010 M KBr
■ potassium bromate(V) solution, 0.0050 M KBrO$_3$
■ acidified methyl orange solution, labelled C, 0.001%
■ white tile
■ thermometer, 0–100 °C
■ 2 beakers, 100 cm^3
■ stopclock or stopwatch
■ sulphuric acid, 0.01 M H$_2$SO$_4$
■ potassium bromate(V) solution, 0.20 M KBrO$_3$
■ methyl orange solution, labelled D, 0.001% in 0.40 M KBr

Procedure – Part A   **Varying the concentration of bromide ions**
1. Prepare the first pair of mixtures in two beakers, as specified in Table 9.3. Use burettes to measure the potassium bromide and phenol solutions and the water; use a measuring cylinder for the others.

Table 9.3

Beaker X		Beaker Y		
Volume of 0.01 M KBr /cm^3	Volume of H$_2$O /cm^3	Volume of 0.005 M KBrO$_3$/cm^3	Volume of solution C /cm^3	Volume of 0.000 10 M phenol/cm^3
10.0	0	10.0	15.0	5.0
8.0	2.0	10.0	15.0	5.0
6.0	4.0	10.0	15.0	5.0
5.0	5.0	10.0	15.0	5.0
4.0	6.0	10.0	15.0	5.0
3.0	7.0	10.0	15.0	5.0

2. Have ready a copy of Results Table 9.9.

Results Table 9.9

Volume of Br$^-$(aq) cm^3	10.0	8.0	6.0	5.0	4.0	3.0
Time t/s						
$\frac{1}{t}$/10^{-2} s^{-1}						
Temperature/°C						

Average temperature of solutions =   °C

3. Pour the contents of beaker X into beaker Y and start the stopclock. Mix the solutions by pouring from one beaker to the other, twice, and place the beaker containing the mixture on the white tile.
4. When the pink colour disappears, stop the clock and record the time in a copy of Results Table 9.9. (As you are looking for a disappearance of colour, this may need a little practice. If in doubt, repeat the reaction once or twice until you get consistent times.) Record the temperature of the solution.
5. Work through the rest of the mixtures in Table 9.3 in the same way, recording each result as you go.

Procedure – Part B

Varying the concentration of bromate(V) ions

6. Follow a similar procedure to that for part A, but keep the volume of bromide solution constant at 10.0 cm^3 and vary the volume of bromate(V) solution as shown in Table 9.4.

Table 9.4

Beaker X		Beaker Y		
Volume of 0.005 M $KBrO_3$/cm^3	Volume of H_2O /cm^3	Volume of 0.01 M KBr /cm^3	Volume of solution C /cm^3	Volume of 0.000 10 M phenol/cm^3
10.0	0	10.0	15.0	5.0
8.0	2.0	10.0	15.0	5.0
6.0	4.0	10.0	15.0	5.0
5.0	5.0	10.0	15.0	5.0
4.0	6.0	10.0	15.0	5.0
3.0	7.0	10.0	15.0	5.0

7. Record your results in a copy of Results Table 9.10.

Results Table 9.10

Volume of BrO_3^-(aq) cm^3	10.0	8.0	6.0	5.0	4.0	3.0
Time t/s						
$\frac{1}{t}$/10^{-2} s^{-1}						
Temperature/°C						

Average temperature of solutions =   °C

Procedure – Part C

Varying the concentration of hydrogen ions

8. For this part of the experiment you need different solutions, as stated in Table 9.5. Follow a similar procedure to that for part A.

Table 9.5

Beaker X		Beaker Y		
Volume of 0.01 M H_2SO_4/cm^3	Volume of H_2O /cm^3	Volume of 0.20 M $KBrO_3$/cm^3	Volume of solution D /cm^3	Volume of 0.000 10 M phenol/cm^3
10.0	0	10.0	15.0	5.0
8.0	2.0	10.0	15.0	5.0
6.0	4.0	10.0	15.0	5.0
5.0	5.0	10.0	15.0	5.0
4.0	6.0	10.0	15.0	5.0
3.0	7.0	10.0	15.0	5.0

9. Record your results in a copy of Results Table 9.11.

Results Table 9.11

Volume of acid/cm³	10.0	8.0	6.0	5.0	4.0	3.0
Time t/s						
$\frac{1}{t}$/10^{-2} s^{-1}						
Temperature/°C						

Average temperature of solutions =   °C

Treatment of results

1. For each part of the experiment, plot a graph of $1/t$ against volume of the reactant under consideration. $1/t$ is proportional to the rate of reaction, and the volume of reactant is proportional to the concentration, since the total volume is constant.
2. Deduce from each graph whether or not the reaction is first order with respect to the reactant under consideration.
3. If you think the reaction is **not** first order, plot another graph, as explained below.
   Suppose that, for a reactant A:

$$\text{rate} = k_1[\text{A}]^n$$

Under the conditions of this experiment, it follows that:

$$\frac{1}{t} = k_2 V^n \quad (V \text{ is the initial volume of reactant})$$

$$\therefore \log \frac{1}{t} = n \log V + \log k_2$$

Plotting $\log (1/t)$ against $\log V$ should therefore give a straight line with slope n.

Questions

1. Write the rate equation for the reaction.
2. Qualitatively compare the rates of the three reactions stated in the introduction.
3. Why does the phenol solution need to be very dilute?

ILPAC

10

BIG MOLECULES

EXPERIMENT 10.1 Chemical properties of carboxylic acids

Aim The purpose of this experiment is to see if carboxylic acids show the typical reactions both of alcohols and of carbonyl compounds.

Introduction You will be carrying out some test-tube reactions on ethanoic acid. Ethanoic acid melts at 17 °C and therefore freezes in cold weather. Because solid ethanoic acid looks like ice, it is often described as 'glacial'. The reactions to be investigated are:
A. pH of aqueous solution.
B. Reaction with sodium hydrogencarbonate solution.
C. Reaction with sodium.
D. Reaction with phosphorus pentachloride.
E. Reaction with 2,4-dinitrophenylhydrazine.
F. Triiodomethane (iodoform) reaction.
G. Action of iron(III) chloride.

Requirements
- safety spectacles and gloves
- 5 test-tubes in rack
- wash-bottle of distilled water
- universal indicator solution
- ethanoic acid, glacial, CH_3CO_2H
- sodium hydrogencarbonate solution, saturated, $NaHCO_3$
- lime-water, $Ca(OH)_2(aq)$
- forceps
- sodium, Na (1 mm cube under oil)
- filter papers
- wood splint
- phosphorus pentachloride, PCl_5
- spatula
- ammonia solution, 2 M NH_3
- 2,4-dinitrophenylhydrazine solution
- iodine solution, 10% I_2 in KI(aq)
- sodium hydroxide solution, 2 M NaOH
- sodium ethanoate (acetate), CH_3CO_2Na
- iron(III) chloride solution, 0.1 M $FeCl_3$
- Bunsen burner and bench mat

HAZARD WARNING

   Glacial ethanoic acid is flammable and corrosive.

  Sodium hydroxide solution is corrosive.

  Sodium and phosphorus pentachloride are extremely reactive, especially with water.

  2,4-Dinitrophenylhydrazine (Brady's reagent) is **toxic**.
Therefore you **must**:
- **wear safety spectacles and gloves;**
- **keep stoppers on bottles as much as possible;**
- **keep bottles of flammable liquids away from flames;**
- **keep sodium and phosphorus pentachloride away from water and moist air.**

Procedure – Part A

pH of aqueous solution

1. Into a test-tube, pour about 2 cm^3 of distilled water and add one drop of universal indicator solution. Shake gently.
2. Add a few drops of glacial ethanoic acid, shake gently and note your observations in a copy of Results Table 10.1.

Results Table 10.1
Reactions of ethanoic acid

Reaction		Observations
A	pH of aqueous solution	
B	Reaction with sodium hydrogen-carbonate solution	
C	Reaction with sodium	
D	Reaction with phosphorus pentachloride	
E	Reaction with 2,4-dinitro-phenylhydrazine	
F	Triiodomethane reaction	
G	Action of iron(III) chloride	

Procedure – Part B

Reaction with sodium hydrogencarbonate solution

3. Into a test-tube, add about 1 cm^3 of sodium hydrogencarbonate solution followed by a few drops of glacial ethanoic acid. Shake gently and test any gas produced.

Procedure – Part C

Reaction with sodium
(Work at a fume cupboard, with your teacher present.)

4. Pour about 2 cm^3 of glacial ethanoic acid into a **dry** test-tube in a rack standing in a fume cupboard.
5. Using forceps, pick up a 1 mm cube of sodium and blot it free of oil on some filter paper.
6. Drop the clean piece of sodium into the glacial ethanoic acid. Test any gas evolved and note your observations. Do not wash away the mixture until you are sure that the sodium has reacted completely. If some sodium remains unreacted, add a little more glacial ethanoic acid; on no account add water.

Procedure – Part D

Reaction with phosphorus pentachloride

7. Pour about 1 cm^3 of glacial ethanoic acid into a dry test-tube in a rack standing in a fume cupboard.
8. A little at a time, carefully add a spatula measure of phosphorus pentachloride. Bring the wet stopper of an ammonia bottle close to the mouth of the tube and note your observations.

Procedure – Part E

Reaction with 2,4-dinitrophenylhydrazine

9. Into a test-tube, pour about 2 cm^3 of 2,4-dinitrophenylhydrazine solution and about five drops of glacial ethanoic acid. Shake gently and note your observations.

Procedure – Part F

Triiodomethane (iodoform) reaction

10. Into a test-tube, place ten drops of iodine solution, and five drops of glacial ethanoic

acid, followed by sodium hydroxide solution added dropwise until the colour of iodine disappears and a straw-coloured solution remains. Shake the tube gently and note your observations.

Procedure
– Part G

Reaction with neutral iron(III) chloride solution
11. Into a test-tube, place about 2 cm^3 of sodium ethanoate solution (this avoids having to neutralise the acid) and a few drops of iron(III) chloride solution. Shake gently and then heat the solution. Note your observations.

Questions
1. Does ethanoic acid more closely resemble hydroxy or carbonyl compounds in its reactions? Explain.
2. Which test indicates that ethanoic acid is a stronger acid than phenol?
3. Explain the fact that ethanoic acid is very soluble in water, whereas benzoic acid, $C_6H_5CO_2H$, a solid, is only slightly soluble in water.

EXPERIMENT 10.2 Chemical properties of ethanoyl chloride

Aim

The purpose of this experiment is to illustrate the chemistry of carboxylic acid derivatives by investigating the reactions of ethanoyl chloride with some nucleophilic reagents.

Introduction

You or your teacher will be carrying out the following reactions of ethanoyl chloride – a typical acyl halide:
A. Reaction with water.
B. Reaction with ethanol.
C. Reaction with ammonia.
D. Reaction with phenylamine.

Since some of the reactions are violent, your teacher may decide to demonstrate this experiment. If you do it yourself, you must take great **care!**

Requirements

■ safety spectacles
■ protective gloves
■ 4 beakers, 100 cm^3
■ wash-bottle of distilled water
■ 4 teat pipettes
■ ethanoyl chloride, CH_3COCl
■ ammonia solution, dilute, 2 M NH_3
■ glass rod
■ universal indicator paper
■ iron(III) chloride solution, 0.1 M $FeCl_3$
■ test-tube
■ sodium carbonate solution, 1 M Na_2CO_3
■ ethanol, C_2H_5OH
■ ammonia solution, concentrated, '0.880' NH_3
■ phenylamine, $C_6H_5NH_2$

HAZARD WARNING

 Ethanoyl chloride gives off a vapour which burns the skin, eyes and respiratory tract. Some of its reactions are violent.

 Phenylamine is very poisonous if inhaled, swallowed or absorbed through the skin.

 Concentrated aqueous ammonia burns the skin and the vapour irritates the eyes.

 Ethanol is flammable. Therefore you **must:**
■ **wear safety spectacles and gloves;**
■ **keep stoppers on the bottles as much as possible;**
■ **perform the experiment in a fume cupboard protected by a safety glass.**

Procedure   The reactions with ammonia and phenylamine are particularly violent. **You must follow the instructions carefully.** Look again at the hazard warning and only perform the tests in a fume cupboard protected by a safety glass.

– Part A   **Reaction with water**
  1. Pour about 5 cm^3 of distilled water into a small beaker placed in the fume cupboard with the front pulled down as far as is practicable.
  2. Wearing safety spectacles, add a few drops of ethanoyl chloride to the water. Bring the moist stopper of a bottle of ammonia (2M NH$_3$, **not** the concentrated 0.880 NH$_3$) solution near to the top of the beaker and note your observations.
  3. Neutralise the solution in the beaker by adding dilute aqueous ammonia (2M NH$_3$, **not** the concentrated 0.880 NH$_3$) dropwise until a drop of the solution from a glass rod gives a neutral colour to universal indicator.
  4. In a test-tube, neutralise about 1 cm^3 of iron(III) chloride solution by adding sodium carbonate solution dropwise until a faint precipitate just remains on shaking.
  5. Add a few drops of the neutral iron(III) chloride to the neutral solution prepared in step 3 and note your observations in a copy of Results Table 10.2.

**Procedure
– Part B**   **Reaction with ethanol**
  6. Repeat steps 1 and 2 of part A using ethanol instead of water in the beaker.
  7. Add sodium carbonate solution until there is no further effervescence and note the smell of the product.

**Procedure
– Part C**   **Reaction with ammonia**
  8. Repeat steps 1 and 2 of part A using concentrated aqueous ammonia instead of water in the beaker. Take special care when you add the ethanoyl chloride a drop at a time. Note your observations.

**Procedure
– Part D**   **Reaction with phenylamine**
  9. Pour five drops of phenylamine in a small beaker placed in the fume cupboard with the front pulled down as far as is practicable.
  10. Wearing safety spectacles, add a few drops of ethanoyl chloride to the phenylamine. Note your observations.

Results Table 10.2

	Reaction	Observations
A	**Reaction with water** Product tested with ammonia Product tested with iron(III) chloride	
B	**Reaction with ethanol** Product tested with ammonia Smell of product	
C	**Reaction with ammonia**	
D	**Reaction with phenylamine**	

Questions

1. Using the general equation for the nucleophilic substitution reactions of carboxylic acid derivatives shown below, together with your observations from the experiment, write equations for the reactions of ethanoyl chloride and the following nucleophilic reagents. Name the products.

$$\underset{\underset{O}{\|}}{R-C}-Y \; + \; HZ \longrightarrow \underset{\underset{O}{\|}}{R-C}-Z \; + \; HY$$

  a Water, H_2O,
  b Ethanol, C_2H_5OH,
  c Ammonia, NH_3,
  d Phenylamine, $C_6H_5NH_2$.

2. Explain the order of reactivity of the four nucleophiles towards ethanoyl chloride.

EXPERIMENT 10.3 Preparation of aspirin

Aim The purpose of this experiment is to prepare a sample of aspirin (2-ethanoyloxy-benzenecarboxylic acid), purify it by recrystallisation, measure its melting point and estimate the yield.

Introduction You prepare aspirin by heating together 2-hydroxybenzoic acid and ethanoic anhydride in the presence of phosphoric(V) acid (catalyst) on a steam bath:

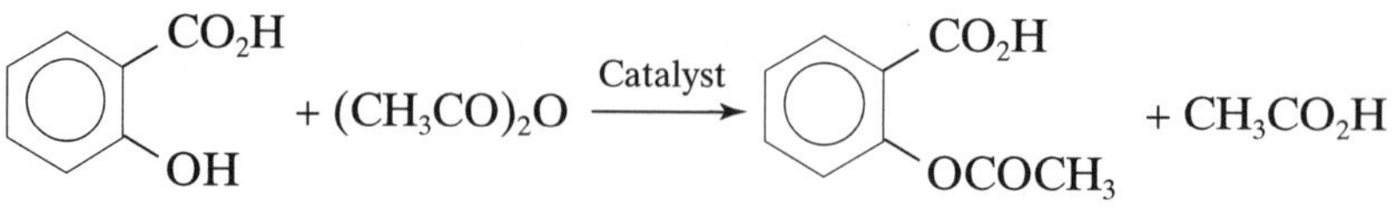

$$+ (CH_3CO)_2O \xrightarrow{\text{Catalyst}}$$

$$+ CH_3CO_2H$$

2-ethanoyloxybenzene-
carboxylic acid
(aspirin)

The product appears as a solid which you purify by filtering and recrystallising from water.

HAZARD WARNING

  Ethanoic anhydride is corrosive and flammable. It is particularly dangerous to eyes.

 2-hydroxybenzoic acid is harmful to eyes, lungs and skin.

 Phosphoric(V) acid (orthophosphoric acid) is corrosive and must be kept in a tray to avoid spillage.

Therefore you **must:**
- **wear safety spectacles and protective gloves.**

Any aspirin that is prepared must **not** be used medicinally.

Requirements – Part A

- safety spectacles and protective gloves
- weighing bottle
- spatula
- ethanoic anhydride $(CH_3CO)_2O$, 4 cm^3
- 2-hydroxybenzoic acid (salicylic acid), 11 g
- phosphoric(V) acid, 85%, a few drops (with teat pipette)
- access to balance, sensitivity 0.01 g
- measuring cylinder, 10 cm^3
- beaker, 250 cm^3
- beaker, 100 cm^3
- reflux apparatus consisting of Liebig condenser and 50 cm^3 pear-shaped flask (Fig. 10.1**a**)
- conical flask, 100 cm^3
- glass rod
- suction filtration apparatus (see Fig. 10.1**b**)
- ice, about half a 250 cm^3 beaker of crushed ice
- wash-bottle of distilled water

Procedure – Part A

Preparation of aspirin

1. Transfer about 2.0 g of 2-hydroxybenzoic acid into a weighing bottle and weigh to the nearest 0.01 g.
2. Into a 50 cm^3 pear-shaped flask pour 4 cm^3 of ethanoic anhydride (**care**) and the bulk of the 2-hydroxybenzoic acid from the weighing bottle.
3. Reweigh the weighing bottle, with any remaining solid, to the nearest 0.01 g.
4. To the mixture in the pear-shaped flask add five drops of 85% phosphoric(V) acid (**care – return to spillage tray with used teat pipette**) and swirl to mix.
5. Fit the flask with a reflux condenser as shown in Fig. 10.1**a** (remember there is no stopper in the top of the condenser) and heat the mixture on the steam bath (beaker of boiling water) for about five minutes. Make sure the solid is carefully swirled at intervals.
6. Without cooling, add 2 cm^3 of water down the condenser. This will hydrolyse any excess ethanoic anhydride and is a vigorous reaction.
7. When the reaction from step 6 has finished pour the mixture into 40 cm^3 of cold water in a 100 cm^3 beaker and allow to cool to room temperature.
8. Complete crystallisation by placing the small beaker and contents into an ice bath. If necessary, scratch the sides of the beaker with a glass rod to induce crystallisation.
9. Collect the product by suction filtration (Fig. 10.1**b**) and wash with a little distilled water.

Figure 10.1

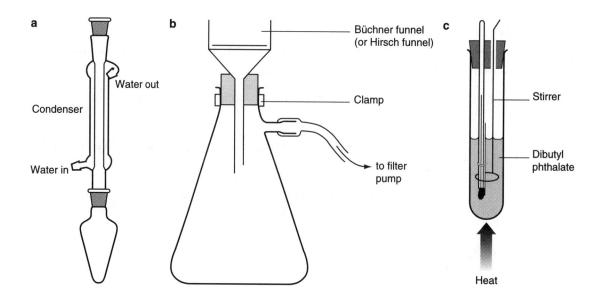

Requirements
– Part B
■ 100 cm³ beaker
■ glass rod
■ water-bath or 250 cm³ beaker
■ Bunsen burner, tripod, gauze and bench mat
■ thermometer, 0–250 °C
■ ice
■ suction filtration apparatus (see Fig. 10.1b)
■ filter papers
■ specimen bottle
■ access to balance, sensitivity 0.01 g

Procedure
– Part B

Recrystallisation

1. Transfer the crystals to a small beaker and cover them with distilled water.
2. Place the small beaker in a beaker of hot water, kept at about 60 °C, and stir with a glass rod.
3. If some solid is still visible, add just enough water to dissolve it completely after stirring.
4. Cool the solution in an ice–water mixture until crystals appear.
5. Filter the crystals through the suction apparatus, using a clean Büchner funnel and filter paper. To avoid losing any solid, break the vacuum and use the filtrate to rinse out the beaker into the funnel.
6. Using suction again, rinse the crystals with about 1 cm³ of cold distilled water and drain thoroughly.
7. Press the crystals between two wads of filter paper to remove excess solvent. Then put the crystals on another dry piece of filter paper placed alongside (not on top of) a Bunsen burner and gauze, turning the crystals over occasionally until they appear dry. Don't let them get too hot or they will melt!
8. Weigh the dry crystals in a pre-weighed specimen bottle and record the mass of your sample of aspirin. Calculate the percentage yield using the expression:

$$\% \text{ yield} = \frac{\text{actual mass of product}}{\text{maximum mass of product}} \times 100$$

Requirements – Part C

- melting-point tubes (at least 2)
- watch-glass
- thermometer, 0–250 °C, long stem
- boiling-tube fitted with cork and stirrer (see Fig. 10.1c) ⎫ or electrical
- dibutylbenzene-1,2-dicarboxylate (dibutyl phthalate) ⎬ melting
- retort stand, boss and clamp ⎪ point
- rubber ring or band ⎭ apparatus

Procedure – Part C

Determination of melting point

1. Take a melting-point tube and push the open end through a pile of aspirin on a watch glass, until a few crystals have entered. If the crystals are large, you may need to crush or grind them first.
2. Tap the closed end of the tube vertically against a hard surface, or rub with the milled edge of a coin, to make the solid fall to the bottom.
3. Repeat the filling and tapping procedure until a total length of 0.2–0.5 cm is compacted at the bottom of the tube. Prepare another tube in this way. If you have an electrical melting point apparatus go to step 7. If not go to step 4.
4. Attach one of the prepared melting-point tubes to the thermometer, as shown in Fig. 10.1c.
5. Half-fill the boiling-tube with dibutyl phthalate and position the thermometer with attached tube and the stirrer through the bung, as shown in Fig. 10.1c.
6. Position the apparatus over a micro-burner (or low Bunsen flame) and gauze and **gently** heat the apparatus, stirring the dibutyl phthalate all the time by moving the stirrer up and down.
7. Keep an eye on the crystals and note the temperature as soon as signs of melting are seen (usually seen as a contraction of the solid followed by a damp appearance). Record the range of temperature over which your sample melts. This first reading gives only a rough melting point but is a guide for the second determination.
8. Remove the burner and the old tube containing aspirin. Allow the temperature to drop about 10 °C before positioning a fresh melting-point tube containing another portion of the aspirin.
9. Repeat the above procedure in order to obtain a more accurate value of the melting point. Raise the temperature very slowly (about 2 °C rise per minute) until the crystals melt (take the formation of a visible meniscus as a sign of melting).
10. Hand in your product suitably labelled, i.e. mass, % yield, melting point, name and date.

Results Table 10.3

Mass of weighing bottle + 2-hydroxybenzoic acid	g
Mass of weighing bottle after emptying	g
Mass of 2-hydroxybenzoic acid	g
Mass of specimen bottle	g
Mass of specimen bottle + aspirin	g
Mass of aspirin	g
Melting point of aspirin	°C

The compounds that you used to prepare aspirin are the same as those used in the actual industrial method of production.

EXPERIMENT 10.4 Identification of two organic compounds

Aim   The purpose of this experiment is to identify the functional groups present in two unknown organic compounds from observations made and inferences drawn from some simple chemical tests.

Introduction   The procedure that follows is taken from two A-level practical examination papers. Since you should preferably work under examination conditions, all the apparatus and chemicals should be provided for you so we have not included a requirements list. However, take note of the hazard warnings.

HAZARD WARNING

 Concentrated hydrochloric acid and solutions of silver nitrate, sodium chlorate(I) (sodium hypochlorite) and sodium hydroxide are all corrosive.

 2,4-Dinitrophenylhydrazine is **toxic** by skin absorption. Therefore you **must**:
■ **wear safety spectacles and gloves throughout.**

 Compound G produces a harmful vapour. Therefore you **must**:
■ **perform experiments with these compounds at a fume cupboard;**
■ **keep tops on bottles as much as possible.**

 Compound G is flammable. Therefore you **must**:
■ **keep this compound away from flames.**

You are provided with two organic compounds, labelled F and G. Each compound contains the elements carbon, hydrogen and oxygen only. You are provided with an aqueous solution of F and a pure sample of G. Carry out the following experiments. Record your observations and inferences in (a larger copy of) Results Table 10.4. Comment on the types of chemical reaction occurring and, where possible, deduce the functional groups present in these compounds. Then answer the questions that follow. Note that the procedure for the triiodomethane reaction in test **d** is different to the one we have followed in previous experiments, but it gives the same result.

Procedure and results

Results Table 10.4

Experiment	Observations	Inferences
a To 2 cm^3 of the solution of F add 2,4-dinitrophenylhydrazine reagent		
b Prepare a sample of Tollens reagent as follows: to 5 cm^3 of aqueous silver nitrate in a test-tube add one to two drops of aqueous sodium hydroxide. Then add dilute aqueous ammonia until only a trace of precipitate remains. Now add five drops of the solution of F and place the tube in hot water. (Pour the contents of the tube down the sink on completion of the test)		
c Add a little of the solution of F to some sodium hydrogencarbonate		
d To 1 cm^3 of the solution of F add 3 cm^3 of aqueous potassium iodide and then 10 cm^3 of sodium chlorate(I) (sodium hypochlorite) solution		
e Place **one** drop of G on an inverted crucible lid and ignite G from above		
f To 1–2 cm^3 of G add 2,4-dinitrophenylhydrazine reagent		
g Prepare a sample of Tollens reagent as in **b**. Add five drops of G, shake the mixture and place the tube in hot water. (Pour the contents of the tube down the sink on completion of the test)		

Questions   1. Comment on the structural features of F.
2. Comment on the structural features of G.

EXPERIMENT 10.5 The glycine/copper(II) complex

Aim The purpose of this simple experiment is to prepare a complex from glycine and copper(II) ions.

Requirements
- safety spectacles
- wash-bottle of distilled water
- test-tube
- spatula
- glycine, $CH_2NH_2CO_2H$
- copper(II) carbonate, $CuCO_3$ (powdered)
- stirring rod
- Büchner funnel (small) or Hirsch funnel
- filter paper
- filter tube with side-arm
- filter pump and pressure tubing
- crystallising dish

Procedure
1. To about 10 cm^3 of distilled water in a test-tube, add about 0.5 g (small spatula-measure) of glycine. Note how easily it dissolves.
2. Slowly add powdered copper(II) carbonate, stirring the contents of the tube between additions. Keep adding the powder until it is in excess.
3. Set up a small Büchner funnel or Hirsch funnel in a side-arm filter tube and filter the mixture.
4. Transfer the filtrate to a crystallising dish and allow it to stand. Note the colour of the solution and whether crystals are formed.

Questions
1. Copper(II) carbonate is only slightly soluble but during the experiment some CO_3^{2-} ions do dissolve. Would you expect this to make the solution slightly acidic, neutral or alkaline? Explain.
2. Bearing in mind your answer to question 1, what form of glycine would you expect to predominate in the solution?
3. How many bonds is each glycine molecule capable of making with Cu^{2+}(aq) under these conditions?
4. Bearing in mind your answers to the questions above, and your knowledge of the types of complex formed by copper(II) ions, suggest a structural formula for the copper(II)/glycine complex.
5. What shape and charge would the complex you described in question 4 have?

EXPERIMENT 10.6 Biuret test for proteins

Aim This experiment is intended to give you practical experience of the biuret test for proteins.

Introduction The biuret test is based on a coloured complex formed between copper(II) ions and the peptide links of neighbouring protein chains. You carry out the test on examples of available protein material.

Requirements
- safety spectacles
- 4 test-tubes in a rack
- spatula
- protein sample(s) (e.g. egg albumin, gelatin, fresh milk)
- wash-bottle of distilled water

■ sodium hydroxide solution, 2 M NaOH
■ teat pipette
■ copper(II) sulphate solution, 0.1 M CuSO₄

HAZARD WARNING

Sodium hydroxide is corrosive. Therefore you **must**:
■ **wear safety spectacles.**

Procedure
1. Take a small amount (enough to cover a spatula tip if solid, about 2 cm³ in the bottom of a test-tube, if liquid) of one of the proteins. Dissolve it in water so that the total volume is no more than a quarter of a test-tube. If necessary, warm the tube.
2. Allow the contents of the tube to cool.
3. Add an equal volume of 2 M sodium hydroxide solution followed by five drops of 0.1 M copper(II) sulphate solution.
4. Leave the tube to stand, if necessary, and note the colour that develops.
5. Repeat steps 3 and 4 using water instead of protein solution. Compare the colour of this 'blank' tube with the colour of your protein solution from step 3. If you don't get a definite colour, try again with a more concentrated protein solution in step 1.
6. Repeat steps 1 to 4 using other protein(s).

Questions
1. How do you think the biuret test might be used to estimate the concentration of a protein in a solution?
2. The biuret test is a test for all compounds containing two peptide links at a suitable separation for use as a bidentate ligand. Given the fact that the Cu^{2+} ion forms 4-coordinate, planar complexes, suggest a possible formula for the complex between Cu^{2+} and portions of two protein chains with the general formula:

$$-\underset{\underset{O}{\|}}{C}-\underset{\underset{H}{|}}{N}-\underset{\underset{R}{|}}{C}-\underset{\underset{O}{\|}}{C}-\underset{\underset{H}{|}}{N}-\underset{\underset{R}{|}}{C}-$$

3. If you hydrolysed a protein sample and converted it completely into its constituent amino acids, would you expect to get a positive biuret test? Explain.

EXPERIMENT 10.7 **Paper chromatography**

Aim
The purpose of this experiment is to illustrate the use of paper chromatography for the separation and identification of amino acids.

Introduction
In this experiment you separate a mixture of three amino acids by means of paper chromatography. From the chromatogram you calculate R_f values for the individual amino acids.

Requirements
■ safety spectacles and protective gloves
■ measuring cylinder, 10 cm³
■ beaker, 400 cm³, tall-form
■ watch glass (big enough to cover beaker)
■ ethanol, C₂H₅OH
■ wash-bottle of distilled water
■ ammonia solution, 0.880 NH₃

- square of chromatography paper, 12.5 cm × 12.5 cm
- pencil and ruler
- sheet of file paper
- 4 melting-point tubes
- aspartic acid solution, 0.01 M
- leucine solution, 0.01 M
- lysine solution, 0.01 M
- mixture of the three amino acids above
- 2 retort stands, bosses and clamps
- 2 paper clips
- hair dryer
- ninhydrin aerosol spray
- oven (105 °C)

HAZARD WARNING

Concentrated ammonia solution is corrosive and gives off harmful vapour. Therefore you **must**:
- **wear safety spectacles and gloves;**
- **keep bottles closed as much as possible.**

Ninhydrin sprays give off **toxic** fumes. Therefore you **must**:
- **work at a fume cupboard;**
- **read the instructions on the aerosol can.**

Procedure

1. In a fume cupboard, prepare the solvent mixture by pouring the following into a 400 cm³ tall-form beaker:

   24 cm³ of ethanol
   3 cm³ of distilled water
   3 cm³ of 0.880 ammonia

2. Cover the beaker with a watch glass. Swirl to mix the liquids and leave to stand.
3. Handling it only by the top edge, place a square of chromatography paper on a clean sheet of file paper. With a pencil (**not** a pen) draw lines and labels as shown in Fig. 10.2.

Figure 10.2

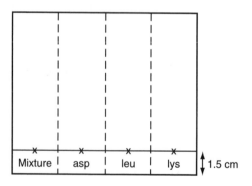

4. Dip a clean melting point tube into the solution of mixed amino acids and then touch it **briefly** on the appropriate labelled cross so that a spot, no more than 5 mm across, appears on the paper.
5. Using a fresh tube each time, repeat step 4 for each of the three solutions of single amino acids.
6. Place a **clean** ruler with its edge along one of the dashed lines and hold it firmly in place with one hand. Without touching it with your fingers, fold the chromatography paper along the line by sliding your hand under the **file paper** and lifting.

7. Repeat the folding procedure for the other two lines so that the opposite edges of the paper almost meet to form a square cross-section.

8. Hold the paper by the edge furthest from the start line, and place it in the beaker so that it does not touch the sides. Replace the cover and leave to stand.
9. Clamp the ruler horizontally at a height of 20–30 cm between two retort stands in a fume-cupboard. This is to support the chromatography paper for drying when the run has finished.
10. While you are waiting, get on with some other work, but look at the paper every ten minutes to see how far the solvent has soaked up the paper.
11. When the solvent has reached nearly to the top of the paper (30–40 minutes) or when you have only 15 minutes laboratory time left, whichever is the sooner, remove the paper from the beaker, open it out and clip it on to the ruler to dry. You can hasten the drying with a hair dryer.
12. When the paper is dry, spray it evenly with ninhydrin solution. Dry it again and then heat it in an oven at 105 °C for five minutes.
13. Remove the paper from the oven and mark with a pencil the positions of the coloured spots.
14. Measure the distances from the origin line to the centres of the spots and record them in a copy of Results Table 10.5.

Results and calculations

Calculate an R_f value for each spot as follows:

$$R_f = \frac{\text{distance travelled by spot}}{\text{distance travelled by solvent}}$$

Results Table 10.5

Amino acid	Distances travelled/cm		
	By solvent	By amino acid	R_f value
Aspartic acid – alone – in mixture			
Leucine – alone – in mixture			
Lysine – alone – in mixture			

Questions

1. For each amino acid, compare your two R_f values with each other and with our specimen results (which you can obtain from your teacher). Why do you think there is some variation?
2. Why do R_f values change when a different solvent is used?
3. Why is it so important to avoid touching the chromatography paper with your fingers?

EXPERIMENT 10.8   Identification of three organic compounds

Aim   The purpose of this experiment is to identify three organic compounds X, Y and Z, which contain the elements carbon, hydrogen and oxygen only, using chemical testing and spectra.

Introduction   In part A of the investigation you carry out some simple chemical tests specified in the results table and record your observations and inferences (about the presence or absence of certain functional groups) in (larger copies of) the tables provided. In part B your teacher will give you percentage elemental analysis data together with mass and IR spectra to not only confirm the functional groups suspected in part A but also to determine the identity of each compound.

Since you should preferably work under examination conditions, all the apparatus and chemicals should be provided for you so we have not included a requirements list. However, you must take a note of the following hazard warning.

HAZARD WARNING

Compounds Y and Z are highly flammable and the vapours are harmful. Therefore you **must**:
- **keep the compounds away from flames;**
- **perform the experiment in a fume cupboard;**
- **wear safety spectacles and gloves.**

2,4-dinitrophenylhydrazine is **toxic** and 2 M sulphuric acid is corrosive. Therefore you **must**:
- **wear safety spectacles and gloves;**
- **do boiling point determinations in the fume cupboard.**

Procedure and results – Part A

Chemical Testing

Results Table 10.6

Test		Observations	Inferences
1.	**a** Burn a small amount of X in a combustion spoon		
	b Shake a small amount of X in a test-tube with 5 cm^3 of water. First try cold water then hot. (Use a hot water-bath)		
	c To a small amount of X in a test-tube add 5 cm^3 of 0.5 M sodium carbonate solution		
	d Determine the melting point of X		
2.	**a** Burn a small volume of Y in a combustion spoon		
	b Shake a small amount (1–2 cm^3) of Y with 5 cm^3 of water in a test-tube. First try cold water then hot. (Use a hot water-bath)		
	c To a few drops of Y in a test-tube, add about 5 cm^3 of a mixture of aqueous potassium dichromate(VI) and 2 M H$_2$SO$_4$ and warm in a hot water-bath		
	d Determine the boiling point of Y in a fume cupboard		
3.	**a** Burn a small volume of Z on a combustion spoon		
	b Shake a small amount (1–2 cm^3) of Z with 5 cm^3 of water in a test-tube. First try cold then hot water		
	c Add a few drops of Z to 5 cm^3 of a solution of 2,4-dinitrophenyl-hydrazine (Brady's reagent) in a test-tube		
	d Determine the boiling point of Z in a fume cupboard		

Complete the following table as far as possible.

Results Table 10.7

Compound	Functional group	Reasoning
X Y Z		

Procedure – Part B

Analysis of mass and IR spectra

Using the results of quantitative analysis, IR and mass spectra from your teacher together with the results from part A, identify, with reasoning, the structures for compounds X, Y and Z. You will also need access to data on melting points and boiling points of organic compounds.

EXPERIMENT 10.9 Preparing phenyl benzoate

Aim

The purpose of this experiment is to prepare a sample of phenyl benzoate, purify it by recrystallisation, and measure its melting point.

Introduction

You prepare phenyl benzoate by shaking phenol with benzoyl chloride in alkaline solution:

$$C_6H_5COCl + C_6H_5OH \rightarrow C_6H_5CO_2C_6H_5 + HCl$$

The product appears as a solid and you purify it by filtering, dissolving in hot ethanol, and cooling to recrystallise the ester. This method is known as the Schotten–Baumann reaction.

HAZARD WARNING

  Benzoyl chloride is lachrymatory (produces tears), is irritating to the skin and can cause burns.

 Phenol vapour is harmful to the eyes, lungs, and skin. Solid and solution are corrosive and poisonous by skin absorption.

 Sodium hydroxide solution is very corrosive. Even when dilute it can damage your eyes.

 Ethanol is flammable.
Therefore you **must**:
- **work at a fume cupboard;**
- **wear safety spectacles and protective gloves;**
- **keep the stoppers on bottles;**
- **keep ethanol away from naked flames.**

Requirements – Part A

- safety spectacles and protective gloves
- weighing bottle
- spatula
- phenol, C_6H_5OH
- access to balance, sensitivity ± 0.01 g
- conical flask, 250 cm^3, with tight-fitting rubber bung
- measuring cylinder, 100 cm^3
- sodium hydroxide solution, 2 M NaOH
- measuring cylinder, 10 cm^3
- benzoyl chloride, C_6H_5COCl
- suction filtration apparatus (see Fig. 10.1b (page 166))
- wash-bottle of distilled water

Procedure – Part A

Preparation of phenyl benzoate

1. Transfer about 5.0 g of phenol into a weighing bottle and weigh it to the nearest 0.01 g.
2. Into a conical flask pour 90 cm^3 of 2 M sodium hydroxide and the bulk of the phenol from the weighing bottle.
3. Reweigh the weighing bottle, with any remaining phenol, to the nearest 0.01 g.
4. In a fume cupboard pour 9 cm^3 of benzoyl chloride into the conical flask.
5. Insert the bung securely and shake the bottle for 15 minutes, carefully releasing the pressure every few minutes as the flask gets warm.
6. Cool the flask under cold, running tap water.

7. Filter the crude product using a suction filtration apparatus (Fig. 10.1**b**, page 166). Use a spatula to break up the lumps of ester on the filter paper, being careful not to puncture the filter paper.
8. Pour more water over the crude ester to destroy any remaining benzoyl chloride.

Requirements
– Part B

- boiling-tube
- ethanol, C_2H_5OH
- glass rod
- water-bath or 250 cm^3 beaker
- Bunsen burner, tripod, gauze and bench mat
- thermometer, 0–100 °C
- ice
- suction filtration apparatus (see Fig. 10.1**b** (page 166))
- filter papers
- specimen bottles
- access to balance, sensitivity ±0.01 g

Procedure
– Part B

Recrystallisation
1. Transfer the crystals to a boiling-tube and just cover them with ethanol.
2. Place the boiling-tube in a water-bath or beaker of hot water, kept at about 60 °C, and stir with a glass rod.
3. If some solid ester is still visible, add **just** enough ethanol to dissolve it completely after stirring.
4. In order to allow the separation of the ester as a solid rather than an oily liquid (phenyl benzoate has a low melting point) add more ethanol to double the volume of solution.
5. Cool the solution in an ice–water mixture until crystals appear.
6. Filter the crystals through the suction apparatus, using a clean Büchner funnel and filter paper. To avoid losing any solid, break the vacuum and use the filtrate to rinse the boiling-tube into the funnel.
7. Using suction again, rinse the crystals with about 1 cm^3 of **cold** ethanol and drain thoroughly.
8. Press the crystals between two wads of filter paper to remove excess solvent. Then put the crystals on another dry piece of filter paper placed alongside a Bunsen burner and gauze, turning the crystals over occasionally until they appear dry. Don't let them get too hot or they will melt!
9. Weigh the dry crystals in a pre-weighed specimen bottle and record the mass of your sample of phenyl benzoate. Calculate the percentage yield using the expression:

$$\% \text{ yield} = \frac{\text{actual mass of product}}{\text{maximum mass of product}} \times 100$$

Requirements
– Part C

- melting-point tubes (at least 2)
- watch-glass
- thermometer, 0–100 °C, long stem
- boiling-tube fitted with cork and stirrer
- rubber ring or band   } or electrical melting
- dibutyl benzene-1,2-dicarboxylate (dibutyl phthalate) } point apparatus
- retort stand, boss and clamp

Procedure
– Part C

Determination of melting point
Follow the procedure that is described in Experiment 10.3 and record the melting point of your sample of phenyl benzoate.
    Hand in your product suitably labelled, i.e. mass, melting point, name and date.

Results Table 10.8

Mass of weighing bottle and phenol	g
Mass of weighing bottle after emptying	g
Mass of phenol	g
Mass of specimen bottle	g
Mass of specimen bottle and phenyl benzoate	g
Mass of phenyl benzoate	g
Melting point of phenyl benzoate	°C

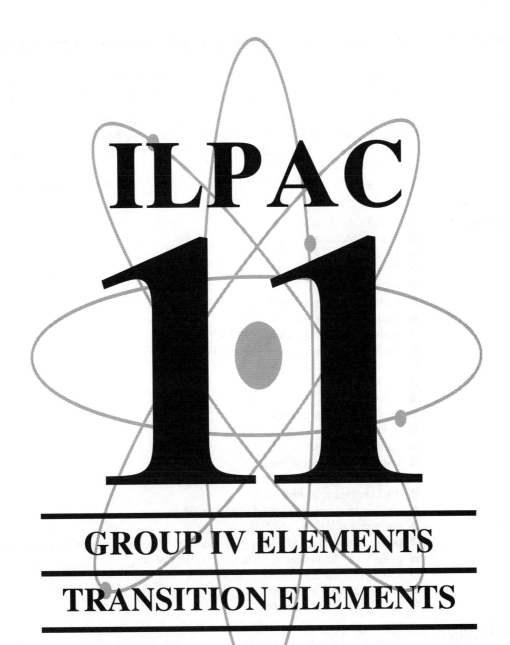

ILPAC

11

GROUP IV ELEMENTS

TRANSITION ELEMENTS

EXPERIMENT 11.1 The reactions of tin and lead and their aqueous ions

Aim

The purpose of this experiment is twofold: to show the reactions of tin and lead with acids, and to familiarise you with some of the common reactions of Pb^{2+}(aq) and Sn^{2+}(aq).

Introduction

In this experiment you find out if the metallic character of tin and lead is evident from their reactions with acids. You treat the elements with two acids: an oxidising agent (nitric acid), and a non-oxidising acid (hydrochloric acid). In each case you attempt to identify any gases evolved.

The reactions of the divalent ions are included here to demonstrate the relative stability of the +2 state in tin and lead.

Requirements

- disposable gloves
- safety spectacles
- 15 test-tubes
- 2 test-tube racks
- test-tube holder
- Bunsen burner and mat
- lead (small pieces)
- hydrochloric acid, dilute, 2 M HCl
- hydrochloric acid, concentrated, HCl
- 3 teat pipettes
- beaker, 250 cm^3
- wood splints
- universal indicator paper
- nitric acid, concentrated, HNO$_3$
- tin (small pieces)
- sticky labels for test-tubes
- 0.1 M solution of Sn^{2+} ions (in dilute hydrochloric acid)
- 0.1 M solution of Pb^{2+} ions
- sodium hydroxide solution, 2 M NaOH
- ammonia solution, 2 M NH$_3$
- potassium manganate(VII) solution, 0.01 M KMnO$_4$ (in dilute ethanoic acid)
- potassium chromate(VI) solution, 0.1 M K$_2$CrO$_4$
- sodium sulphide solution, 0.02 M Na$_2$S
- potassium iodide solution, 0.1 M KI
- access to fume cupboard

HAZARD WARNING

  Lead compounds are harmful if ingested or absorbed through the skin.

   Sodium sulphide is **toxic** and corrosive and evolves highly poisonous hydrogen sulphide gas on contact with acids.

 Concentrated hydrochloric acid is very corrosive.

 Sodium hydroxide is corrosive, even in 2 M solution.

  Concentrated nitric acid is very corrosive and a powerful oxidant.
Therefore you **must**:
- **wear protective gloves and safety spectacles;**
- **use sodium sulphide in the fume cupboard.**

Procedure
1. Place a small piece of lead in each of three test-tubes.
2. To one test-tube add about 2 cm^3 of dilute hydrochloric acid and heat gently. Can you see or detect a gas? If not, repeat the experiment carefully using about 2 cm^3 of concentrated hydrochloric acid.
3. In the remaining test-tube carefully add about 2 cm^3 of concentrated nitric acid to the lead and heat gently.
4. Place a small piece of tin in each of two test-tubes and repeat steps 2 and 3.
5. Record your results in a larger copy of Results Table 11.1.
6. Add approximately 2 cm^3 of the Sn^{2+} solution to each of seven test-tubes.
7. Add approximately 2 cm^3 of the Pb^{2+} solution to each of seven test-tubes.
8. Add each of the following reagents to separate portions of the Sn^{2+} and Pb^{2+} solutions:
   a Dilute sodium hydroxide solution, initially drop-by-drop, and then to excess.
   b Ammonia solution, initially drop-by-drop, and then to excess.
   c About 2 cm^3 of dilute hydrochloric acid, heat the mixtures and then cool them under running cold water.
   d About 2 cm^3 of acidified potassium manganate(VII) solution.
   e About 1 cm^3 of potassium chromate(VI) solution.
   f Five drops of sodium sulphide solution (do this in the fume cupboard and dispose of the mixture by pouring into the fume cupboard sink).
   g About 2 cm^3 of aqueous potassium iodide.
9. Record your observations in a larger copy of Results Table 11.2.

Results Table 11.1

Acid	Tin	Lead
Dilute hydrochloric acid		
Concentrated hydrochloric acid		
Concentrated nitric acid		

Results Table 11.2

Reagent	Sn^{2+}(aq) (acidified)	Pb^{2+}(aq)
a Sodium hydroxide solution		
b Ammonia solution		
c Dilute hydrochloric acid		
d Acidified potassium manganate(VII) solution		
e Potassium chromate(VI) solution		
f Sodium sulphide solution		
g Potassium iodide solution		

Questions
1. Copy and complete the following equations:
   Pb(s) + HCl(aq) →
   Sn(s) + HCl(aq) →

2. Are the reactions between the elements and hydrochloric acid typical of metals? Explain your answer.

3. Reactions with nitric acid tend to be complex and equations are not generally required. The questions illustrate some general points.

   a Which gas did you detect when nitric acid reacted with tin and lead?

   b Do other metals behave in a similar way with nitric acid? Give one example.

   c Why does nitric acid behave differently from hydrochloric acid?

4. Use your textbook(s) to complete and balance the equations in a larger copy of Table 11.1. In the comments column you should describe the type of chemical reaction occurring and any other important feature(s).

Table 11.1

Equations	Comments
$Sn^{2+}(aq) + OH^-(aq) \rightarrow$ $Sn(OH)_2(s) + OH^-(aq) \rightarrow$	The precipitate dissolves in excess NaOH to form a stannate(II) ion*, $Sn(OH)_6^{4-}$
$Pb^{2+}(aq) + OH^-(aq) \rightarrow$ $Pb(OH)_2(s) + OH^-(aq) \rightarrow$	
$2MnO_4^-(aq) + 16H^+(aq) + 5Sn^{2+}(aq) \rightarrow$	
$Pb^{2+}(aq) + 2Cl^-(aq) \rightarrow$	Simple precipitation reaction. Precipitate soluble in hot water
$Cr_2O_7^{2-}(aq)^{**} + H^+(aq) + Sn^{2+}(aq) \rightarrow$	
$Pb^{2+}(aq) + CrO_4^{2-}(aq) \rightarrow$	
$Pb^{2+}(aq) + S^{2-}(aq) \rightarrow$	
$Sn^{2+}(aq) + S^{2-}(aq) \rightarrow$	
$Pb^{2+}(aq) + I^-(aq) \rightarrow$	

*Various formulae have been proposed for the stannate(II) ion, ranging from SnO_2^{2-} for the anhydrous form to $Sn(OH)_4^{2-}$ and $Sn(OH)_6^{4-}$ for the hydrated forms. $Sn(OH)_6^{4-}$ seems the most probable. Similar variations have been proposed for the plumbate(II) ion, $Pb(OH)_6^{4-}$. **The solution of Sn^{2+} is acidic and chromate(VI), CrO_4^{2-}, changes to dichromate(VI), $Cr_2O_7^{2-}$, when acidified:

$$2CrO_4^{2-}(aq) + 2H^+(aq) \rightleftharpoons Cr_2O_7^{2-}(aq) + H_2O(l)$$

5. In the experiment, potassium manganate(VII) solution was acidified with dilute ethanoic acid and not, as is usual, dilute hydrochloric acid or dilute sulphuric acid. With the aid of your textbook(s), explain why you think this change was made. Give any relevant equations in your answer and state what you would observe if the MnO_4^- solution were acidified with $HCl(aq)$ or $H_2SO_4(aq)$.

6. By reference to your results, suggest which of the divalent ions (Sn^{2+} or Pb^{2+}) is more stable.

EXPERIMENT 11.2   The preparations and reactions of tin(IV) oxide and lead(IV) oxide

Aim

The purpose of this experiment is to prepare tin(IV) oxide and lead(IV) oxide and compare their reactions and relative stabilities.

Introduction

In Parts A and B of this experiment you react tin and lead with concentrated nitric acid. However, although this acid oxidises tin to tin(IV) oxide, it oxidises lead only to the +2 state. In order to reach the +4 state, you add a stronger oxidising agent to the lead(II) compound (e.g. sodium chlorate(I) solution (sodium hypochlorite) in alkaline solution) to form lead(IV) oxide.

Since the preparation of lead(IV) oxide involves more than one stage, we ask you to calculate the percentage yield in order to test the efficiency of the method and your practical techniques.

In Part C of this experiment you compare the effect of heat on tin(IV) oxide and lead(IV) oxide and the effect of various reagents on these two oxides.

Requirements

- disposable gloves
- safety spectacles
- access to fume cupboard
- access to balance
- granulated tin
- evaporating basin
- Bunsen burner, mat, tripod and gauze
- measuring cylinder, 10 cm^3
- measuring cylinder, 100 cm^3
- nitric acid, concentrated, HNO_3
- 3 teat pipettes
- glass rod
- spatula
- suction filtration apparatus (see Fig. 10.1**b** on page 166)
- distilled water
- 2 specimen tubes
- sticky labels
- lead foil
- conical flask, 250 cm^3
- sodium hydroxide solution, 2 M NaOH
- sodium chlorate(I) solution (hypochlorite), 1.5 M NaClO
- nitric acid, 2 M HNO_3
- propanone, CH_3COCH_3
- tin(IV) oxide, SnO_2
- lead(IV) oxide, PbO_2
- 10 test-tubes
- test-tube holder
- wood splints
- hydrochloric acid, dilute, 2 M HCl
- hydrochloric acid, concentrated, HCl
- blue litmus paper
- sodium hydroxide solution, 8 M NaOH
- potassium iodide solution (acidified), 1 M KI

Procedure – Part A

Preparation of tin(IV) oxide

1. Weigh about 1.5 g of granulated tin and place it in an evaporating basin in the fume cupboard.
2. Carefully pour 5 cm^3 of concentrated nitric acid over the tin. Warm the mixture, if necessary, until the reaction is proceeding moderately.
3. As the evolution of gas subsides, stir the contents of the basin carefully with a glass rod.
4. When the reaction appears to be complete, add a few drops of concentrated nitric acid and warm carefully. If brown fumes are evolved, the reaction is not complete, in which case add a few more drops of concentrated nitric acid and warm until the brown fumes cease.
5. When cool, transfer the contents of the basin (mainly solid) to the suction filtration apparatus.
6. Wash the precipitate thoroughly with distilled water until there is no sign of a yellow coloration.
7. Transfer the precipitate (hydrated tin(IV) oxide) to an evaporating basin and heat (gently to start with, in order to avoid 'spitting', and then strongly).
8. When cool, record the appearance of the solid in a copy of Results Table 11.3 and transfer the solid to a labelled specimen bottle.

Procedure – Part B

Preparation of lead(IV) oxide

9. Weigh about 5 g of lead (small pieces of foil), record the mass, and place it in a conical flask.
10. Pour 10 cm^3 of distilled water into the flask followed by 10 cm^3 of concentrated nitric acid.
11. Heat the flask gently **in the fume cupboard** until the reaction proceeds at a moderate rate.
12. Gradually add about 5–10 cm^3 of distilled water to replace any water lost by evaporation.
13. When all the lead has reacted, allow the mixture to cool to room temperature.
14. If crystals (of lead(II) nitrate) appear on cooling, add a little distilled water to dissolve them.
15. Add dilute sodium hydroxide solution using a teat pipette and swirl the contents until a **permanent** faint white precipitate appears.
16. Pour in a further 50 cm^3 of sodium hydroxide solution followed by 30 cm^3 of sodium chlorate(I) solution (sodium hypochlorite) and carefully bring the contents of the flask to the boil.
17. Allow the precipitate to settle and carefully pour off the clear liquid.

18. Add 100 cm^3 of distilled water, shake and again pour off the clear liquid.
19. Add 20 cm^3 of dilute nitric acid followed by 50 cm^3 of distilled water and shake again.
20. Filter the precipitate at the pump and wash thoroughly with distilled water, followed by two 5 cm^3 portions of propanone.
21. Draw air through the solid for about five to ten minutes to allow the propanone to evaporate.
22. Leave the solid in a warm place for a day or two and, when you are satisfied that it is completely dry, weigh it.
23. Record your results in a copy of Results Table 11.3 and calculate the percentage yield based on the lead used.

Results Table 11.3

Mass of Pb used	
Maximum possible mass of PbO$_2$ obtainable	
Mass of PbO$_2$ obtained	
% yield	
Appearance of PbO$_2$	
Appearance of SnO$_2$	

Procedure – Part C

Reactions of tin(IV) oxide and lead(IV) oxide

Carry out the following tests on separate samples of the oxides which you have already prepared, and record your results in a copy of Results Table 11.4. We suggest that you also use tin(IV) oxide prepared by the manufacturers for the tests with the concentrated acids and alkalis since the oxide prepared by the above method is particularly insoluble.

a Heat a spatula-measure of each oxide separately in a test-tube. Identify any gases given off.
b To half a spatula-measure of each oxide (approximately 0.1 g) add about 1 cm^3 of dilute hydrochloric acid in the fume cupboard. Identify any gas given off.
c i) Add approximately 0.1 g of lead(IV) oxide to 1 cm^3 of concentrated hydrochloric acid **in the fume cupboard**, identify the gas evolved and note the colour of the final solution.
   ii) Add half a spatula-tip (or less) of tin(IV) oxide to 1 cm^3 of concentrated hydrochloric acid and very cautiously warm the mixture in the fume cupboard. Does any of the solid dissolve?
d Add half a spatula-tip (or less) of each oxide separately to 1 cm^3 of concentrated sodium hydroxide (8 M NaOH) and very cautiously warm the mixture in the fume cupboard.
e Add approximately 0.1 g of each oxide separately to 2 cm^3 of acidified KI solution.

Results Table 11.4

Test	Tin(IV) oxide	Lead(IV) oxide
a Heat		
b Dilute hydrochloric acid		
c Concentrated hydrochloric acid		
d Concentrated sodium hydroxide		
e Acidified potassium iodide		

Questions

1. Write an equation for the effect of heat on lead(IV) oxide.
2. What is happening in the reactions between:
   a lead(IV) oxide and dilute hydrochloric acid,
   b lead(IV) oxide and acidified potassium iodide?
3. Find out from your textbook(s) the identity of the yellow liquid formed when lead(IV) oxide reacts with concentrated hydrochloric acid.
4. Write equations for the reactions between:
   a tin(IV) oxide and concentrated sodium hydroxide,
   b lead(IV) oxide and concentrated sodium hydroxide.
5. What is the acid–base nature of tin(IV) oxide and lead(IV) oxide? (Bear in mind that concentrated sulphuric acid will attack tin(IV) oxide to form tin(IV) sulphate.)
6. Dilead(II) lead(IV) oxide (red lead), Pb_3O_4, behaves in many respects as a mixture of lead(II) oxide and lead(IV) oxide, and the formula $Pb_2^{II}Pb^{IV}O_4$ (or $2PbO \cdot PbO_2$) is often recommended. Predict the effect of heat on the substance and write the chemical equation.
7. Predict the effect of heating separate samples of tin(II) oxide and lead(II) oxide. Find out what actually happens and write equations.

EXPERIMENT 11.3 Observation and deduction exercise 4

Aim The purpose of this experiment is to give you further practice in the investigation of unknown substances.

Introduction The procedure which follows is taken from two separate A-level practical examination papers. Since the format of each paper is slightly different, we have divided this experiment into two parts. In the first part you carry out tests on a powder Q, and in the second part you test a solution of a compound H and also a solid I. Note that in the examinations, candidates were not told that this experiment referred to Group IV.

Requirements
- safety spectacles
- 10 test-tubes in rack
- test-tube holder
- sample of powder Q
- spatula
- Bunsen burner and mat
- wood splints and litmus papers
- wash-bottle of distilled water
- funnel and filter paper
- nitric acid, dilute, 2 M HNO_3
- potassium iodide solution, 0.1 M KI
- sodium hydroxide solution, 2 M NaOH
- solution of substance H
- silver nitrate solution, 0.02 M $AgNO_3$
- iron(III) chloride solution (neutralised), 0.3 M $FeCl_3$
- potassium thiocyanate solution, 0.5 M KSCN
- sample of solid I
- 1 boiling-tube
- sulphuric acid, dilute, 2 M H_2SO_4
- potassium chromate(VI) solution, 0.5 M K_2CrO_4
- other chemicals are available from your teacher

HAZARD WARNING

Sodium hydroxide solution is corrosive, even at 2 M concentration. Therefore you **must**:
- **wear safety spectacles throughout.**
Powder Q is harmful if ingested.

Procedure – Part A

Tests on Q
Test the powder Q as follows:

1. Heat a portion in a test-tube until reaction ceases. Test any gas evolved.
2. Warm a portion with dilute nitric acid. Filter if necessary. Retain the solution or filtrate for step 3.
3. Test portions of the solution or filtrate from step 2 with:
   a aqueous potassium iodide,
   b aqueous sodium hydroxide.

Carefully observe what happens, and report fully. What tentative inferences do you draw from these experiments? Carry out and report on **one** further experiment which tests your inferences. This experiment can be made on Q or on the products of the above reactions. Full credit will not be given unless your answer discloses the method (including the scale of your experiments), careful observations, and some comment on the type of chemical reactions involved in the experiments.

The record of your work must be made in larger copies of Results Tables 11.5 and 11.6.

Results Table 11.5
Tests on Q

Test	Method	Observations	Inferences
1. Heat			
2. Dilute nitric acid			
3. Test portions of solution or filtrate from step 2 with: **a** Potassium iodide solution **b** Sodium hydroxide solution			

Results Table 11.6
Experiment to test inference

Inference	Test and observations	Conclusion

Procedure – Part B

Tests on H and I

You are provided with a solution of a compound H and a solid I. Carry out the following tests and record your observations and inferences in a larger copy of Results Table 11.7.

Results Table 11.7
Tests on H and I

Test	Observations	Inferences
1. To 1 cm^3 of the solution of H add aqueous silver nitrate followed by dilute nitric acid		
2. To 1 cm^3 of the solution of H add aqueous sodium hydroxide until in excess		
3. To 1 cm^3 of aqueous iron(III) chloride add a few drops of aqueous potassium thiocyanate. To this solution add some of the solution of H		
4. Heat some of solid I in a Pyrex boiling-tube. Allow to cool. Add 8–10 cm^3 of dilute nitric acid to the residue and boil the mixture for one or two minutes. Filter if necessary and use portions of the cool solution for the following tests: a To 1 cm^3 of the solution add aqueous sodium hydroxide b To 1 cm^3 of the solution add dilute sulphuric acid c To 1 cm^3 of the solution add aqueous potassium chromate(VI)		

Now answer the following question.

Question   Comment on the nature of the metal contained in H and on the oxidation states of this metal in the compounds involved in reactions 2 to 3 in Results Table 11.7.

EXPERIMENT 11.4   Illustrating the oxidation states of vanadium

Aim   The purpose of this experiment is to illustrate the presence of several different oxidation states for vanadium, and to show how it is possible to change from one oxidation state to another.

Introduction   Starting with a solution containing vanadium(V) in acid conditions, you use powdered zinc as a reducing agent. Colour changes indicate the formation of other oxidation states. After this first series of reactions you perform some changes between oxidation states by using a variety of oxidising and reducing agents.

Requirements   ■ disposable gloves
■ safety spectacles
■ conical flask, 100 cm^3
■ spatula

- ammonium polytrioxovanadate(V), NH_4VO_3 (ammonium metavanadate)
- measuring cylinder, 25 cm^3
- sulphuric acid, dilute, 1 M H_2SO_4
- sulphuric acid, concentrated, H_2SO_4
- 5 test-tubes and holder
- test-tube rack
- zinc powder, Zn
- Bunsen burner, tripod, gauze and bench mat
- filter funnel and paper
- potassium manganate(VII) solution, 0.02 M $KMnO_4$ (permanganate)
- sodium sulphite, Na_2SO_3
- potassium iodide solution, 0.05 M KI
- sodium thiosulphate solution, 0.1 M $Na_2S_2O_3$
- wash-bottle of distilled water

HAZARD WARNING

  Concentrated sulphuric acid is corrosive and reacts violently with water. Therefore you **must**:
- **wear safety spectacles and gloves;**
- **when diluting, add acid to water, not water to acid;**
- **mop up small spillages with excess water.**

Procedure

First complete a copy of Table 11.2 to assist you in identifying the different oxidation states of vanadium.

Table 11.2

Ion (hydrated)	*VO_2^+	VO^{2+}	V^{3+}	V^{2+}
Colour	Yellow	Blue	Green	Violet
Oxidation state				
Name				

*The VO_3^- ion in the ammonium salt is converted to VO_2^+ by acid:
$$VO_3^-(aq) + 2H^+(aq) \rightleftharpoons VO_2^+(aq) + H_2O(l)$$

1. Place about 0.25 g (one spatula-measure) of ammonium trioxovanadate(V) in a conical flask and add about 25 cm^3 of dilute sulphuric acid. Carefully add about 5 cm^3 of concentrated sulphuric acid and swirl the flask until you obtain a clear yellow solution.
2. Pour about 2 cm^3 of this vanadium(V) solution into each of two test-tubes ready for later tests.
3. To the conical flask add 1–2 g (one spatula measure) of zinc powder, a little at a time. Swirl the flask at intervals and record any observed colour changes in a copy of Results Table 11.8.
4. When the solution has become violet (you may need to heat the flask for this final change), filter about 2 cm^3 into each of three test-tubes.
5. To one of the three tubes add, a little at a time, an excess of acidified potassium manganate(VII) solution, shaking after each addition, until no further change is observed.
6. Keep the other test-tubes of solutions for later tests. Answer the first two questions (page 191) and complete Results Table 11.8 as far as you can before doing further tests.

7. To one of the tubes containing vanadium(V) add a little sodium sulphite and shake. Filter if cloudy. Now boil carefully (at a fume cupboard) to remove excess sulphur dioxide and add about the same volume of the vanadium(II) solution. Record your observations.
8. To the second of the tubes containing vanadium(V), add about 2 cm^3 potassium iodide solution and mix. Then add about 2 cm^3 of sodium thiosulphate solution. Record your observations.
9. Keep the last tube of vanadium(II) solution for a final experiment you may wish to do after answering question 7.

Results Table 11.8

Test	Observations	Summary of reaction
Ammonium vanadate + acid	White solid turned red and dissolved to a yellow solution	$\overset{+5}{V}O_3^- \rightarrow \overset{+5}{V}O_2^+$
Vanadium(V) + zinc		
Vanadium(II) + manganate(VII)		
Vanadium(V) + sulphite Add vanadium(II)		
Vanadium(V) + iodide + thiosulphate		
Vanadium(II) + . . .		

Questions

1. How do you explain the **first** appearance of a green colour in the solution?
2. What are the subsequent changes in colour and why do these changes occur?

You will need the following electrode potentials* in order to answer some of the remaining questions:

$$Zn^{2+}(aq) + 2e^- \rightleftharpoons Zn(s) \qquad\qquad E^\ominus = -0.76 \text{ V}$$
$$V^{3+}(aq) + e^- \rightleftharpoons V^{2+}(aq) \qquad\qquad E^\ominus = -0.26 \text{ V}$$
$$VO^{2+}(aq) + 2H^+(aq) + e^- \rightleftharpoons V^{3+}(aq) + H_2O(l) \qquad E^\ominus = +0.34 \text{ V}$$
$$VO_2^+(aq) + 2H^+(aq) + e^- \rightleftharpoons VO^{2+}(aq) + H_2O(l) \qquad E^\ominus = +1.00 \text{ V}$$
$$SO_4^{2-}(aq) + 4H^+(aq) + 2e^- \rightleftharpoons H_2SO_3(aq) + H_2O(l) \qquad E^\ominus = +0.17 \text{ V}$$
$$I_2(aq) + 2e^- \rightleftharpoons 2I^-(aq) \qquad\qquad E^\ominus = +0.54 \text{ V}$$

* If you have not yet studied electrode potentials in detail, you can regard $E^\ominus$ as a sort of equilibrium constant. The larger (more positive) the value of $E^\ominus$, the more likely the reaction is to go from left to right. In order to predict (or explain) which overall reactions are likely to occur, two half-equations can be combined in such a way that the one with the more positive $E^\ominus$ goes from left to right, the one with the more negative $E^\ominus$ goes from right to left, and equal numbers of electrons are exchanged. Ask your teacher for help if necessary.

3. What did you observe when you added iodide ions to vanadium(V)? What caused this colour?
4. Why did you add sodium thiosulphate?
5. Why does reduction with iodide not give the same result as reduction with zinc?
6. What did you observe when you added sulphite ions to acidified vanadium(V) solution? Does this result correspond with a prediction made using the $E^{\ominus}$ values? (Hint: sulphite ions and acid react to give what?)
7. How would you set about finding a suitable oxidising agent for the oxidation of vanadium(II) to vanadium(III) and no further? Does one appear in the table above?

EXPERIMENT 11.5   Illustrating the oxidation states of manganese

Aim and introduction

The purpose of this experiment is to make samples of some of the less common oxidation states of manganese. There are three parts, with questions following each.

Requirements

- disposable gloves
- safety spectacles
- 6 test-tubes and rack
- potassium manganate(VII) (permanganate) solution, 0.01 M KMnO₄
- sulphuric acid, dilute, 1 M H₂SO₄
- sodium hydroxide solution, 2 M NaOH
- manganese(IV) oxide (manganese dioxide), MnO₂
- spatula and stirring rod
- wash-bottle of distilled water
- filter funnel and 3 papers
- manganese(II) sulphate-4-water, MnSO₄ · 4H₂O
- sulphuric acid, concentrated, H₂SO₄

HAZARD WARNING

 Sodium hydroxide is corrosive, even in dilute solution.

  Concentrated sulphuric acid is corrosive and reacts violently with water. Therefore you **must**:
- **wear safety spectacles and gloves;**
- **when diluting, add acid to water, not water to acid;**
- **mop up small spillages with excess water.**

Procedure – Part A

$E^{\ominus}$ values enable us to predict that it should be possible to make Mn(VI) from Mn(VII) and Mn(IV).

1. Put about 5 cm³ of potassium manganate(VII) solution in each of three test-tubes.
2. To one of the three tubes add about 3 cm³ of dilute sulphuric acid, to another add about 3 cm³ of sodium hydroxide solution, and to the third add about 3 cm³ of distilled water.
3. To each of the three tubes add a little solid manganese(IV) oxide and stir for about a minute.
4. Filter enough of each mixture into a clean tube to see the colour of the filtrate clearly. Use a fresh filter paper for each mixture.
5. One of the tubes should now have in it a clear green solution of Mn(VI). Add to this a little dilute sulphuric acid.

Questions
– Part A

1. Explain why only one of the three mixtures reacted to give green Mn(VI).
2. What happened when acid was added to Mn(VI)? Explain.

Procedure
– Part B

$E^{\ominus}$ values enable us to predict that it should be possible to make Mn(III) from Mn(II) and Mn(VII).

6. Dissolve about 0.5 g of manganese(II) sulphate in about 2 cm^3 of dilute sulphuric acid in a test-tube.
7. **Carefully** add about ten drops of concentrated sulphuric acid and cool the tube under a running tap.
8. Add a few drops of potassium manganate(VII) solution to obtain a deep red solution of Mn(III).
9. Dilute the red solution with about five times its volume of water, wait a few moments, and note any colour change.

Question
– Part B

3. Explain what happened when the Mn(III) solution was diluted.

Procedure
– Part C

$E^{\ominus}$ values enable us to predict that it should also be possible to make Mn(III) from Mn(II) and Mn(IV).

10. In each of two test-tubes, dissolve a little manganese(II) sulphate in water and add an equal volume of sodium hydroxide solution to obtain a precipitate of manganese(II) hydroxide.
11. To one of the two tubes, add a little manganese(IV) oxide and stir.
12. Let both tubes stand for a few minutes, and note any changes.

Questions
– Part C

4. Can you see any sign of Mn(III) in the tubes?
5. What is different about the conditions of this experiment (part C) compared with the last (part B) which makes its success less likely?
6. What happens in the test-tube which had no manganese(IV) added? Suggest an explanation. (Hint: is the change greater in the upper part of the mixture?)

EXPERIMENT 11.6   Relative stabilities of some complex ions

Aim

The purpose of this experiment is to test predictions of ligand replacement reactions made using stability constants.

Introduction

In a series of test-tube reactions you examine a number of ligand replacement reactions. One type, in which charged and uncharged ligands are represented as lig$^-$ and LIG respectively, can be represented:

$$Cu(LIG)_4^{2+} + 4\,lig^- \rightleftharpoons Cu(lig)_4^{2-} + 4\,LIG$$

You use stability constants to predict the outcome before mixing suitable pairs of solutions.

Requirements

- disposable gloves
- safety spectacles
- 6 test-tubes
- test-tube rack
- copper(II) sulphate solution, 0.20 M CuSO$_4$
- wash-bottle of distilled water

- sodium chloride solution, saturated NaCl
- sodium ethanedioate solution, 0.20 M $(CO_2Na)_2$ (sodium oxalate)
- 1,2-diaminoethane solution, 0.10 M $(CH_2NH_2)_2$
- edta solution (sodium salt), 0.10 M $C_{10}H_{14}O_8N_2Na_2$

HAZARD WARNING

Sodium ethanedioate is **toxic**. Therefore you **must**:
- **wear safety spectacles and disposable gloves.**

Procedure
1. Complete the four prediction columns (headed 'P') in a copy of Results Table 11.9, using the stability constants given. Use a '✓' to indicate 'replacement' and a '✗' to indicate 'no reaction'.
2. Place about 1 cm³ of copper sulphate solution in each of five test-tubes.
3. To the first tube add about 5 cm³ of distilled water. This tube is for colour comparison with the others.
4. To the second tube add about 5 cm³ of sodium chloride solution a little at a time, noting any colour changes.
5. To the third tube add about 5 cm³ of sodium ethanedioate in the same way.
6. Similarly, to the fourth and fifth tubes add diaminoethane and edta solutions respectively.
7. The colours in the five tubes are predominantly due to the five complex ions shown in Results Table 11.9. Write down the colours in your table, and fill in the first results column (headed 'R'). Again, use a '✓' or a '✗' to show whether or not replacement of ligands has occurred.

Note that, in addition to the abbreviation edta, we use 'ox' to represent the ethanedioate (**ox**alate) ligand and 'en' to represent the 1,2-diaminoethane ligand (**e**thylenediami**n**e).

Results Table 11.9

Ligand	H_2O	Cl^-	$C_2O_4{}^{2-}$ = ox	$NH_2C_2H_4NH_2$ = en	$C_{10}H_{12}O_8N_2{}^{4-}$ = edta
Complex ion	$Cu(H_2O)_4{}^{2+}$	$CuCl_4{}^{2-}$	$Cu(ox)_2{}^{2-}$	$Cu(en)_2{}^{2+}$	$Cu(edta)^{2-}$
Colour					
Stability constant	–	4.0×10^5 $mol^{-4}\ dm^{12}$	2.1×10^{10} $mol^{-2}\ dm^6$	–	6.3×10^{18} $mol^{-1}\ dm^3$

	Predictions (P) and results (R) ✓ = replacement, ✗ = none									
Test	P	R	P	R	P	R	P	R	P	R
Add H_2O										
Add Cl^-										
Add ox										
Add en										
Add edta										

8. Divide the solution containing $CuCl_4^{2-}$ ions into four parts. To each of these add an excess of one of the other four ligands in turn – use the original ligand solutions and not the complex ion solutions you have made. Complete the second results column according to whether or not you think replacement has occurred.
9. Repeat step 8 for the remaining complex ion solutions and complete the remaining results columns.

Questions
1. Could you have made any tentative predictions without knowing stability constants?
2. Estimate the approximate stability constant for $Cu(en)_2^{2+}$.
3. One of the ligand exchange reactions appeared to be readily reversible. Which one was this?
4. Calculate the ratio $[Cu(H_2O)_4^{2+}(aq)]/[CuCl_4^{2-}(aq)]$ for the following values of $[Cl^-(aq)]$:
   a 5.0 mol dm^{-3} (in saturated NaCl),
   b 0.050 mol dm^{-3} (in dilute NaCl).
   How do these ratios help to explain the reversible nature of the ligand exchange?

EXPERIMENT 11.7   Determining the formula of a complex ion

Aim
The purpose of this experiment is to use colorimetry to find the formula of the complex ion formed from copper(II) ions and ammonia. The same method can be used for many other complex ions.

Introduction
Using different proportions of copper(II) ions and ammonia you prepare mixtures and examine them in a colorimeter. The mixture which shows the most intense colour (and, therefore, the greatest absorbance) indicates the proportions of Cu^{2+} and NH_3 in the complex ion.

Requirements
■ disposable gloves
■ safety spectacles
■ 3 beakers, 100 cm^3
■ 3 burettes, 50 cm^3 **or** 3 graduated pipettes, 10 cm^3
■ 3 small funnels for filling burettes
■ 8 test-tubes (to fit colorimeter) in test-tube rack
■ 8 corks or bungs to fit test-tubes
■ distilled water
■ ammonium sulphate solution, 2.0 M $(NH_4)_2SO_4$
■ copper(II) sulphate solution, 0.10 M $CuSO_4$
■ ammonia solution, 0.10 M NH_3
■ colorimeter, with filters

Procedure
1. Prepare a different mixture in each of eight test-tubes by running in from burettes or graduated pipettes the volumes of the three solutions shown in Results Table 11.10. Cork each tube and shake to mix thoroughly.

Results Table 11.10

Tube number	1	2	3	4	5	6	7	8
Volume of $(NH_4)_2SO_4$/cm^3	15	5	5	5	5	5	5	5
Volume of $CuSO_4$/cm^3	0.0	1.0	1.5	2.0	2.5	3.0	4.0	5.0
Volume of NH_3/cm^3	0.0	9.0	8.5	8.0	7.5	7.0	6.0	5.0
Colorimeter reading	0.00							

2. Choose a suitable filter for this experiment. If you are not quite sure which filter to use, look at the notes at the end of this procedure section.
3. With the filter in position, put tube 1 into the colorimeter, cover it to exclude stray light, and turn the adjusting knob so that the meter shows zero absorbance (or, on some colorimeters, 100% transmission).

   Ideally, this should set the intensity of the light reaching the tubes for the whole experiment but, because simple colorimeters tend to give a light intensity which is not constant, you should repeat this step immediately before each reading you take.
4. Still with tube 1 in the colorimeter, check for constancy of meter reading with the tube rotated and moved to slightly different positions. Mark the tube so that you can replace it in such a way as to get the same reading each time.

   If necessary, change the tube until you are satisfied. (With some of the simplest colorimeters, it may not be possible for you to be too fussy!)
5. Immediately after setting zero with tube 1, replace it with tube 2 and take a reading of absorbance (or % transmission). To minimise errors due to irregular tube diameter and position, rotate the tube and take an average reading. (If you are lucky enough to be using matched tubes, put the mark in the same position each time.)

   Also, check the zero again after the reading and repeat if necessary. Record the average reading in a copy of Results Table 11.10.
6. Repeat steps 3 and 4 before taking further colorimeter readings for each of the remaining coloured solutions in turn.
7. Plot a graph of meter reading against volume of reactants as shown in Fig. 11.1. If your meter shows absorbance, the graph will show a peak; if it shows transmittance, the graph will show a trough.

Figure 11.1

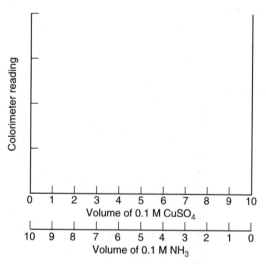

8. From the graph, determine the volumes of $CuSO_4$ and NH_3 corresponding to the peak (or trough if you are working with transmittance). These volumes may not necessarily be those used in any of the tubes, but should give a simple whole number ratio.
9. Use the simple whole number ratio obtained from the graph to write the formula for the complex ion.

Choosing a filter

Ideally, the filter lets through **only** light of the particular wavelength which is absorbed by the complex ion. So for a blue complex ion, which absorbs yellow light, you need a yellow filter – yellow is the complementary colour to blue. See Fig. 11.2.

Figure 11.2

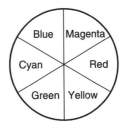

If you are not clear which filter has the complementary colour of the solution you are using, then follow the detailed procedure below.

1. Put any one of the available filters into the slot in the colorimeter, and insert tube 1, covering it to exclude stray light. Turn the adjusting knob so that the meter shows zero absorbance (or, on some colorimeters, 100% transmission). Mark the rim of the tube so that you can replace it in the same position.
2. Replace tube 1 with tube 5 and take a reading of absorbance (or of % transmission). Mark this tube too so that you can replace it in the same position.
3. Repeat steps 1 and 2 above for all the filters in turn.
4. Choose the filter which gives the greatest absorbance (or least transmission) and go back to step 3 of the procedure section.

Questions

1. What is the function of the ammonium sulphate in this experiment? If you do not know the answer, try adding ammonia solution to copper sulphate solution without any ammonium sulphate present. If you are not in the laboratory, or if you still need a clue, look up the common ion effect in textbooks.
2. Why does the absorbance **decrease** after the peak while the amount of added copper ions **increases**?
3. Why does the absorbance **increase** up to the peak while the amount of added ammonia **decreases**?
4. How would your results be affected by using the wrong filter?
5. How would your results be affected by using no filter at all?

Extension

The method described above can be used with very little modification (if any) to find the formulae for many other complex ions. You may wish to try, for example, using a solution of diaminoethane (ethylenediamine) in place of the ammonia in the experiment above. If you do this, the ammonium sulphate is not necessary and should be replaced with water.

Other complexes you might try are those made from:

nickel(II) ions and edta
iron(III) ions and thiocyanate ions

Note that the volumes given in Results Table 11.10 may need adjusting for different complexes. Ask your teacher for advice.

EXPERIMENT 11.8 Some redox chemistry of copper

Aim and introduction

The purpose of this experiment is to prepare three copper(I) compounds by reduction of copper(II). Different conditions are used in parts A, B, C and D.

Requirements

- safety spectacles
- boiling-tube and holder
- spatula
- copper turnings, Cu
- copper(II) chloride-6-water, $CuCl_2 \cdot 6H_2O$
- sodium chloride, NaCl
- wash-bottle of distilled water
- Bunsen burner and mat
- beaker, 250 cm^3
- 4 test-tubes
- test-tube rack
- sodium sulphite-7-water, $Na_2SO_3 \cdot 7H_2O$
- copper(II) sulphate solution, 0.10 M $CuSO_4$
- potassium iodide solution, 0.10 M KI
- sodium thiosulphate-5-water, $Na_2S_2O_3 \cdot 5H_2O$
- Fehling's solutions, 1 and 2

Procedure – Part A

1. Put one spatula measure of copper turnings, two of copper(II) chloride and two of sodium chloride in a boiling-tube and add about 10 cm^3 of distilled water.
2. Heat the tube till the contents **just** boil, and maintain this temperature, swirling the tube from time to time, for several minutes until the solution appears not to be darkening in colour any further.
3. Allow the tube to cool a little, and pour the solution into about 50 cm^3 of fresh distilled water in a beaker.
4. Put the beaker on one side while you do part B of the experiment and then re-examine it.

Procedure – Part B

5. Dissolve one spatula-measure of copper(II) chloride in water in a test-tube about one-third full.
6. Dissolve one spatula-measure of sodium sulphite in water in another test-tube about one-third full.
7. Mix the two solutions and allow to stand for a few minutes.
8. If necessary, pour off the solution to examine the white solid.

Questions – Parts A and B

1. What is the white solid produced in each case, and why has it no colour?
2. What is the reducing agent in each case?
3. Why was heat required in part A and not in part B?
4. What is the function of the excess of chloride ions in part A?
5. What causes the dark brown colour in part A?
6. Why does the solution in contact with the white solid in part A slowly turn blue on standing?

Procedure – Part C

9. Mix a little copper(II) sulphate solution in a test-tube with about twice the volume of potassium iodide solution and allow to settle.
10. Add a crystal of sodium thiosulphate and shake the tube until no further change is observed.

**Questions
– Part C**

7. What do you observe in step 9?
8. Explain the change in appearance after step 10.
9. Why is the solution no longer blue after step 10?
10. What, therefore, is the creamy white solid?

**Procedure
– Part D**

11. Mix 2 or 3 cm³ of Fehling's solutions 1 and 2 in a boiling tube.
12. Add half a spatula-measure of glucose (or other reducing sugar) and stand the tube in a beaker of boiling water. Observe and record any colour changes over the next few minutes.

**Questions
– Part D**

11. Fehling's solution 1 is simply aqueous copper(II) sulphate. Fehling's solution 2 is an alkaline solution of sodium potassium 2,3-dihydroxybutanedioate. Suggest an explanation for the colour change you observed when 1 and 2 are mixed.
12. Glucose does not reduce Fehling's solution 1 alone. Suggest a reason why it does react with a mixture of 1 and 2. Suggest a formula for the red solid product, bearing in mind that the solution is alkaline.

Summarise the whole experiment in a copy of Results Table 11.11.

Results Table 11.11

		Method	Observations	Equation(s)
A	Preparation of			
B	Preparation of			
C	Preparation of			
D	Preparation of			

The experiment illustrates some important points about copper(I) compounds:

1. $Cu^+(aq)$ can exist in only very low concentrations, because it readily disproportionates:

$$2Cu^+(aq) \rightleftharpoons Cu^{2+}(aq) + Cu(s)$$

2. The copper(I) state can be stabilised by:
   a the formation of complex ions,
   b the precipitation of insoluble compounds such as CuCl, CuI and Cu_2O.
3. The reduction of copper(II) to copper(I) via complex ions can be achieved by reducing agents other than copper(0), and this forms the basis of a test for organic reducing agents using Fehling's solution.

EXPERIMENT 11.9 Investigating the use of cobalt(II) ions as a catalyst

Aim The purpose of this experiment is to test whether cobalt(II) ions will catalyse the oxidation of 2,3-dihydroxybutanedioate ions by hydrogen peroxide and to look for evidence of intermediate compound formation.

Introduction In this short experiment, you simply mix the hot reactants and add the potential catalyst. If you see a coloured intermediate, you can attempt to stabilise it by cooling the mixture quickly.

Requirements
- disposable gloves
- safety spectacles
- beaker, 250 cm^3
- distilled water
- spatula
- potassium sodium 2,3-dihydroxybutanedioate, $CO_2K(CHOH)_2CO_2Na \cdot 4H_2O$ (also known as potassium sodium tartrate or Rochelle salt)
- Bunsen burner and mat
- tripod and gauze
- thermometer, 0–100 °C
- measuring cylinder, 25 cm^3
- hydrogen peroxide solution, 20-volume H_2O_2
- 2 test-tubes and rack
- cobalt(II) chloride, $CoCl_2 \cdot 6H_2O$
- stirring rod
- teat pipette

HAZARD WARNING

  Hydrogen peroxide is corrosive and an oxidant. Therefore you **must**:
- **handle with care**.

Procedure
1. Dissolve about 1 g of potassium sodium 2,3-dihydroxybutanedioate in about 50 cm^3 of water in a beaker.
2. Heat the solution to about 70 °C.
3. Add about 20 cm^3 of hydrogen peroxide solution, heat again to about 70 °C and then remove from heat. At this stage there should be little or no sign of reaction.
4. Dissolve a few small crystals (about 0.25 g) of cobalt(II) chloride in a little water (about 5 cm^3) in a test-tube and add this to the hot solution. There will be an induction period before a reaction starts, so be patient! The length of the induction period decreases with increasing concentrations of reactants and catalyst and with increasing temperature. These can be varied if necessary.

5. As soon as the solution appears to be dark green, quickly transfer about 5–10 cm^3 by teat pipette to a test-tube and cool it under the tap. If the green colour has disappeared before you have cooled the tube, repeat the experiment in such a way that the reaction proceeds more slowly.

Questions
1. The gas given off when the reaction starts has two components. What are these?
2. What is the dark green solution and why does the colour return to pink?
3. Why does cooling the test-tube preserve the green colour for a while?

EXPERIMENT 11.10   Catalysing the reaction between iodide ions and peroxodisulphate ions

Aim
The purpose of this experiment is to find and test suitable catalysts, from a range of readily available transition metal ions, for the reaction:

$$S_2O_8^{2-}(aq) + 2I^-(aq) \rightarrow 2SO_4^{2-}(aq) + I_2(aq)$$

Introduction
You can make predictions about the suitability of possible catalysts by assuming that the mechanism of catalysis consists of two stages, either of which can be the first:

i) higher oxidation state of catalyst oxidises I^-,
ii) lower oxidation state of catalyst reduces $S_2O_8^{2-}$.

You then perform a number of experiments, each with fixed starting concentrations of I^-, $S_2O_8^{2-}$ and possible catalyst. Thiosulphate ions and starch are also added to enable you to measure the rate of reaction, and thus test your predictions.

As the reaction proceeds, any iodine formed immediately reacts with the thiosulphate:

$$I_2(aq) + 2S_2O_3^{2-}(aq) \rightarrow S_4O_6^{2-}(aq) + 2I^-(aq)$$

When all the thiosulphate has reacted, the free iodine gives a deep blue colour with the starch. If t is the time taken for the blue colour to appear, then $1/t$ is a measure of the initial rate of reaction.

Requirements
- safety spectacles
- 4 test-tubes and rack
- potassium iodide solution, 0.2 M KI
- sulphuric acid, dilute, 1 M H$_2$SO$_4$
- potassium manganate(VII) solution, 0.1 M KMnO$_4$
- potassium chromate(VI) solution, 0.1 M K$_2$CrO$_4$
- iron(III) chloride solution, 0.1 M FeCl$_3$
- potassium peroxodisulphate solution, 0.2 M K$_2$S$_2$O$_8$
- manganese(II) sulphate solution, 0.1 M MnSO$_4$
- chromium(III) chloride solution, 0.1 M CrCl$_3$
- iron(II) sulphate solution, 0.1 M FeSO$_4$
- 4 burettes and stands ⎫
- 4 beakers, 100 cm^3 ⎬ shared with other students
- 4 small funnels   ⎭
- starch solution, 0.2%
- sodium thiosulphate solution, 0.01 M Na$_2$S$_2$O$_3$
- conical flask, 150 cm^3
- boiling-tube
- stopclock
- distilled water

Procedure

1. In a copy of Results Table 11.12 write the appropriate electrode potentials from your data book.
2. Use the electrode potentials to predict the feasibility of each step in the proposed mechanism. You should wait until these steps have been tested before predicting the overall feasibility.

Results Table 11.12

Transition element		Chromium	Manganese	Iron
Oxidation states used		Cr(VI) Cr(III)	Mn(VII) Mn(II)	Fe(III) Fe(II)
Electrode potential/V (higher ox. state $\rightleftharpoons$ lower)				
Electrode potential/V ($I_2 + 2e^- \rightleftharpoons 2I^-$)				
Electrode potential/V ($S_2O_8^{2-} + 2e^- \rightleftharpoons 2SO_4^{2-}$)				
Does higher ox. state oxidise I^-?	Prediction			
	Practically			
Does lower ox. state reduce $S_2O_8^{2-}$?	Prediction			
	Practically			
Do you expect catalysis?				
Time for blue colour to appear t/s				

3. In a test-tube, mix a few drops of potassium iodide solution with a few drops of dilute sulphuric acid. Add a few drops of one of the solutions containing a transition element in a higher oxidation state. Look for evidence of reaction and fill in your table accordingly.
4. In a test-tube, mix a few drops of potassium peroxodisulphate solution with a few drops of a solution containing the same transition element in a lower oxidation state. Look for evidence of reaction and fill in your table accordingly.
5. Repeat steps 3 and 4 for the other two transition elements. From your results predict which of the given solutions are likely to be catalysts.

To check whether catalysis actually occurs, proceed as follows. (If you do not have time to check every prediction, share your results with other students.)

6. Fill four burettes with one each of the following solutions:
   - potassium iodide,
   - starch,
   - potassium peroxodisulphate,
   - sodium thiosulphate.
7. From the burettes run into a conical flask these volumes:
   - 10 cm^3 of potassium iodide solution,
   - 10 cm^3 of sodium thiosulphate solution,
   - 5 cm^3 of starch solution.
8. Run 20 cm^3 of potassium peroxodisulphate solution into a boiling-tube.
9. Quickly pour the contents of the boiling-tube into the flask and start the stopclock. Swirl the flask twice to mix the contents and then stand it on the bench while you look for the appearance of a blue colour.

10. As soon as the solution turns blue, stop the clock and record the time taken.
11. Repeat steps 7 to 10, but in addition to the first three reagents, add five drops of a solution containing a transition metal ion.
12. If you have time to repeat the procedure before trying another possible catalyst then, of course, your results should be more reliable.

Questions

1. For one of the three transition elements you used, **all** of the predictions were confirmed by experiment. Which one was this? Describe briefly a possible mechanism (without equations) for catalysis involving this element.
2. One of the three transition elements did **not** catalyse the reaction. Which one was this? Why could it not function as a catalyst?
3. One of the three transition elements worked well as a catalyst, even though its lower oxidation state did not appear to react with peroxodisulphate. Which one was this? Suggest a possible explanation. (Hint: look at Experiment 11.5.)
4. Two students performed this experiment on different days using the same equipment and solutions. They found that the times they recorded did not agree very well. Suggest an explanation.

EXPERIMENT 11.11 Observation and deduction exercise 5

Aim and introduction

This experiment is intended primarily for students preparing for a practical examination, but your teacher may wish to use it to assess your skills in observation, recording and interpretation. Ideally, it should be done under examination conditions. We do not include a requirements list here because we assume that all the materials you need will be provided for you.

HAZARD WARNING

Sodium hydroxide and sulphuric acid are corrosive, even in dilute solution.

Hydrogen peroxide is corrosive and an oxidant.
Therefore you **must**:
■ **wear safety spectacles throughout;**
■ **heat solutions with care, to avoid spurting.**

You are provided with two salts C and D. Carry out the following tests and record your observations and inferences in a copy of Results Table 11.13. Then answer the question which follows the table.

	Test	Observations	Inferences
Procedure and results **Results Table 11.13**	1. Warm three-quarters of your sample of C with 4–5 cm^3 of aqueous sodium hydroxide		
	2. Add approximately 10 cm^3 of dilute sulphuric acid to the remainder of your sample of C in a boiling-tube and warm the mixture in order to dissolve the solid. Use portions of the solution for the following tests: **a** To 1–2 cm^3 of the solution of C add an equal volume of aqueous potassium iodide. Then add, dropwise, aqueous sodium thiosulphate until there is no further change **b** To 2 cm^3 of the solution add a little copper powder and warm **c** To 3–4 cm^3 of the solution add a little zinc powder and allow the mixture to stand. It is suggested that you make observations for about five minutes and then allow the mixture to stand for a further 30 minutes, making observations from time to time. During this time you should proceed with other tests		
	3. Carry out a flame test on substance D		
	4. Dissolve some D in the minimum quantity of distilled water and use portions of the solution for the following tests: **a** Add a few drops of this solution to a mixture of 1–2 cm^3 of aqueous potassium iodide with an equal volume of dilute sulphuric acid. Then add aqueous sodium thiosulphate dropwise **b** To 1 cm^3 of the solution of D add aqueous sodium hydroxide. Then add dilute sulphuric acid until in excess **c** To about 2 cm^3 of the solution of D add an equal volume of dilute sulphuric acid. Then add hydrogen peroxide solution drop-wise until there is no further change **d** Transfer the solution from **c** to a boiling-tube and add about 10 cm^3 of aqueous sodium hydroxide and 1 cm^3 of hydrogen peroxide solution. Heat the resulting solution		

Question The anion in D contains oxygen and a metal. Give the oxidation states of the metal which are indicated in the reactions in **4a**, **4b** and **4d**.

ILPAC

12

p-BLOCK ELEMENTS

EXPERIMENT 12.1 Reactions of aluminium

Aim The purpose of this experiment is to show how aluminium foil reacts with dilute acids and alkalis and, when reactions do occur, to carry out tests on the resulting solutions.

Introduction In your studies of the Periodic Table, you have learned that aluminium oxide is amphoteric. Other metals with amphoteric oxides such as beryllium and zinc tend to react with acids and alkalis, so you might also expect aluminium to react in a similar way.

In addition to observing the reactions of aluminium with dilute acids and alkalis, you also attempt to interpret some reactions of the resulting solutions.

Requirements
- ■ safety spectacles
- ■ 6 pieces of aluminium foil, 3 cm × 3 cm
- ■ 10 test-tubes
- ■ test-tube rack
- ■ test-tube holder
- ■ sodium hydroxide solution, 2 M NaOH
- ■ hydrochloric acid, dilute, 2 M HCl
- ■ Bunsen burner and bench mat
- ■ beaker, 100 cm^3
- ■ copper(II) chloride solution, 0.1 M CuCl$_2$
- ■ mercury(II) chloride solution, 0.1 M HgCl$_2$
- ■ wash-bottle of distilled water
- ■ filter funnel
- ■ filter paper
- ■ sulphuric acid, dilute, 1 M H$_2$SO$_4$
- ■ sodium carbonate solution, 1 M Na$_2$CO$_3$
- ■ red and blue litmus papers

HAZARD WARNING

 Sodium hydroxide solution is corrosive, even in dilute solution.

 Mercury(II) chloride is highly **toxic** by ingestion and by skin absorption. Therefore you **must**:
- ■ **wear safety spectacles and protective gloves;**
- ■ **work with great care.**

(Your teacher may choose to demonstrate the use of mercury(II) chloride in this experiment.)

Procedure – Part A

Reactions of aluminium foil

1. Tear one of the sheets of aluminium foil into smaller pieces and place them in a test-tube containing 3–4 cm^3 of dilute sodium hydroxide solution. Identify any gas given off and record your observations in a copy of Results Table 12.1. Keep the resulting solution for further tests.
2. Repeat step 1 using dilute hydrochloric acid instead of sodium hydroxide solution. If no reaction occurs, heat the mixture gently.
3. Place 3 pieces of aluminium in a small beaker and just cover them with copper(II) chloride solution. On a fourth piece of aluminium, place 3 separate drops of mercury(II) chloride solution.
4. After about 2 minutes, pour away the copper(II) chloride solution and rinse the foil with distilled water. Leave one piece exposed to the air. Put the others in 2 test-tubes and add sodium hydroxide and dilute hydrochloric acid respectively. Compare what happens with the results of steps 1 and 2.

5. Rinse away the drops of mercury(II) chloride solution with distilled water and leave the foil exposed to the air. Examine it after a few minutes and compare it with the foil treated with copper(II) chloride.

Results Table 12.1
Reactions of aluminium foil

Reagent	Observations	Identity of any gas given off
Sodium hydroxide solution		
Sodium hydroxide solution after immersion in $CuCl_2$(aq)		
Dilute hydrochloric acid		
Dilute hydrochloric acid after immersion in $CuCl_2$(aq)		
Air after immersion in $CuCl_2$(aq)		
Air after immersion in $HgCl_2$(aq)		

Procedure – Part B

Reactions of the resulting solutions

6. Filter the resulting solutions from steps 1 and 2 (if necessary) and test the filtrates as follows:
7. To separate 1 cm³ portions of the filtrates from step 6 add, as appropriate, the following reagents, a little at a time, until they are present in excess:
   a dilute sulphuric acid (to the solution in NaOH only),
   b dilute sodium hydroxide solution (to the solution in HCl only),
   c sodium carbonate solution (to the solution in HCl only).
8. Record your observations in a copy of Results Table 12.2. If no reaction occurs write **none** in the appropriate box.

Results Table 12.2
Reactions of the solutions

Reagent	Observations using solutions of	
	Al in NaOH	Al in HCl
Dilute sulphuric acid		
Sodium hydroxide solution		
Sodium carbonate solution		

You may need to refer to your textbook(s) in order to answer the following questions.

Questions

1. Untreated aluminium has a wide variety of uses which depend, in part, on its resistance to corrosion in normal conditions. However, standard electrode potentials suggest that aluminium is more reactive than iron, which corrodes badly. Explain briefly.
2. How does treatment with a solution of copper(II) chloride or mercury(II) chloride reveal the true reactivity of aluminium?
3. Suggest a reason for the fact that mercury(II) chloride is more effective than copper(II) chloride in promoting a reaction between aluminium and air.
4. Why should you not use washing soda or some special oven-cleaners on aluminium kitchenware?
5. Write equations for the reactions of aluminium with
   a dilute acids **b** alkalis.
6. Explain, as far as possible, the observations you have made in Results Table 12.2 and name the precipitates formed. (Hint: aluminium carbonate is not known.)

EXPERIMENT 12.2 Reactions of the oxoacids of nitrogen and their salts

Aim
The purpose of this experiment is to illustrate some of the redox reactions of nitric acid, nitrates, nitrous acid and nitrites by means of simple small-scale tests.

Requirements
- safety spectacles
- protective gloves
- 6 test-tubes
- 1 cork or bung to fit the test-tubes
- copper turnings, Cu

- nitric acid, concentrated, 16 M HNO_3
- wash-bottle of distilled water
- Bunsen burner and bench protection mat
- magnesium ribbon, Mg
- nitric acid, dilute, 2 M HNO_3
- wood splints
- 2 boiling-tubes
- sodium hydroxide solution, 2 M NaOH
- Devarda's alloy (Cu 50%, Al 45%, Zn 5%)
- aluminium foil, Al
- sulphuric acid, dilute, 1 M H_2SO_4
- beaker, 250 cm^3
- ice
- spatula
- sodium nitrite, $NaNO_2$
- potassium iodide solution, 0.5 M KI
- potassium manganate(VII) solution, 0.02 M $KMnO_4$
- iron(II) sulphate, $FeSO_4 \cdot 7H_2O$

HAZARD WARNING

Concentrated nitric acid is corrosive.

Nitrogen dioxide is a **toxic** gas, which may be produced in reactions of nitrogen compounds and is a powerful oxidising agent.

Sodium hydroxide solution is corrosive, even in dilute solution.
Therefore you **must**:
- **wear safety spectacles and protective gloves;**
- **work at a fume cupboard.**

Procedure – Part A

Reactions of nitric acid

1. Place a single copper turning in a test-tube and carefully add a few drops of concentrated nitric acid. Record your observations in a copy of Results Table 12.3 and identify the gas evolved.
2. Pour about 2 cm^3 of concentrated nitric acid into a test-tube and carefully dilute it with an equal volume of distilled water. Drop in 2–3 copper turnings. Identify the gas evolved by observing its colour over the whole length of the test-tube. You may need to warm the tube **gently** to speed up the reaction.
3. Add about 4 cm^3 of 2 M nitric acid to a 4 cm piece of magnesium ribbon in a test-tube. Cork the tube **loosely** and attempt to identify the gas or gases evolved.
4. Add about 3 cm^3 of distilled water to a 4 cm piece of magnesium ribbon in a test-tube and add 1 cm^3 of 2 M nitric acid. Cork the tube **loosely** and attempt to identify the gas evolved.
5. In a boiling-tube, mix 1 cm^3 of 2 M nitric acid and 2 cm^3 of 2 M sodium hydroxide solution. Add a spatula-measure of Devarda's alloy and warm **gently**. Identify the gas given off.
6. Repeat step 5 using a small piece of aluminium foil instead of Devarda's alloy. Complete your copy of Results Table 12.3.

Results Table 12.3
Reactions of nitric acid and
nitrates

Reactants	Observations	Identity of gas
1. Copper and 16 M HNO_3		
2. Copper and 8 M HNO_3		
3. Magnesium and 2 M HNO_3		
4. Magnesium and 0.5 M HNO_3		
5. Devarda's alloy and a nitrate in alkali		
6. Aluminium and a nitrate in alkali		

**Procedure
– Part B**

Reactions of nitrous acid

7. Prepare a solution of nitrous acid, as follows. Pour about 15 cm^3 of dilute sulphuric acid into a boiling-tube and stand it in an ice-bath for about 5 minutes. Dissolve about 1.5 g of sodium nitrite in the minimum quantity of distilled water and cool in the ice-bath. Mix the two cooled solutions.

8. Transfer about 2 cm^3 of the nitrous acid solution to a test-tube and warm gently. Record your observations and try to identify the gas evolved.

9. In another test-tube add a few drops of potassium iodide solution to approximately 2 cm^3 of nitrous acid solution.

10. Repeat step 9 using a few drops of potassium manganate(VII) solution instead of potassium iodide.

11. Dissolve a few small crystals of iron(II) sulphate in about 2 cm^3 of cold distilled water.

    a To half of this solution add dilute aqueous sodium hydroxide.

    b Add the other half of the iron(II) sulphate solution to an equal volume of nitrous acid solution. Heat the mixture until the colour lightens and then cool. Add sodium hydroxide solution and compare the result with what happened in **a**.

12. To a little solid sodium nitrite add 1–2 cm^3 of aqueous sodium hydroxide and a small piece of aluminium foil. Heat the mixture and test any gases evolved. Complete your copy of Results Table 12.4.

Results Table 12.4
Reactions of nitrous acid and nitrites

Reactants in solution	Observations	Identity of coloured product(s)	Oxidation or reduction of NO_2^-
7. Sodium nitrite and sulphuric acid		HNO_2 or perhaps N_2O_3	
8. Warm nitrous acid			
9. Potassium iodide and nitrous acid			
10. Potassium manganate(VII) and nitrous acid			
11.**a** Iron(II) sulphate and sodium hydroxide			
11.**b** Iron(II) sulphate, nitrous acid and sodium hydroxide			
12. Aluminium and a nitrite in alkali			

Questions

To help you with your answers you may need to refer to your textbooks.

1. Write equations for the reactions between copper and nitric acid of different concentrations. Explain your observations of these reactions.
2. Describe and explain the difference between the reactions of magnesium with dilute and very dilute nitric acid.
3. Aluminium is the most powerful reducing agent of the three metals in Devarda's alloy. Suggest reasons why the alloy is more effective than aluminium foil.
4. Write an equation for the thermal decomposition of nitrous acid. What type of redox reaction is this? Why does nitric acid not undergo the same type of reaction?
5. Which of the reactions in the experiment may be used to distinguish:
   a nitrates and nitrites from most other compounds,
   b nitrates from nitrites?

EXPERIMENT 12.3   Investigating reactions of the oxosalts of sulphur

Aim
The purpose of this experiment is to illustrate the redox reactions of some oxoanions of sulphur, some of which can be used as tests for these ions.

Introduction
You are asked to carry out some simple test-tube reactions on solutions and solid samples of the following salts:
- sodium sulphite, Na_2SO_3,
- sodium sulphate, Na_2SO_4,
- sodium thiosulphate, $Na_2S_2O_3$,
- sodium peroxodisulphate, $Na_2S_2O_8$ (sodium persulphate).

In some cases you may not be able to interpret the reactions fully, but be sure to record your observations clearly and precisely. Ask your teacher which of the reactions you need to learn.

Requirements
- safety spectacles
- protective gloves
- 10 test-tubes in rack
- sodium sulphite solution, 0.2 M Na_2SO_3
- sodium sulphate solution, 0.2 M Na_2SO_4
- sodium thiosulphate solution, 0.2 M $Na_2S_2O_3$
- sodium peroxodisulphate solution, 0.2 M $Na_2S_2O_8$ (persulphate)
- hydrochloric acid, dilute, 2 M HCl
- Bunsen burner and bench protection mat
- wash-bottle of distilled water
- wood splints
- potassium dichromate(VI) solution, acidified, 0.1 M $K_2Cr_2O_7$
- strips of filter paper
- silver nitrate solution, 0.1 M $AgNO_3$
- 'silver residues' bottle
- iodine solution, 0.2 M I_2 in KI(aq)
- potassium iodide solution, 0.5 M KI
- iron(III) chloride solution, 0.5 M $FeCl_3$
- sodium hydroxide solution, 2 M NaOH
- test-tube holder
- spatula
- sodium sulphite-7-water, $Na_2SO_3 \cdot 7H_2O$
- sodium sulphate-10-water, $Na_2SO_4 \cdot 10H_2O$
- sodium thiosulphate-5-water, $Na_2S_2O_3 \cdot 5H_2O$
- sodium peroxodisulphate, $Na_2S_2O_8$
- boiling-tube
- sulphur, powdered, S
- filter funnel and papers

HAZARD WARNING

Aqueous sodium hydroxide is corrosive.

Silver nitrate is corrosive and **toxic**.

Sodium peroxodisulphate is a powerful oxidant.
Therefore you **must**:
- ■ wear safety spectacles and protective gloves;
- ■ work at a fume cupboard (for test 1, which produces a toxic gas);
- ■ smell gases cautiously (especially if you suffer from asthma).

Procedure   Perform tests 1 to 5 on separate portions (about 1 cm³) of **solutions** of the four oxosalts provided.

1. Working at a fume cupboard, add an equal volume of dilute hydrochloric acid, a few drops at a time. Warm **gently** (do not boil) and test any gas that you can see or smell. Record your observations in a copy of Results Table 12.5 and infer what you can from them.

2. Add about 2 cm³ of silver nitrate solution, a few drops at a time. Pour residues into the bottle provided.

3. Add a few drops of iodine solution.

4. Add a few drops of potassium iodide solution.

5. Add two drops of iron(III) chloride solution, followed by a few drops of dilute hydrochloric acid. Warm gently (do not boil) for half a minute and then add sodium hydroxide solution.

6. Heat small separate portions (about 0.5 g) of the **solid** oxosalts in a series of clean test-tubes. Test any gases evolved. Record your observations and inferences in your copy of Results Table 12.5.

7. Place about 0.5 g of finely powdered sulphur in a boiling tube and add about 10 cm³ of sodium sulphite solution. Boil the mixture for 2–3 minutes and then filter.

8. Perform tests 1 to 5 on portions of the filtrate from step 7. Record your observations in the last column of Results Table 12.5 and attempt to identify the new species, X, in the filtrate.

Results Table 12.5

Test	Na$_2$SO$_3$	Na$_2$SO$_4$	Na$_2$S$_2$O$_3$	Na$_2$S$_2$O$_8$	X
1. Dilute hydrochloric acid. Warm	a	b	c	d	
2. Silver nitrate solution	e	f	g	h	
3. Iodine solution in aqueous potassium iodide	i	j	k	l	
4. Potassium iodide solution	m	n	o	p	
5. Iron(III) chloride solution. Acidify warm, add alkali	q	r	s	t	
6. Effect of heat on solid	u	v	w	x	

Questions
1. With the aid of your textbook(s) interpret your observations as far as you can, writing equations where possible, especially for **a**, **c**, **i**, **k**, **l** and **q**. Insert oxidation numbers for sulphur in the equations.
2. Which of the reactions illustrate(s) disproportionation?
3. Which of the oxosalts is:
   i)   the strongest oxidising agent,
   ii) the strongest reducing agent, and
   iii) the most stable salt?

4. Apart from the reactions used in the experiment, describe, from your previous knowledge, how you would distinguish between sodium sulphite and sodium sulphate.

5. What is the identity of the new species, X, produced by heating sodium sulphite solution with sulphur?

EXPERIMENT 12.4   Anodising aluminium

Aim

The purpose of this experiment is to demonstrate the effect of anodising aluminium on its electrical conductivity and behaviour towards dyes.

Introduction

Aluminium is anodised by making it the anode during the electrolysis of a solution which normally releases oxygen – you will use dilute sulphuric acid. Instead of oxygen, aluminium ions are released and these are immediately hydrolysed to give a layer of hydrated oxide. After electrolysis you compare anodised and unanodised aluminium by testing their conductivities and immersing them in a dye solution.

Requirements

- safety spectacles
- 2 pieces of sheet aluminium, 7 cm × 3 cm, mounted on wooden bars
- 2 beakers, 100 cm^3
- forceps or tweezers
- cotton wool
- propanone, CH_3COCH_3
- sulphuric acid, dilute, 1 M H_2SO_4
- Bunsen burner, tripod, gauze and bench mat
- thermometer, 0–100 °C
- d.c. supply, 12 V
- ammeter, 1 A
- rheostat, 10 Ω, 4 A
- 4 connecting leads, two with crocodile clips at one end
- 2 large pins
- dye solution, e.g. alizarin red

HAZARD WARNING

Propanone is flammable. Therefore you **must**:
- **keep the bottle away from flames and return its stopper as soon as possible.**

Dilute sulphuric acid is corrosive. Therefore you **must**:
- **wear safety spectacles.**

Procedure – Part A

Anodising

1. Mark one of the wooden supports for the electrodes with a 'plus' sign. This carries the piece of aluminium to be used as the anode.

2. Working at a fume cupboard, remove any grease from the surface of the anode by swabbing with cotton wool soaked in propanone and held in forceps or tweezers. From now on, hold the anode only by its wooden support.

3. Pour about 75 cm^3 of dilute sulphuric acid into a small beaker, heat to about 40 °C and stand it on the bench.

4. Place the electrodes in the beaker and set up the circuit shown in Fig. 12.1. Make sure the clean anode is connected to the positive terminal of the supply.

5. Switch on the d.c. supply and adjust the rheostat to give a current of 0.3 A. Maintain this current for at least 15 minutes (longer if it is convenient), adjusting the rheostat if necessary to keep the current constant.

6. Switch off the supply. Disconnect the electrodes, remove them from the beaker and wash them with distilled water. Has their appearance changed?

Figure 12.1

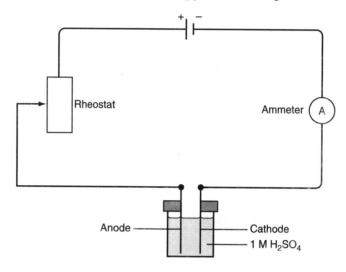

**Procedure
– Part B**

Conductivity testing

7. Clip a large pin to each of the leads you had previously connected to the electrodes. Adjust the rheostat so that when the two pins touch each other, the current is no greater than 1 A.
8. Touch each pin **lightly** on the surface of the cathode and note the ammeter reading. Repeat for the anode. Is there any difference? Now press the pins more firmly on to the anode surface. If this does not change the ammeter reading, try scratching the surface with the pins.

**Procedure
– Part C**

Dyeing

9. Place spots of dye solution on both anode and cathode and leave for 2–3 minutes. (If you have enough dye, you can immerse the electrodes.) Rinse the electrodes with water and inspect them.

Questions

1. How does anodising affect aluminium with regard to its:
   a appearance,
   b conductivity,
   c susceptibility to dyes?
2. You probably noticed that you had to reduce the variable resistance during the electrolysis in order to prevent the current from falling. Suggest two reasons for this.
3. In what applications might anodising be:
   a an advantage,
   b a disadvantage?

EXPERIMENT 12.5   Observation and deduction exercise 6

Aim and introduction

You are provided with aqueous solutions, labelled B, C and D, of three salts. They are compounds of the same three elements.

Carry out the following experiments. Safety spectacles should be worn throughout. Record your observations and inferences in (a copy of) Results Table 12.6, commenting on the types of chemical reactions involved.

Procedure and results

Results Table 12.6

Test	Observations	Inferences
1. To 2 or 3 cm^3 of solution B add a few drops of dilute hydrochloric acid. Now add a few drops of aqueous barium chloride		
2. To 2 or 3 cm^3 of solution B add a few drops of aqueous lead ethanoate (lead acetate). Now add an excess of ammonium ethanoate (ammonium acetate) and shake the mixture		
3. To about 5 cm^3 of solution C in a boiling-tube add about 10 cm^3 of dilute hydrochloric acid. Allow the mixture to stand for a minute or two. Cautiously smell the mixture. Warm, if necessary, and test the gas evolved. Describe below how you performed this test **Method**		
4. **a** In a small beaker place 2 or 3 cm^3 of aqueous copper(II) sulphate. Acidify with two drops of dilute sulphuric acid. Now add about 5 cm of aqueous potassium iodide **b** To the mixture obtained in **4a** add solution C until in excess, swirling well		
5. **a** In a small beaker mix about 2 cm^3 of aqueous sodium chloride with an equal volume of aqueous silver nitrate **b** To the mixture obtained in **5a** add solution C until in excess, swirling well		
6. Dissolve about 1 g of iron(II) sulphate crystals in dilute sulphuric acid and add a few drops of aqueous potassium thiocyanate. Now add a few drops of solution D		
7. **a** In a small beaker place about 5 cm^3 of aqueous potassium iodide and a few drops of dilute sulphuric acid. Now add about 5 cm^3 of solution D. Warm this mixture **b** To the mixture obtained in **7a** add solution C until in excess, swirling well		
8. Evaporate a small quantity of solution B to dryness and perform a flame test on the residue. Describe below how you do this **Method**		